BUSH VS. THE BELTWAY

Laurie Mylroie

ReganBooks

An Imprint of HarperCollins*Publishers*

BUSH

VS.

How the CIA and the State Department
Tried to Stop the War on Terror

THE BELTWAY

HarperCollins books may be purchased for educational, business, or sales promotional use. For information please write: Special Markets Department, HarperCollins Publishers Inc., 10 East 53rd Street, New York, NY 10022.

FIRST EDITION

Designed by Judith Abbate/Abbate Design

Printed on acid-free paper

Library of Congress Cataloging-in-Publication Data has been applied for.

ISBN 0-06-058012-7

03 04 05 06 07 WBC/RRD 10 9 8 7 6 5 4 3 2 1

*In loving memory of my grandparents Victor and Erna Koerner Knopf,
who found a new home in America, and to the family members
who died in the Holocaust:*

*Anna Koerner; Dezoe and Margaret Koerner Eisner and their children,
Erninko and Magda; Emile Koerner; Rose Koerner Klein and her children,
Hilda and Rudy; and Rudolph Spoller along with his son Maxie*

Woe unto those who call evil good and good evil, who turn darkness into light and light into darkness.

CONTENTS

INTRODUCTION

F IT IS TRUE that generals have a tendency to fight the last war, so too do antiwar protesters. While there was certainly room for serious debate about the wisdom of engaging in war with Iraq, many observers were struck by the incongruity of some of the positions taken in opposition to the war. On the one hand there was the frightening, if unfounded, image of indiscriminate U.S. bombing causing "thousands" (or even "hundreds of thousands") of civilian deaths; on the other hand it was rarely acknowledged that the existing state of "peace" already entailed very real civilian suffering, without any hope of relief, as well as a substantial (and widely resented) U.S. military presence in the Persian Gulf region that could not be withdrawn until the threat had been eliminated.

Most striking, however, was the easy dismissal, on the part of many commentators as well as protesters, of the idea that U.S. policy-makers might have serious concerns about an Iraqi threat, either imminent or long-term. President George W. Bush's commitment to disarming Iraq was seen as reflecting (pick one): his cowboy mentality; or his ties to big oil; or the pernicious influence of his hawkish neoconservative advisers. The war against Iraq was treated as a distraction from the war on terrorism, rather than as a key element of it.

Dismissing the Threat

SOME OF THE criticisms had the quality of wishful thinking. The Carnegie Endowment for International Peace assured us that we needn't fear biological or chemical terrorism because Saddam could be counted on not to share his "crown jewels"—his weapons of mass destruction—with terrorist agents. Along the same lines, others held that he would unleash such weapons only if he faced certain military defeat.

It is hard to imagine any president staking the security of American cities on reasoning of this sort. For President Bush, the first duty of the office was to protect the country's security. He certainly did not have the option of ignoring the strategic landscape: Saddam Hussein's project included his unrelenting push to develop and conceal weapons of mass destruction; his use of chemical warfare during the 1980s; his successful drive to end weapons inspections in the 1990s; his blatantly imperialist aspirations, invading first Iran and then Kuwait and threatening Saudi Arabia too (not to mention raining thirty-nine missiles down on Israel); and his avowed hostility to the United States throughout the period since the 1991 Gulf War.

Nor could any policy-maker, particularly after September 11, 2001, disregard the possibility of innovative, nonmilitary methods of delivery of chemical or biological weapons—botulism, smallpox, or deadly nerve agents such as sarin, mustard gas, or VX. Anthrax, after all, had arrived through the mail, and passenger planes had become deadly missiles.

This seems an obvious enough point, so obvious that it's difficult to understand why so many commentators not only dismissed such concerns, but also could not fathom that *anyone* actually took them seriously.

The Party Is *So* Over

IT'S HARD TO RECALL just how giddy and dizzying the 1990s were. We had won the 1991 Gulf War handily, finally laying to rest (it seemed) the ghost of Vietnam. The Soviet Union, our great antagonist, suddenly collapsed from its own inner weakness. Bill Clinton ran—and won—on the slogan "It's the economy, stupid," and the longest period of sustained economic growth in U.S. history followed. America had peace and prosperity.

Both the peace and the prosperity contained elements of illusion, we now recognize. The security bubble burst in one day, with the attacks of September 11, 2001. The economic bubble was already deflating, more gradually. The stock market decline, which began in 1999, deepened over the next year and a half; the dramatic rebound of the second half of 2001 turned to a full rout at the beginning of 2002, no doubt exacerbated by the economic fallout from the terrorist attacks. The bankruptcies of such established companies as Enron and WorldCom introduced the term "creative accounting" into the American lexicon and shook our faith in U.S. business leadership, as did the evidence that a number of prestigious Wall Street brokerage firms had been flogging overvalued shares of the corporations they brokered, making hefty commissions at the expense of their credulous clients.

The illusory peace bubble had something in common with this inflated impression of prosperity. As we'll see in chapter 6, many of the members of U.S. government foreign policy agencies—the bureaucracies—tend to serve interests as narrowly defined as those of the Wall Street brokerage firms. The interests of the public must be championed by elected officials, since such interests rarely register on the "radar screens" of unelected bureaucrats.

Where Were the Checks?

IN SOME WAYS, America's Founding Fathers held a rather pessimistic view of human nature. Because they believed that power was bound to be abused, they established a system of government in which power is fractured, in a set of opposing forces we know as "checks and balances." It is no great surprise to learn that some individuals or agencies in Washington have been prone to behavior comparable to Wall Street's "sins of commission"—and that such behavior can have an impact on the public interest and on national security. Ironically, though, individuals in the private sector are far more likely than those in government to be held to account for egregiously inappropriate behavior, even though the consequences of government officials' actions can be much more damaging.

"Everyone must do what he must do for his career," I was told by a highly regarded Middle East expert back in 1998. "The times are very cynical," he claimed, and so behavior that was very self-serving became acceptable, irrespective of its possible implications for the country's security. Like most of his colleagues at the time, he evidently shared the mentality of the now-disgraced Wall Street firms. And the cynically constructed policy analysis offered by most of the Iraq experts during the 1990s directly reflected the entrenched cynicism of the bureaucracies, which is where the greatest problem lay.

The Decision for War

THE DECISION FOR WAR with Iraq was made soon after the September 11 attacks, far above the bureaucratic level.[1] On the afternoon of September 11, with the Pentagon still burning and rescue workers still engaged in the grim task of pulling bodies from the rubble, Secretary of Defense Donald Rumsfeld—who himself could have been among the casualties had the hijacked plane hit another part of the building—ordered the Defense Department's intelligence agencies to search for evidence that Baghdad, as well as al Qaeda, was linked to the attacks. Rumsfeld also ordered the military to start working on plans for striking Iraq.[2] Critics of the war, both in and outside government, have suggested that Rumsfeld and others in the Pentagon, as well as in the vice president's office, used the September 11 attacks as a vehicle to promote a prior, unrelated project: overthrowing Saddam. But this suggestion reflects a fundamental misunderstanding. What these critics had no way of knowing was that the Pentagon had just completed a review of counterterrorism policy, and Rumsfeld already had some reason to suspect that Iraq may have been involved.[3]

On September 17, 2001, following a weekend meeting with his senior advisers at Camp David, Bush told a National Security Council meeting, "I believe Iraq was involved, but I'm not going to strike them now. I don't have the evidence at this point." Bush had already decided to target Osama bin Laden, al Qaeda, and the Taliban, but he also told the Pentagon to keep working on plans for attacking Iraq, and he signed off on the outline of a war plan that included Iraq.[4]

In early 2002, as the war in Afghanistan was winding down, Bush directed the CIA to begin a major, covert program to topple Saddam. Expectations were low—yet even if it did not succeed, it would help prepare the way for military action, as the agency identified targets and intensified its intelligence gathering.

On January 28, during his State of the Union speech, Bush denounced the "Axis of Evil," putting Iraq at the top of the list. It was Bush's first public indication that Iraq could be the next target in the war on terrorism

On April 4, 2002, Bush told a British television journalist, "I made up my mind that Hussein needs to go." Pressed for further detail, Bush would only say, "The policy of my government is that he goes."[5] Bush also told National Security Adviser Condoleezza Rice that it was time to figure out "what we are doing about Iraq."[6] Serious military planning began around the same time.

Nonetheless, three months later, in July, Richard Haass, director of policy planning in the State Department, suggested to Rice that they should discuss the pros and cons of confronting Iraq. Rice replied that there was no point; the president had already decided.[7] Critics within the bureaucracies would later complain that they did not learn of the decision until it had already been made.

This book is, from one point of view, the story of Bush's battle with the bureaucracies of the U. S. government, particularly the CIA and the State Department.

While the September 11 strikes changed everything for Bush—

imposing the inescapable responsibility to prevent a future recurrence—they had no comparable impact on the bureaucracies. Within these bodies, individual responsibilities are often very narrowly defined, and there is great sensitivity to so-called political constraints. To show any serious concern for the larger policy implications of one's limited task is generally considered "naive": the "sophisticates" avoid thinking above their pay grade.

There was a general inability within the bureaucracies to comprehend the danger that the president recognized after September 11. In fact, to have recognized the problem would have been tantamount to acknowledging that the existing policy analyses, supplied by the same agencies, had left the country exposed to a great danger.

Specifically, these agencies had rationalized away the threat of bioterrorism and related terrors. Stunning revelations had emerged in 1995 about Iraq's ongoing weapons programs—biological, chemical, and nuclear—from evidence provided by the Iraqi regime after Saddam's son-in-law Hussein Kamil (who had actually supervised those programs) defected to Jordan. Not only many public commentators, but also much of the national security bureaucracy itself maintained that Saddam would not use those weapons, or commit other major acts of aggression against the United States, because (they claimed) he was a rational actor, interested above all in his own survival, and because the threat he feared above all others was retaliation by the United States.

This view represented the position held by the CIA and the State Department during the Clinton administration: Saddam was "in his box." That assessment had in fact changed very little in 2002 and 2003, even as the United States prepared for war. In October 2002, the consensus among CIA analysts was still that Saddam was *unlikely* to commit acts of terrorism—whether using weapons of mass destruction or even conventional attacks, under the current circumstances. The one situation in which Saddam's calculations were likely to change, according to these analysts, would be if the United States went to war to depose him. Then, they argued, the chances were very high that he would strike back in a ferocious way.[8]

Why, then, did President Bush make the apparently risk-laden decision to go to war? Why not let a sleeping dog lie? The danger was indeed acute that Saddam would lash out with an unconventional terrorist attack as the United States took him down, and the United States was extremely fortunate that nothing of the sort occurred. That Bush had apparently steeled himself to incur that risk underscores that he not only understood something the CIA analysts did not, but that he also accepted a burden of responsibility that they were unwilling to share.

A Fatally Flawed Concept

THIS BOOK IS ALSO the story of a massive intelligence failure that occurred in the 1990s. In that comfortable decade, given America's demonstrated power and might, it was presumed that no rational actor would challenge us. What existed, to borrow a phrase from Clinton's National Security Council Adviser, Anthony Lake, were a handful of "backlash states," a small group of rogues including Iraq and North Korea, which had not decided to get with the program. These were not major states, however, and their numbers were small—and so it was assumed, conveniently, that their ability to cause serious harm was limited.

If major dangers existed, we were told, they were more likely to come from nonstate actors, particularly religious extremists such as Osama bin Laden. They alone did not march to the drum of reason. To begin with, they were fanatics, with followers ready to die in pursuit of their hatreds. And they appeared to enjoy a unique exemption from the constraint of deterrence: they could act against the United States without fear of massive, focused retaliation. The war in Afghanistan in fact demonstrated that this was not really so, and that even bin Laden and al Qaeda had a territorial base that could be denied to them by military action.

There was also a far more serious flaw in this general assessment. The implicit syllogism ran as follows: a terrorist attack by a state against the United States would invite retaliation; to invite retaliation is irrational;

states are (now) rational; therefore no state would engage in terrorism against the United States. What this logic failed to acknowledge was the possibility that a state (such as Iraq) might attempt to evade deterrence by evading detection—that is, by concealing its activities behind one of these irrational nonstate actors. In that case, a state might well take the risk of committing an assault—even a massive assault—on the United States.

Clearly, any such attempt at concealing terrorist activity and evading detection would represent a direct challenge to U.S. intelligence capabilities. The assertion, often repeated over the past year, that Iraq had been "successfully contained" reflected a confidence in our intelligence capabilities—as well as a certainty that no significant "third-party" terrorist activity could be successfully concealed—that is not justified by the facts, as we shall see in later chapters.

Similarly, the sustained diplomatic effort called the "Middle East Peace Process," which began with the 1993 Oslo accords, was premised on the conviction that "rational" actors like Hafiz al Assad and Yasser Arafat must recognize that, with the loss of the Soviet Union (their superpower patron), they had "no choice" but to make peace with Israel, given its close ties with the world's sole remaining superpower. The only actors who would not recognize this new reality and accommodate themselves to it were the more marginal (and irrational) players—the Islamic militants, the "enemies of peace."

Events would prove, however, that this distinction was not quite so sharp or clear. Arafat could, and did, work with the Islamic organization Hamas, at least on a tactical level; and elements of the PLO, like the Al-Aqsa Martyrs Brigades, certainly had Islamic leanings. Syria, moreover, served as the base for the Palestinian Islamic Jihad and also supported Hizbollah, the Shi'a militant organization in Lebanon. And neither Arafat nor Assad ever made peace, despite the increasingly generous territorial concessions offered by Israel in this period. There was little reason to believe Saddam Hussein would hesitate to play the same game of using proxies for his terrorist aims.

Confronting a Grave Threat

AMERICANS GENERALLY did not understand the peril that developed during the 1990s, and which only grew more acute as we went to war in Afghanistan and then in Iraq. In part, this was because of the Bush administration's efforts to avoid causing panic by revealing in detail Iraq's potential for terror. But the president did explain the threat in general terms in early March 2003, on the eve of war:

> Saddam Hussein has a long history of reckless aggression and terrible crimes. He possesses weapons of terror. He provides funding and training and safe haven to terrorists, terrorists who would willingly use weapons of mass destruction against America, and other peace-loving countries. . . .
> I think the threat is real, and so do a lot of other people in my government. And since I believe the threat is real, and since my most important job is to protect the security of the American people, that's precisely what we will do.[9]

Bush was not the first president to recognize the unique threat to the country posed by Iraq's potential for covert use of unconventional weapons. Bill Clinton had spoken of it in 1998:

> Think how many can be killed by just a tiny bit of anthrax, and think about how it's not just that Saddam Hussein might put it on a Scud missile, an anthrax head, and send it on to some city he wants to destroy. Think about all the other terrorists and other bad actors who could just parade through Baghdad and pick up their stores if we don't take action.[10]

Clinton, however, did not take action. And in the absence of presidential leadership, nothing would be done to address the danger. It would require a determined presidential commitment to overcome the inertia, narrow agendas, and mutual mistrust of the bureaucracies.

No Choice but War

GEORGE W. BUSH was absolutely right: there was no choice but war. The danger was enormous. Not only was there the possibility of more large and undefendable attacks on the order of September 11; the possibility of unconventional terrorism, and particularly biological terrorism, was very real. That was suggested not only by the anthrax letters that followed the September 11 attacks, but also by an evident (and alarming) interest in crop dusters on the part of some hijackers and their unidentified companions.

Warfare often involves deception; history is filled with stunning and successful ruses. The failure of the bureaucracies to consider, let alone investigate, the possibility that deception was involved in the September 11 attacks (as well as previous terrorist assaults) reveals these agencies' limitations in understanding and assessing not only the threat posed by Iraq, but potential future threats as well.

Immediately after the September 11 strikes, there was widespread public speculation about Iraq's involvement. The appearance of the anthrax letters a few weeks later certainly fueled that speculation. But in late 2001, with the United States still engaged in Afghanistan, unattributed leaks began to appear in the media designed to systematically discredit any information that might suggest an Iraqi link to al Qaeda or terrorism. The leaks continued to flow in the spring of 2002 and reached a crescendo in the fall, as the administration began to make its case for war.

In fact, substantial evidence *did* exist to tie Iraq to al Qaeda, and to suggest that Iraq was involved in the September 11 attacks. That evidence, along with the bureaucratic campaign to undercut it, is crucial to understanding both the war itself and the challenges posed in the post-Saddam era.

The International Context

THE QUESTION OF TERRORISM was not the only Iraq-related issue con-
tested by the hidebound American bureaucracy. There was also the problem of how to overthrow Saddam and what would replace him. As long ago
as 1991, the CIA had been persuaded (possibly because of Iraqi disinformation) that Saddam would be overthrown in a military coup; when the
Gulf War brought on massive popular uprisings against Saddam, the first
President Bush was advised to allow Saddam to suppress them—on the
perverse, and tragically misguided, argument that this would spark an
internal coup. Twelve years later, the CIA was still dealing with the same
Iraqi exiles who had promised, and failed, to deliver such a coup. Similarly, the State Department generally looked to Iraq's old guard—the
Ba'athists—to provide the basis for a new regime, despite the president's
stated objective of establishing a democratic government in Iraq.

The ability of any president to impose his policies on the bureaucracies of his government is far more constrained than we tend to think.
The bureaucracies tend to see themselves as a permanent government:
presidents and their cabinets, after all, come and go. And they have their
own indirect ways of imposing constraints, working with selected allies
in the think tanks and media to fight their perennial Beltway battles.

Among the more astonishing bureaucratic feats in this regard is the
successful suppression of substantial information that could tie Iraq to
at least two major acts of terrorism against the United States: the 1993
bombing of New York's World Trade Center, masterminded by the individual known as Ramzi Yousef; and the audacious 1995 plot—mercifully
derailed—to bomb a dozen U.S. passenger aircraft, in which Yousef participated along with Khalid Shaikh Mohammed, the man who would go
on to mastermind the September 11 attacks six years later.

Indeed, over the course of the post-9/11 investigation into al Qaeda,
an odd picture emerged. Mohammed is said to be Yousef's uncle; two of
Yousef's brothers are high-ranking al Qaeda figures, as is one of his
cousins.[11] Moreover, one of Yousef's childhood friends was arrested,

along with Yousef, in the unsuccessful plot to bomb U.S. airplanes. Thus, the claim of U.S. investigators is now essentially that one family—Yousef, his uncle, two brothers, a cousin, and a childhood friend—constitute the core of the astonishingly ambitious and lethal Islamic terrorism that has targeted the United States over the past decade.

This is an intriguing scenario, worthy of a spy thriller, and we naturally want to know more about these people and where they come from. Ever since the 1993 World Trade Center bombing, I've followed the case as best I could—turning for guidance to Jim Fox, who headed the New York FBI and directed the investigation in New York at that time. We generally shared the same view of that attack, including a fascination with the problem of Ramzi Yousef.

Who was this mysterious figure who had entered late into the plot and transformed it from a routine terrorist bomb scare to a staggeringly ambitious plan to bring down the Twin Towers (a goal it did not, of course, achieve)? Much of the information about his purported identity did not add up (as we'll see in chapter 7), and he seemed to come from a different world than the militant Islamists with whom he was associated.

The discovery of the 1995 airplane plot revealed that there was in fact another distinct, and very lethal, terrorist "network" that appeared to center on Yousef, confirming our view of the importance of this man's identity. The Washington bureaucracies had not simply dropped the ball; in effect, they had chosen to kneel on the ball and run out the half.

There is another odd point. All these individuals are said to be Pakistanis, born and raised in Kuwait (save perhaps the "cousin," who may have grown up elsewhere). The little we really know about their identities is based on files in Kuwait that *predate* Kuwait's liberation. Yet because Iraq occupied Kuwait for nearly seven months, the reliability of those files is open to serious suspicion. Iraqi intelligence had ample time to tamper with them.

It is more than likely that the Kuwaiti records on which the identities of these terrorist masterminds are based belonged to individuals who died (possibly during the Iraqi occupation). The files would then have been doctored to create false identities—"legends," as they're called in intelligence circles—for the Pakistani terrorists, as we shall discuss. The alternative hypothesis is that a single family was the moving force behind the most lethal and sophisticated terrorist campaign ever waged. No known terrorist organization has a family at its core; such a claim is without precedent.

And Iraqi intelligence, of course, is the only party that reasonably could have tampered with those files—during Iraq's occupation of Kuwait. To demonstrate that these Pakistani terrorists are not the individuals they claim to be—and that the Kuwaiti files were tampered with—would thus be tantamount to demonstrating Iraq's sponsorship of their terrorism.

That demonstration is most easily carried out with the individuals in custody, such as Yousef himself, who was arrested in February 1995. Yousef's identity is indeed based on a corrupted Kuwaiti file. The same is probably true of Khalid Shaikh Mohammed, who was arrested in March 2003. Demonstrating that Mohammed is not who he claims to be, and that a file in Kuwait was tampered with to create his legend would establish a direct connection between Iraq and the September 11 attacks, as chapter 7 explains.

Finally, chapter 8 addresses the issue of the war's legality, among the most misunderstood dimensions of the war. I am indebted to Professor Robert F. Turner, cofounder of the Center for National Security Law at the University of Virginia, for a cogent and comprehensive analysis of the case in international law. As he makes clear, there are three distinct principles that can be invoked to argue the legality of the action. Principle number one, factually supported by the broad line of argument of this book, is the right of states to self-defense. Principle number two is the narrower (and less conclusive) legal argument that Iraq's repeated violations of the terms of the cease-fire resolution (which were the subject of repeated warnings by the Security Council) in effect vitiated the resolution. Principle number three, equally strong as the case for self-defense, is the argument that gross violations of human rights (themselves the subject of United Nations condemnation) by their very nature give other states the right to intervene.

In the public debate going into the war, it was sometimes argued that the administration's invocation of humanitarian grounds somehow detracted from the persuasiveness of its claims regarding imminent threat. Turner presents a broader view, invoking the "totality of circumstances" and pointing to the need for legal standards to adapt to contemporary values—such as, for example, the concept of popular rather than monarchical sovereignty (as in the broadly though not legally recognized right of self-determination).

In fact, there is arguably an inherent connection between the two broad principles in the case—the threat of terrorism against other states, and the urgency of the humanitarian situation within Iraq. Both involve the threat or use of terror against a civilian population, foreign in the first instance and domestic in the second. As in other infamous historical cases, terrorism—as the inverse of charity—appears to begin at home.

Two overarching considerations must also be kept in view. First, in the case of Iraq's violation of the cease-fire agreement, the key legal obstacle to war arose from the fact that the 1991 Gulf War was concluded without a formal agreement signed by all parties, thus giving the Security Council (rather than the coalition) the sole right to assert that Iraq's increasingly flagrant violations did in fact nullify the agreement.

And second, the bureaucracies' sustained campaign to suppress and invalidate the evidence of Iraq's role in terrorism, traced throughout this book, had the effect of systematically undercutting the administration's most compelling and urgent grounds for war—as a necessary action of self-defense against further terrorist attacks of potentially far greater magnitude.

How Did We Get Here?

DURING THE 1990S, international affairs tended to be viewed through the same prism that had worked rather well in dealing with the Soviet

Union during the Cold War: despite the inevitable differences of ideology and narrow interests, nations were viewed as part of a system in which competing interests could be traded, adjusted, or otherwise made to balance. Leadership at the national level could be counted on to adhere to a kind of realism, and to provide a counterweight to the sorts of fantasies and fanaticisms that might characterize subnational organizations and networks.

This narrow realism was undoubtedly one of the factors at work in the general bureaucratic evasion of responsibility that constituted the U.S. investigation of terrorism. The same attitude shaped, with tragic results, the U.S. attempts to bring peace to the Middle East (chapter 5).

But humans and their motives are complex, and in the often astonishing train of events and actions recounted here, there is no single "root cause" of error and misjudgment. There is certainly, on the other hand, a structural weakness, pointed to in chapter 6.

And there is an actual hero, in the person of a president who could not be rolled, spun, or otherwise diverted from his most solemn obligation.

Punishing the Deed

IF NO GOOD DEED goes unpunished, a heroic deed can expect some serious bruising. Soon after the war the daily press returned to politics as usual—with a generous helping of bureaucratic revenge as critics accused the administration of exaggerating, even manufacturing, evidence regarding Iraq's weapons programs.

But in all the impassioned debate leading up to the war, there was never any serious question among experts on the issue of proscribed weapons. Not only was it generally agreed that Iraq *had* such weapons programs in flagrant violation of the U.N.-sponsored cease-fire, it was also understood they included a large biological program.

Once President Bush had made the decision for war, admittedly, he ran a little roughshod over those who wouldn't accept that it was imprudent to leave Saddam Hussein in power in a country he had terrorized for more than thirty years, with a hidden biological weapons program and a record of deceiving inspectors repeatedly to protect it.

But when U.S. forces failed to find proscribed weapons at once, the media, prodded by antagonists in the bureaucracies and Congress, launched an immediate counteroffensive: the intelligence, they claimed, had been "politicized." The weapons would never be found, they said; previous evidence of their existence was not merely flawed but cooked. The resentment grew so intense that some highly distorted accounts, originated on the Internet or in left-wing publications overseas, entered mainstream discourse, often endorsed by present and former U.S. officials. The *Wall Street Journal*'s Robert Bartley rightly denounced extreme reports appearing in the *New York Times* and *The New Yorker* as "off the deep end." Critics ignored realistic explanations for the missing material: it was well hidden; it had been moved to another country; it may have been destroyed in a final, cunning act of revenge. And critics ignored this crucial point: *none* of those circumstances would have diminished the case for war.

Polls show, however, that most Americans are not seriously bothered by the failure to find such weapons. The war, they feel, was justified.

This book gives some context to the media witch hunt that followed this quick, successful conflict, which removed a brutal tyrant with minimal casualties. The story begins with a crucial failure of intelligence (and policy) in the 1990s. The bureaucracies—who had rationalized the inadequate policy of "containment"—proved unable to accept a perspective different from the one to which they had become committed. To save face, they could *only* protest that officials who drew different conclusions from the intelligence had "politicized" the issue.

What the media melee obscured were the central issues behind the war in Iraq: the safety of the American people, and the nature of the terrorist threat. These issues, traced through the tangle of information and disinformation, are the primary concern of *Bush vs. the Beltway*.

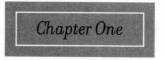

Chapter One

THE ANTHRAX PROBE

MORE THAN ANY OTHER assault experienced by America—more, even, than the attacks of September 11, 2001—the anthrax letters that *followed* those strikes perfectly illustrated the danger apprehended by the president and other senior administration officials as the United States contemplated war with Iraq. American civilians had been exposed to a lethal biological agent, delivered through nonmilitary means, without a single solid clue to its origins or sponsorship.

The Perfect Terrorist Crime

AGAIN AND AGAIN, in late 2002 and early 2003, the administration would point with genuine alarm to the threat of terrorism involving weapons of mass destruction—and, in particular, to the threat of biological agents that could not be traced back to their source.

The FBI has steadfastly adhered to its own theory that the anthrax letters were the work of a lone American, but there is substantial reason to doubt that explanation. High-level U.S. national security officials favor the more likely theory that the anthrax was produced by a terrorist state, and Iraq is the most likely candidate. Precisely because this was a biological attack, silent and stealthy, it is virtually impossible, however, to determine its origins with any certainty. In this sense, a biological attack can represent the "perfect" terrorist crime.

The Anthrax Attacks

SEPTEMBER 2001 MARKED the first experience in the United States of a biological attack on a civilian population. More than one type of anthrax was employed, the spores exhibiting varying degrees of processing—from clumpy material that looked like "dog chow"[12] under the microscope to spores that had been fully "weaponized."

The delivery system used in the September attack was technologically as simple as can be imagined: a quantity of anthrax spores was sealed in a prestamped envelope, addressed, and sent through the U.S. mail. All the envelopes shared common features: the same handwriting; photocopied messages with nearly identical wording, and in some cases, identical postmarks.

Assaults on the American News Media

On September 27, a sixty-three-year-old man named Robert Stevens became ill, complaining of fatigue and fever. A British-born photo editor, Stevens worked for American Media, Inc. (publisher of five major tabloids, including the *National Enquirer*). Five days later, Stevens was taken to the emergency room at Palm Beach County Hospital. The initial diagnosis was meningitis, and Stevens was treated with a course of antibiotics. Further consultations, however, yielded the correct diagnosis: inhalational anthrax, the most deadly form of the disease. Stevens died just three days later.

The 66,000-square-foot American Media office building was found to be completely contaminated with anthrax spores. All American Media employees were subsequently administered nasal swab tests and a sixty-day course of antibiotics. Anthrax spores were indeed found in the nasal cavities of two other employees, both of them mailroom workers. One, a seventy-three-year-old man, was hospitalized with inhalational anthrax and recovered. The second, a thirty-six-year-old woman, did not become ill. Follow-up blood tests revealed that five additional employees had been exposed but remained in good health.

Just before the events at American Media, on September 25, security officials at NBC News in New York had notified the FBI that they had received two suspicious letters postmarked September 18, from Trenton, New Jersey—one of them filled with white powder. The *New York Post* received an identical letter, with the same postmark. The identical photocopied letters were dated "09-11-01." The letters warned, in five lines of block-written letters, "This is next. Take penacilin [*sic*] now." They concluded with the refrain, "Death to America, Death to Israel, Allah is great." The FBI picked up the letters from NBC the next day.

The envelope delivered to NBC had been opened by Erin O'Connor, a thirty-eight-year-old assistant to Tom Brokaw (to whom both letters were addressed). On September 28, O'Connor developed a strange sore on her chest and consulted a doctor specializing in infectious diseases. The doctor suspected cutaneous anthrax. On October 6, the New York City Health Department was notified, and the powder remaining in the envelope was sent to the Centers for Disease Control, which confirmed that it was indeed anthrax. A month later, it was learned that a second NBC news employee had developed cutaneous anthrax.

The letter at the *New York Post* had not been opened: it was addressed simply to "Editor" and contained no return address. It lay around unnoticed until October 19. Three employees of the *Post* nevertheless developed cutaneous anthrax.

On September 28, the seven-month-old son of a woman who worked in New York as an assistant to ABC News anchor Peter Jennings was brought to the ABC newsroom by the boy's baby-sitter. The infant soon developed cutaneous anthrax, but no letter was discovered, and the source of the infection remains unknown.

On October 1, a staffer for anchor Dan Rather at CBS News learned that she had developed cutaneous anthrax on her cheek. Again, no suspect letter was found.

In addition, two postal workers in Trenton, New Jersey, developed cutaneous anthrax.

At this point, American Media, Inc., the *New York Post*, plus all three major U.S. television networks had suffered mysterious anthrax attacks. With the exception of the letter to American Media, however, the attacks did little actual harm.

But this was only the beginning of America's experience with anthrax. Before the siege was over, there would be twenty-two cases of anthrax in the United States, including five fatalities.

Attacks on Senators Leahy and Daschle

On October 7, the U.S. bombing of Afghanistan began. This was the first phase of the U.S. response to the September 11 attacks, and it would soon result in the fall of the Taliban and the defeat of al Qaeda. Just two days later—October 9 is the date of the postmark—two anthrax-laced letters were mailed to Democratic Senators Tom Daschle (then Senate majority leader) and Patrick Leahy.[13]

The letter to Daschle was opened on October 15, immediately bringing about a complete quarantine of U.S. government mail. The letter to Leahy was thus only discovered a month later, on November 16.

The two letters appeared identical. They were addressed in the same sloping handwritten block letters as those to NBC News and the *New York Post*. There were, again, identical photocopied notes in the envelopes. These too carried the date "09-11-01," but the message was now slightly different. It consisted of four lines: "You can not stop us; We have this anthrax; You die now; Are you afraid?" Then the familiar refrain: "Death to America; Death to Israel; Allah is great."

The senators' letters each contained two grams of a far more lethal and sophisticated form of anthrax than had been sent to the media. These anthrax spores were just one to three microns in diameter, small enough to be inhaled into the lungs. And they were stunningly "slippery."

Ordinarily, anthrax spores carry an electrostatic charge (static electricity) that makes the microscopic spores stick together in clumps that are too big to be inhaled into the lungs. But these spores had been coated with a Teflon-like substance containing silica, as sophisticated analysis of the spores would later reveal. The coated spores did not clump together and therefore became airborne at the slightest motion. When U.S. Army experts tried to examine them, the spores refused to stay put on the glass microscope slide. An imperceptible current of air was enough to carry them off. It behaved like no sample the army scientists had ever seen. (Apart from the mystery of its processing, this raised another perplexing aspect: as one Defense Department scientist asked, given the way the anthrax floated around, like a gas, how did they get the material into the letters?)

This weightless, almost gaseous quality made this batch of anthrax particularly effective as a weapon. Twenty-eight people tested positive for exposure to anthrax in the Senate. In addition to individuals in

Daschle's office, some of Senator Dianne Feinstein's staffers tested positive, as did several Capital Hill police officers. The anthrax also spread to other offices on Capitol Hill (perhaps also through contaminated mail), and a substantial part of the U.S. Congress was closed down for three months, beginning in October 2001.

Senator Leahy warned that the tiny amount of anthrax in just one of the letters was sufficient to cause 100,000 deaths.

The army's premier anthrax expert, John Ezzell, was especially worried. The evident level of expertise involved in the production of this weaponized anthrax powder suggested that the United States had been attacked by a sophisticated, ruthless, and formidable foe.[14]

Little Is Known Even Now

EVEN NOW, nearly two years later, astonishingly little is known about the source of this first biological attack in modern U.S. history. The FBI has not yet identified the source of the anthrax spores retrieved from the letters and from the bodies of the victims, the laboratory and equipment used to produce and weaponize the anthrax, or the copier used to copy the warning letters. And, needless to say, the FBI has not developed the evidence to bring charges against even one individual.

On March 1, 2003, FBI Director Robert Mueller stated that the FBI had not determined "which of the nation's research laboratories may have been the source of the anthrax," adding that "we are not focused on one facility or a series of facilities." Scientists at the Institute for Genetic Research (TIGR), using "genetic fingerprints" (unique markers), have tried without success to trace the anthrax samples to a source facility.

The FBI investigation has not even narrowed the source of the anthrax to a single country. The virulent Ames strain that was used in the attacks is known to be held by laboratories in three countries: United States, Canada, and Britain. But key U.S. and British facilities were partly privatized (including to an Arab investor), creating the possibility of the unauthorized diversion of at least a very small quantity of spores—a quantity sufficient to generate much more, as it is simply a matter of growing the material in a suitable environment.

And apart from their biological characteristics, the processing of the spores shows evidence of sophisticated laboratory work:

> Anthrax probers fret that "some of our best scientific minds" haven't been able to copy the powder that killed five in attacks more than 18 months ago. Investigators hope that knowing how it was made will point to a suspect.[15]

Indeed, after nearly two years' worth of effort, the FBI, working with the country's top scientific experts, has proved unable to produce anthrax spores in the extraordinarily lethal form in which they were sent to Senators Tom Daschle and Patrick Leahy.

"Their failure so far," the *Wall Street Journal* reported, "suggests a person or group with high skills."[16]

Specifications

For anthrax to be lethal in its inhalational form, it must be breathed into the lungs, where it can enter into the bloodstream. The spores must be one to five microns in diameter (a micron is a tenth of a millimeter). Spores that are bigger than that will be filtered out by the body's natural defenses. Spores that are too small will be exhaled instead of settling into the lungs.[17]

To produce material to these narrow specifications—material invisible to the naked eye—requires a high degree of expertise. It requires specialized equipment as well, along with elaborate, somewhat cumbersome internal safeguards. The inability of the FBI to find such a laboratory, despite a massive investigation, is significant.

Dissemination

If skillfully disseminated, a biological agent such as anthrax can cover an area ten thousand times larger than the equivalent weight of chemical agents. Moreover, biological agents are ideally suited for a stealthy attack, to get in "under the radar" of the target population even when it is on high alert. A biological attack could go undetected until a great deal of damage had already been inflicted: people would seek treatment only after they had developed symptoms, by which time medical treatment might be too late. That, of course, assumes that the biological agent had not been engineered to be antibiotic-resistant, in which case there might be no treatment at all.

And in the case of an infectious agent such as smallpox (but not anthrax), the process of contagious spread could at that point be well under way.

The perpetrators of a biological attack would accordingly have the opportunity to escape before the attack had been detected. This sort of attack would not be a suicide mission.

The most lethal method of disseminating a biological agent is a plane equipped with a spraying device such as a crop duster, flying upwind of the target city and perpendicular to the wind. An anthrax assault expertly carried out could achieve fatalities on the scale of a nuclear attack. Official estimates of the probable casualties range from 100,000 to a few million—dwarfing, by far, the terrible atrocities of September 11.[18]

The 9/11 Hijackers

ZACARIAS MOUSSAOUI, a thirty-three-year-old French Muslim, had aroused the suspicion of flight instructors in Minnesota. Although he had virtually no experience as a pilot, he wanted to learn to fly a Boeing

747—and he was interested in learning only how to operate the controls in flight, but not in taking off or landing the plane. Moussaoui was detained on August 17, on immigration charges.

Among his possessions, investigators discovered a manual on crop dusting.

Thus it was that, in a commendable instance of the government's right hand paying attention to its left hand, even after the general post-September 11 ban on airplane flights had been lifted, the ban on crop dusters (along with other small planes) remained in effect for several additional days.

And after the crop duster ban had been lifted, on September 17, it was reinstated just six days later when the FBI learned of the visits of hijacker Mohammed Atta and several other Middle Eastern men to a crop-dusting firm called South Florida Crop Care. As Attorney General John Ashcroft told the U.S. Congress thirteen days after the September 11 attacks, the administration now feared that crop dusters might be used to distribute biological or chemical weapons. Ashcroft noted that Atta had been compiling information on such planes, and that a search of Moussaoui's computer had revealed that he had downloaded a "significant amount" of information from the Internet about "aerial application of pesticides or crop-dusting."[19]

South Florida Crop Care

BETWEEN FEBRUARY 2001 and August 2001 an undetermined number of Middle Eastern men paid repeated visits to an obscure airport in rural Florida, the single-runway Belle Glade State Municipal Airport, to talk with J. D. Lee, the general manager of South Florida Crop Care. On some occasions, the group included Mohammed Atta, the presumed leader of the September 11 attacks.

The men always came in groups of two or three, and Lee told the FBI investigators that he would probably not have recognized repeat visitors: "I've probably seen twelve, fifteen, or eighteen different ones, but some might have been the same." Lee's report was chilling in retrospect: "They asked about how big a load [the crop duster] could haul, how much fuel it could carry, how fast it could go."[20] The Middle Eastern men often had video or still cameras, and took pictures of the planes.

Atta, we know, was a terrorist, not a farmer. The likeliest explanation for the group's interest in crop dusters was as a means for the covert dispersal of chemical or—far deadlier—biological agents.

Atta himself would presumably not be part of whatever group was planning to implement a crop duster attack. The dramatic assault in which he would be a key participant was already in the works. It seems safe to conclude, however, that he and the others were exploring the possibility of an additional assault, and that this assault was intended to have a devastatingly lethal biological component.

The Hijacker's Mysterious Ailment

AHMED AL-HAZNAWI was one of the four hijackers of United Flight 93 (whose passengers, showing extraordinary heroism, succeeded in bringing the doomed plane down in a field in rural Pennsylvania). A short time after his arrival in the United States on June 8, 2001, al-Haznawi had visited the emergency room of Holy Cross Hospital in Fort Lauderdale, Florida. Al-Haznawi, a twenty-two-year-old Saudi, spoke little English, but he was accompanied by Ziad Jarrah (the presumed pilot-hijacker of that flight), who was well traveled and far more knowledgeable than the other hijackers.[21] Al-Haznawi showed the attending doctor an angry-looking infection on his lower leg, which he said had developed from bumping into a suitcase two months before.

The emergency room physician, Dr. Christos Tsonas, examined the wound—a one-inch black lesion with raised round edges—cleaned it, and prescribed a common antibiotic. He did not think about it again until some FBI agents, having found that prescription among al-Haznawi's effects, came to interview him in October 2001. Tsonas, like many other American doctors, had by that time familiarized himself with the previously all but unknown symptoms of anthrax. As the agents read him his own notes of al-Haznawi's emergency room visit, Tsonas recognized that his description sounded very much like cutaneous anthrax. (Cutaneous, or skin, anthrax, arising from skin contact with anthrax spores, is far less lethal than pulmonary, inhaled anthrax.)

The FBI, however, did not pursue the question of the hijacker's ailment very vigorously. Almost two months later, in January 2002, a concerned FBI official bypassed the normal bureaucratic channels to consult two biodefense experts at Johns Hopkins University in Baltimore, Maryland. After consulting other medical experts, they reported back that the diagnosis of cutaneous anthrax was in fact "the most probable and coherent interpretation of the data available."[22]

While the evidence is less than conclusive, based as it is on the notes of a single emergency room visit, as circumstantial evidence it certainly raises serious suspicion. Tsonas and the Johns Hopkins group both concurred that the best explanation for al-Haznawi's unusual wound was anthrax infection.

Establishing a Return Address

To SENIOR U.S. national security officials, the sophistication of the processing of the anthrax spores in the letters to the senators indicated that a state must have been involved in the attacks. Bob Woodward reports that at a crucial National Security Council meeting on October 17, CIA Director George Tenet suggested that the source of the attack was al Qaeda, *with the backing of a state:* "I think there's a state sponsor involved. It's too well refined."[23]

Another attendee, Scooter Libby, Dick Cheney's chief of staff, also thought that the attacks were state sponsored. He strongly advised against suggesting that al Qaeda was responsible: "If we say it's al Qaeda, a state sponsor may feel safe and then hit us thinking they will have a bye, because we'll blame it on al Qaeda."

Tenet's reply did not directly respond to Libby's telling point. "I'm not going to talk about a state sponsor," he asserted. Vice President Dick Cheney agreed: "It's a good thing that we don't, because we're not ready to do anything about it."[24]

The United States was at that point already engaged against the Taliban in Afghanistan. *It could not afford to acknowledge—much less confront—a second major enemy, whether or not a foreign state had just launched a sophisticated biological attack on the United States,* with possibly more to come.

Downplaying the Threat

DESPITE THE VERY SERIOUS concerns of national security officials, a mere four days after the discovery of the Daschle letter, other U.S. officials were taking pains to deflect press attention from the sophistication of the anthrax involved. One official told the *New York Times* that government leaders were consciously trying to minimize public fears. "There has been an effort to downplay and not promote the ability of the people who are doing this."[25]

That may have been part of the reason why the FBI very quickly suggested that the anthrax had been produced by a lone American terrorist, even formally naming its investigation "Amerithrax"—a title that certainly seemed to prejudge the outcome of the investigation.

Like Tenet, Libby, and a number of other U.S. officials involved in national security affairs, some nonofficial commentators also believed that a state must have been behind the attacks. In late October 2001, the *Washington Post* suggested that only three countries were capable of making such sophisticated anthrax: the United States, the former Soviet Union, and Iraq.[26] ABC's *World News Tonight* ran three stories suggesting Iraq had produced the anthrax—only to encounter ferocious opposition from the White House.[27]

With the U.S. engaged in Afghanistan, the White House (as Cheney's reported remark indicated) may have been trying to squelch speculation about Iraq, as there was nothing the administration could do at that moment to respond militarily to what would have to be regarded as an act of war. Moreover, to suggest that Iraq was behind the attacks would have added to the general alarm, instead of calming public fears.

For the FBI, however, there may also have been more strictly bureaucratic reasons for adhering to its "home-grown" terrorism theory.

Only Loners Need Apply

FBI HEADQUARTERS IN WASHINGTON readily endorsed the new view of terrorism that emerged in the 1990s: major attacks were no longer state sponsored but were now carried out by individuals, or "loose networks." Indeed, the Bureau was specifically allergic to the suggestion of Iraqi involvement in terrorism.[28] Apart from Saddam Hussein's attempt to assassinate former President Bush, in April 1993, the FBI had managed to avoid making a finding of Iraqi responsibility for any major act of terrorism since the 1991 Gulf War.

The notes in the anthrax letters explicitly linked them to the September 11 attacks: they featured the date "09-11-01" prominently at the top, and they presented, however crudely, the position of a Muslim activist angry at the United States. The FBI, however, focused on the image of a lone American perpetrator, who had surreptitiously developed and produced that anthrax and then (according to this theory), in the wake of the September 11 attacks, decided to send the material through the U.S. mail, using those attacks as a cover. But how likely is it that a deranged terrorist just chanced to have a variety of anthrax spores on hand—some made with such extraordinary skill that even U.S. government scientists cannot reproduce them—and then took advantage of the September 11 strikes to do something with them?

The more straightforward explanation is that whoever carried out the elaborately planned September 11 attacks was also behind the sophisticated anthrax attacks that followed soon afterward. Nonetheless, in early November, the FBI held a press conference in which it reported that "based on case studies, handwriting and linguistic analysis, forensic data and other evidence, authorities do not believe at this point in their five-week investigation that Osama bin Laden's Al Qaeda network was behind the anthrax attacks."[29] (The possibility that a state was responsible did not even arise.) The FBI explained that a "lone individual" had produced the anthrax; that he had "some" science background; and that the spores could have been weaponized in a basement laboratory for as little as $2,500.[30] The Bureau's analysis suggested that the sender "is a non-confrontational person, at least in his public life. He lacks the personal skills necessary to confront others." And he "prefers being by himself more often than not."[31]

The "science" behind that assessment was extremely dubious; the FBI itself would later conclude that genuine expertise was necessary. Following this extraordinary press conference, one former Pentagon official remarked in dismay that the Bureau was unlikely to solve the case until it brought in the psychics.

Tracking Anthrax

SINCE THE FBI initially assumed that almost any American male (the profile excluded women) could have carried out the attack, the investigation focused on analysis of the anthrax itself—its organic properties as well as its processing, including its "slippery" coating—to determine where it might have come from. The result of that approach underscored just how difficult it is to use strictly forensic methods to fix responsibility for a biological terrorist attack.

It was quickly learned that all the anthrax was of the Ames strain (one of eighty-nine anthrax strains), so called because it was first isolated from a diseased cow near Ames, Iowa, in 1932. A nonvirulent form of this strain had been relatively widely distributed. A virulent form of Ames anthrax had been sent to army researchers in 1980, to use on animals for the purpose of developing a more effective anthrax vaccine. An analysis at Northern Arizona University in Flagstaff determined that the DNA of the anthrax used in the attacks was indistinguishable from the sample provided by the U.S. Army Medical Research Institute of Infectious Diseases (located outside Washington in Fort Detrick, Maryland).

However, the same strain had also been sent, for the same purpose, to Fort Detrick's British counterpart, the Chemical Defense Establishment at Porton Down (near Salisbury, England). Porton Down had shared the strain with a few other laboratories.

Questions began to emerge, moreover, regarding the security of anthrax samples even in Britain. The public health agency associated with Porton Down (called the Center for Applied Microbiology and Research) had been producing anthrax vaccine, and in 1993 it had been partly privatized through an agreement that licensed Porton Products, Ltd., to sell the vaccine.

But who was Porton Products? In fact, the company was owned (through an intermediary) by a shell company, which was in turn partly owned by Fuad El Hibri, an Arab of Lebanese origin who held joint German-U.S. citizenship. El Hibri had also purchased a U.S. company that produced anthrax vaccine, Michigan Biological Products Institute (formerly owned by the state of Michigan). Like Porton Down, MBPI had obtained the virulent Ames strain of anthrax in order to perfect its own vaccine.[32]

El Hibri's interest in the anthrax vaccine may have arisen from his commercial ties with Saudi Arabia. The Saudis were interested in obtaining an anthrax vaccine to counter Iraq's biological warfare capabilities, and the United States had refused to provide it.

As it turned out, Iraq itself had tried to obtain the Ames strain from Britain in the late 1980s. Although Baghdad was officially rebuffed in that effort, in view of the relatively lax controls over the transfer of pathogens like anthrax at that time, some experts believe that Iraq indeed managed to acquire the Ames strain. As one microbiologist who has studied Ames remarked, "The probability that they don't have the strain is near zero."[33]

Whoever had engineered the anthrax attacks on the United States would presumably have wanted to ensure that responsibility for the attacks could not be traced. It would have made perfect sense for the attacker to use an anthrax strain that had been distributed internationally, at least to some extent, and particularly a strain associated with the U.S. military program.

The FBI's Dead End

RICHARD SPERTZEL, in testimony before Congress, expressed strong disagreement with the FBI's conclusion that the anthrax letters came from a lone domestic source. Retired from the U.S. Army, Spertzel had served as the chief investigator on biological weapons for the U.N. Special Commission (UNSCOM), the commission initially responsible for finding and destroying Iraq's proscribed weapons. In his testimony, Spertzel explained that the quality of the anthrax in the letters to the senators was superior even to that developed in the U.S. biological weapons (BW) program, ended in 1969, or to that of the Soviet BW program.[34] He disputed the FBI profile, dismissing it as "a lot of hokum," and stated flatly, "I don't think that an individual is capable of doing it."[35]

Indeed, as the FBI would later conclude, making that anthrax required considerable expertise. Only a small number of people, whose identities were well known, had the requisite scientific backgrounds to be considered even possible candidates. The FBI had the capability of investigating each and every one of them. An intense, narrowly focused investigation of such an individual should have produced concrete evidence linking him to those attacks, if he were involved. (The FBI has fingered one scientist, Stephen Hatfill, as a "person of interest," but beyond establishing that Hatfill has a quirky background, the Bureau has produced no serious evidence to support its suspicions.)

Moreover, the FBI should be able to identify the facility in which the anthrax was made. To prevent anthrax spores from leaking into the outside air, such a facility would require highly specialized construction. Yet any contractor who had built a facility to the exacting airtight specifications required for a BW lab would presumably have contacted the FBI, if only for the $2 million reward. Alternatively, the terrorist-scientist could have purchased a "clean room," an esoteric item used by electronic firms—but, that too would have been easy enough for the FBI to trace.

To avoid the very serious problems that leaking anthrax spores would create (including the likelihood of discovery), a more ordinary facility could have been located in an extremely remote site. Yet to achieve the high degree of purity of tiny spores found in the anthrax sent to the senators, an industrial-grade centrifuge (costing $30,000 to $50,000) would have been necessary, and the considerable electricity required to run the centrifuge would have provided a red flag for investigators.

Thus, if that facility were indeed located in the United States, it would have to have been in an established laboratory—but the FBI could easily investigate established laboratories for this sort of rogue activity. In fact, it did and found nothing. That the FBI, by now, has not been able to discover the laboratory that produced the anthrax is because almost certainly it is located abroad.

In the end, the FBI's theory, that the anthrax spores were made by a lone American, has borne virtually no results. Indeed, the FBI has failed to produce a single piece of tangible evidence that the anthrax was manufactured in the United States, whether by a lone American or by anyone else.

Iraq's Weapons Program

THE DEFECTION OF HUSSEIN KAMIL, Saddam's son-in-law, in August 1995, marked a crucial turning point in understanding the threat that Iraq posed after the 1991 Gulf War. Kamil had supervised Iraq's unconventional weapons programs. Until he defected, it was assumed that most of Iraq's proscribed programs had been destroyed during the war, and that since the war UNSCOM had been slowly mopping up what remained. To the extent that Iraq was considered an international threat, the problem existed at some future point, after sanctions had been lifted, when Saddam would again be in the business of producing weapons of mass destruction.

Kamil's defection, however, made clear that Iraq was a very serious *present* danger. Concerned about what Kamil might reveal, Iraq now took the approach of trying to control the flow of information itself. In essence, Iraq now officially explained that *all* its proscribed weapons programs were much larger than it had ever acknowledged to UNSCOM; essentially, the materials that Iraqi officials had been turning over to UNSCOM were the least important elements of those programs.

The most disturbing revelations involved Iraq's nuclear and biological programs. The nuclear program appeared to be ongoing; the only component Iraq lacked to produce a bomb was the fissile material, which it might obtain on the international black market, or so UNSCOM concluded. As the United States went to war with Iraq in 2003, however, the nuclear program was still a future danger. The biological program was another story.

The Biological Weapons Program

IRAQ'S BIOLOGICAL WEAPONS program was the immediate threat. It was the program that Baghdad had taken the most pains to hide from

UNSCOM, both before and after Kamil's defection: Iraq did not even acknowledge it had a BW program until July 1995, more than four years after UNSCOM began its work in Iraq. Even then, the Iraqis concealed most of it—as became clear a month later, when Kamil defected.

Following Kamil's defection, Iraq acknowledged not only that it had produced anthrax and botulinum in far greater quantities than it had previously admitted, but also that these biological agents had been manufactured in a more advanced and lethal form than the Iraqis had acknowledged—i.e., they had been weaponized. Iraq also confessed to having worked with odd, dangerous, and exotic viruses, including ebola, as well as camelpox. UNSCOM, seeing no plausible reason for Iraq to work on a disease of camels, concluded that this was probably a cover for smallpox research.

Iraqi officials claimed to have unilaterally destroyed their BW stockpile. They could provide no documentation to support that claim, nor could they credibly account for the disposition of that material. UNSCOM did not believe them and remained convinced that the banned material was still in Iraq's possession.

Smallpox

ANTHRAX IS CERTAINLY FRIGHTENING, but smallpox—because it is contagious—is even more so. Smallpox could be used as an effective BW agent in its natural "wet" form, with little processing required. It could be distributed by aerosolizing it—i.e., spraying from any device that dis-perses droplets in the air. That could be something as small as a cologne atomizer, or as large as a crop duster. Indeed, the Iraqis developed, tested, and produced so-called drones of death, unmanned planes to which sprayers were attached to deliver chemical and biological agents—essentially, crop dusters intended for war.

On the eve of the war's start in 2003, most informed experts believed that Iraq possessed smallpox. There was less agreement, however, about whether Iraq had managed to weaponize it, by producing it in a dry, powdered form. Once weaponized, smallpox could be dispersed like weaponized anthrax.

Moreover, if Iraq did not yet have the capability to produce weaponized smallpox, it would have developed the capability with time. Given even more time, Iraq could probably develop a strain of smallpox genetically engineered to be resistant to the available vaccine.

UNSCOM's work in Iraq ended in December 1998. Iraqi officials had not yielded any of the biological stockpile they had acknowledged producing after Kamil's defection. Nor did they release any of it in late 2002 and early 2003, when the newly reconstituted inspections organization UNMOVIC[36] provided the regime its final chance to cooperate in destroying banned materials.

After the war, as U.S. forces searched for evidence of Iraq's proscribed weapons programs, it soon became apparent that much had been hidden, destroyed, or spirited away. However, relatively early on, two mobile BW labs were found, much like the mobile labs described by Secretary of State Colin Powell in his presentation to the U.N. Security Council in February 2003. Significantly, a date on the fermenting machine in one truck showed that it had been manufactured just one month before—in January 2003.[37] As Secretary of Defense Donald Rumsfeld earlier explained, "Iraq has designed its programs in a way that they can proceed in an environment of inspections . . . they are skilled at denial and deception."[38]

The Logic Behind the Letters?

HAD THE ANTHRAX terrorists wanted to inflict many more casualties, they could easily have done so. If, for example, the letter to Senator Daschle had not stated that it contained anthrax, whoever opened it would probably have paid little attention to the white powder it contained. The prophylactic application of antibiotics triggered by that warning almost certainly saved a significant number of lives, particularly given that once symptoms are advanced, anthrax is difficult to treat.[39]

Moreover, simple alternatives were available for dispersing the weaponized anthrax in such a way as to cause much more harm. Because the spores had been made "slippery," disseminating them did not require that they be aerosolized; any air current would have sufficed to disperse that material. A pound of anthrax, tossed into an enclosed space (such as the subway of a major city, or the ventilation system of a large building), could have produced a horrific number of fatalities, as many or more than the toll of September 11.

Nor would it have been difficult to produce anthrax that was resistant to antibiotics, such that no medical treatment would have been available. If grown in proximity to an antibiotic, most anthrax spores will be killed, but those few that survive can be cultured to produce anthrax that cannot be treated by that particular antibiotic. By mixing several such resistant batches (which have been developed by using various antibiotics), a "cocktail" of spores can be created such that no combination of medicines will be effective.

What, then, could have been the logic behind an anthrax attack seemingly designed to produce far fewer than the maximum possible number of casualties?

Iraqi Commentary

On September 27, 2001—shortly before news of the anthrax attacks began to break in the United States—*Babil*, an Iraqi newspaper owned by Saddam's son Uday, carried a piece in its "Hot Articles" section titled "Scenarios of a Coming War." Uday often writes in that section, and the column was very likely his own.

Speculating on how the United States would respond to the September 11 attacks, the paper anticipated a U.S. invasion of Afghanistan: "They cannot retreat; the sound of their gunfire and the rattle of their military equipment must be heard. . . . There will be an extensive U.S. strike against Afghanistan." The article went on to speculate about three alternative scenarios for the U.S., including "the Afghan quagmire." *Babil* continues:

> At this stage it is possible to turn to biological attack, where a small can, not bigger than the size of the hand, can be used to release viruses that affect everything. This attack might not necessarily be launched by the Islamists. It might be done by the Zionists *or any other party through an agent.* The viruses easily spread by air, and people are affected without feeling it [emphasis added].

Thus, as *Babil* explained, a prolonged U.S. war in Afghanistan could provide the occasion for *any other party* to attack the United States with biological weapons (and it would not be "the Zionists"). If U.S. authorities had jumped to the conclusion that al Qaeda was behind the anthrax attacks (as they were evidently meant to do), why—especially with the United States bogged down in Afghanistan and focused solely on the struggle with al Qaeda—would anyone think that an entirely extraneous third party, like Iraq, had become involved?

The FBI, of course, had come up with a completely different explanation for the anthrax letters—their elusive lone American—and the Iraqi regime appeared unhappy with that theory. In late October 2001, Saddam Hussein himself tried to suggest al Qaeda was behind the attacks, mocking the FBI's theory:

> We have heard in the news, recently, that American officials think that the source of anthrax is probably [in] the US itself. Is this conclusion, or information, just a tactic to divert the attention of those who were terrorized to hear that bin Laden is the source of the anthrax?[40]

Iraq has long had the ability to carry out biological terrorist attacks against the United States, but what it has always needed is a cover. Given Iraq's huge biological program (prior to March 2003, among the largest in the world); Saddam's attachment to it; and his avowed hatred for the United States, Iraq would invariably be a suspect after any major attack against American targets.

If, however, Iraq could cause the United States to believe that another party, like al Qaeda, were involved in biological terrorism against it, then Baghdad could carry out such terrorism under the cover of the widespread assumption that this was all al Qaeda's work.

Probing U.S. Assumptions

For Iraq, then, a crucial piece of information was to be gained in the aftermath of the anthrax attacks. Would the al Qaeda association indeed divert official U.S. attention away from Iraq's known biological weapons program?

The administration was aware that if it announced that al Qaeda was responsible for the anthrax letters it might be walking into a trap. As Dick Cheney's chief of staff warned, blaming al Qaeda might amount to giving a state sponsor a "bye"—carte blanche—to carry out further attacks.[41] The attacks of September 11 had already raised considerable speculation about Iraq's possible involvement, most significantly from senior U.S. officials including the secretary of defense. When the anthrax attacks occurred, Iraq's biological warfare capability came immediately under widespread suspicion, even though U.S. officials never publicly voiced their own suspicions.

If Iraq hoped to be able to implement a major bioterrorist attack with impunity, it presumably would need a more robust alternative scenario than the FBI's theory of a lone American scientist.

The anthrax letters are probably best understood as a test, a dry run. When this limited anthrax operation—with a relatively low number of casualties and an apparently simple delivery system—produced widespread speculation about Iraqi involvement, the lesson would have been

clear: any further biological attacks, particularly one that produced
large casualties, might well be attributed to Iraq. That would be particularly troublesome to Iraq in light of the unexpectedly rapid U.S. military
victory in Afghanistan. In the end, Saddam—barely, perhaps—failed to
develop the necessary cover for bioterrorism.

The President's Burden

AMERICA MAY WELL have dodged a bioterrorist bullet. The country was
(and remains) enormously vulnerable to biological terrorism, and Iraq
had developed the means to inflict a major bioterrorist attack. Yet Baghdad required a further crucial element: a plausible cover for terrorist
activity.

Following September 11, the sustained focus on al Qaeda's operation came uncomfortably close to providing Iraq just such a cover—and
the FBI appeared determined to provide yet another one, with its focus
on domestic terrorism. In the end, however, the question of the origins
of such finely milled, "teflonized" anthrax material proved too problematic to be swept aside.

In the fall of 2002, as President Bush prepared the nation for conflict, he repeatedly stressed the threat posed by Iraq's biological
weapons program. His most complete statement was made that October:

> In 1995, after several years of deceit by the Iraqi regime, the head of
> Iraq's military industries defected. It was then that the regime was
> forced to admit that it had produced more than 30,000 liters of
> anthrax and other deadly biological agents. The inspectors, however,
> concluded that Iraq had likely produced two to four times that
> amount. This is a massive stockpile of biological weapons that has
> never been accounted for and is capable of killing millions. . . . And
> of course, sophisticated delivery systems aren't required for a chemi-
> cal or biological attack. All that might be required are a small con-
> tainer and one terrorist or Iraqi intelligence operative to deliver it.

And that is a source of our urgent concern about Saddam Hussein's links to international terrorist groups.[42]

In the debate over war with Iraq, the opinion was widely voiced that such an action would be a dangerous "distraction" from the war on terrorism, as if Iraq were not part of the terrorist threat. Anthrax had been inflicted on American civilians, and in a sophisticated, weaponized form. It was well known that Iraq had pursued its biological weapons program with unparalleled determination. (Scarcely noticed, however, were the explicit references to its use that had appeared in the official Iraqi media.)

From this point of view, the greater danger was that an extended engagement in Afghanistan would distract the United States from the terrible threat presented by Iraq's biological weapons.

The problem arose more acutely on the eve of the Iraq war. There was every reason to believe that as Saddam went down, he would lash out at his enemies. After all, the Iraqis themselves had told UNSCOM (after Kamil defected) that during the 1991 Gulf War, they had taken out to remote airfields twenty-five SCUD missiles, tipped with biological warheads, and given their officers orders to fire them on targets in Israel and Saudi Arabia if the coalition marched on Baghdad and the regime fell.

As the United States prepared for war, thwarting such scenarios was an integral part of the military planning. However, that still left a great vulnerability on the home front: biological terrorism. On February 7, the nation's terrorist alert status was raised from yellow to orange ("high risk"). Reportedly, Khalid Shaikh Mohammed, mastermind of the September 11 attacks, was planning another attack (he would be arrested three weeks later).

Biological terrorism was prominent among the concerns of U.S. officials in these days. Shortly before the alert was issued, Vice President Dick Cheney convened an interagency group of counterterrorism experts, and pushed them on their preparations for a biological attack. "At the end of the day," the vice president warned, "we have to be able to ask ourselves: Did we do everything we could?"[43]

Already, flights in airspace around the nation's capital were restricted. Within a fifteen-mile radius, special restrictions applied to private planes flying below 18,000 feet: to file flight plans in advance and to maintain communications with ground air control as they passed through that space. When the country's alert status was raised, the restricted area was expanded to a thirty-mile radius. In addition, key subway stations were equipped with devices to detect a chemical or biological attack, and the Pentagon issued 80,000 masks (costing $150 each) to enable its employees to exit buildings, if they were attacked by chemical or biological agents.[44]

After the war, an intriguing item was found in Baghdad, outside the Iraqi intelligence headquarters: a section of a manual with details about how the U. S. Department of Homeland Security planned to defend the country against unconventional terrorism. It had been faxed to Baghdad from Iraq's U.N. mission in New York.[45]

Thankfully, no such attack occurred. But the potential danger was acute, and no one could have known whether it would in fact materialize. President Bush decided to confront Baghdad decisively in spite of the threat:

> The price of doing nothing exceeds the price of taking action. . . . The price of the attacks on America, the cost of the attacks on America on September the 11th were enormous. They were significant. And I am not willing to take that chance again.[46]

Few people understood that the dangers were even greater than the president's words suggested—not only the threat of terrorism that existed on the eve of war, but also the dangers that the war was intended to avert.

Chapter Two

DECEPTION AND
SELF-DECEPTION

O N SEPTEMBER 11, much of America was convinced that the
shock and horror we suffered that day had been the work of
Osama bin Laden and his al Qaeda network. Most commentators were drawing on their prior "knowledge" that the terrorist assaults of the past decade, starting with the 1993 bombing of the
World Trade Center, had been inflicted by Islamic militants, epito-
mized by the bin Laden organization.

A few, however, suspected the existence of another actor: not only al
Qaeda but also Saddam Hussein might have been involved in the attacks
of September 11. These observers too were drawing on their prior
understanding of the terrorist attacks of the past decade.[47]

Most notable was the order issued that afternoon by Donald Rumsfeld, instructing Pentagon intelligence agencies to search broadly for
information linking Iraq to the attacks rather than focus narrowly on al

Qaeda. Notes taken that day and leaked to the press a year later summarize the order: "Judge whether [intelligence] good enough hit S.H. [Saddam Hussein] at same time. Not only UBL [Usama bin Laden]."[48]

Rumsfeld's other strategic move that afternoon was to issue an order to prepare military plans to strike Iraq.

CBS News criticized these commands as inconsistent with the existing intelligence: a mere five hours after the attacks, they pointed out, all the intelligence pointed toward bin Laden. As any serious investigator must be aware, however, the most readily available intelligence may simply be the information that was intended for easy discovery. As we've seen with the anthrax case, the willingness of the American media to accept simple and convenient (if flawed) explanations is matched only by the willingness of self-interested U.S. government agencies to promote such explanations—even in the face of disturbing evidence to the contrary.

Masterpieces of Deception

DECEPTION IN WAR is a well-known force multiplier. If you can trick your enemy, you can fight him with fewer resources. Deception is probably as old as war itself—certainly as old as the Trojan War.

As every schoolchild once knew, when the Greek forces attacking the city of Troy were unable to breach its walls, they resorted to a trick. They built a large, handsome wooden horse and left it as a gift, before (apparently) sailing away. When the Trojans woke in the morning, they discovered this tribute left by the Greeks and triumphantly wheeled the wooden horse into the city. While the city slept that night, a band of Greek soldiers concealed in the wooden horse emerged to open the gates of Troy to their waiting army.

During World War II, the British and American allies ran a vast deception campaign against enemy forces.[49] In an operation known as the Double-Cross System, the British managed to gain control of the

Germans' entire spy network within Britain, disrupting their intelligence flow and feeding false information to the German high command.[50]

The key objective of this Anglo-American deception campaign was to make possible the extraordinarily dangerous mission of crossing the British Channel to enter occupied France. Prime Minister Winston Churchill understood clearly that the crucial event of the war would be the day when Allied forces would sail from Britain across the twenty-two-mile channel separating Britain from France. The most dangerous moment would be the actual landing, D day, when the disembarking troops would become an easy target for waiting enemy forces. There was no possibility of concealing those forces, or disguising the overall thrust of the Allied plan. The key to success would be "misdirection"—to throw the enemy off guard by providing false information (or "disinformation").

The Allies therefore devised an elaborate plan of deception to convince the Germans that the landing would occur at Pas de Calais, the point on the French coast closest to England. To aid the deception, an entire false army was created in East Anglia, just across the channel from Pas de Calais. Called the FUSAG (First U.S. Army Group), it was commanded by General George Patton, for whom the Germans had high regard. They would fully expect such a crucial maneuver to be led by someone of his caliber.

Yet the only thing that was real about the entire FUSAG enterprise was Patton himself. Patton was, indeed, in England, but the rest of his enormous force was an illusion. Intensive planning had gone into Operation Fortitude, devising the multiplicity of information that the German monitors were expected to seize on, in order to fix in the minds of the German high command the notion that the landing would take place two hundred miles away from the actual site.

False radio signals simulated the existence of a real army, discussing all the myriad details about which an actual military unit would communicate, from logistics planning to complaints about drunken soldiers. Carefully planted items in the British press announced the occasional engagement of an American soldier and his girlfriend, while American Forces Network broadcast songs to the troops, requested by fictitious women. Rubber tanks, rubber trucks, and plywood airplanes constituted the "equipment" of this force, with Hollywood crews enlisted to help construct it. And, of course, everything had been camouflaged—just ineffectively enough to reward German espionage efforts. (And, since the British controlled the airspace over their country, German reconnaissance planes saw only what they were meant to see.) Finally, Double-Cross spies were enlisted to feed the Berlin command false information, to reinforce the erroneous information they were gathering and "intercepting."

The plan worked with astounding success. The German command, and above all Hitler, now "knew" that Calais was the intended landing point. Even after the Normandy landing was already under way, the Germans dismissed it as a diversion, *relying on their prior "knowledge" in preference to the facts on the ground.* The real assault, they were convinced, was still to come—at Calais.

Even so, when the largest amphibious force in military history landed on the beaches of Normandy on June 6, 1944, they sustained brutally heavy casualties—twelve thousand men. That they were able to advance at all was attributable to the deception of Operation Fortitude. The Allies continued the disinformation campaign even after the landing, in order to put off as long as possible the moment when the Germans would recognize that this was indeed *the* landing, and the start of the campaign to retake Europe. The longer the Allies could keep the Germans under the impression that this had not been the "actual" crossing of the Channel, some significant number of German forces would remain pinned down, waiting for the expected attack.

How well did the ruse work? The head of Germany's most important intelligence office was still insisting, even *after* Normandy, that the major attack was yet to come. "Not a single unit of the First United States Army Group [the phony FUSAG]," he reported, "which comprises twenty-five large formations north and south of the Thames, has so far been committed."[51] For another five weeks, until mid-July, Hitler still expected the main Allied force to arrive at Pas de Calais, and there-fore held back crucial forces. Operation Fortitude proved to be the most successful deception campaign in military history.

The United States used a similar strategy in the 1991 war with Iraq. Centcom fed false information to the Iraqis to create the impression that the main thrust of the attack would be "straight up the middle," with U.S. forces supposedly preparing to march directly from Saudi Arabia into Kuwait. Accordingly, U.S. Army forces were based initially in the Wadi al Batin area, which comprises Kuwait's western border with Iraq as well as its southern frontier with Saudi Arabia.

But the real thrust of the U.S. attack was to be an innovative "Left Hook" (also termed the "Hail Mary," after the famous Notre Dame foot-ball play). In an operation that resembled Fortitude, the Army troops were discreetly moved far to the west, where they were reinforced by additional troops, totaling some 300,000 soldiers. While the Iraqis continued to expect an attack from Kuwait, the actual offensive came as a flanking attack through the forbidding Iraqi desert.

As U.S. forces at Wadi al Batin stole westward, small units or "deception cells" were left behind to create the impression that nothing had changed. False radio signals were broadcast in code, knowing that the Iraqis would continue to perform "traffic analysis" of signals (to glean information from such factors as the frequency, time, and length of communications). "Visual signatures" were produced using smoke generators, while "loudspeaker teams along the border would broadcast tape recordings of tanks and trucks repositioning" themselves under cover of darkness. There were also dummy helicopters and Humvees, plus "elaborate tank decoys costing some $4,000 each"—which actually emitted the infrared heat signature of an M1 Abrams tank.[52]

Like the army, the marines employed deception to conceal their positions and lines of attack, engineered by a deception team named Task Force Troy (symbolized, with marine panache, by a wooden camel on wheels). Their deception on land was complemented by deception at sea. They conducted exercises landing large numbers of troops, first in

Saudi Arabia and then in Oman, making sure that the maneuvers received extensive press coverage. The result was that the Iraqis shifted several divisions to the Kuwaiti beaches.

The coordinated campaign of false information was accompanied by a rigorous block on real information. All commercial satellites were prohibited from flying over the war zone, lest Iraq obtain pictures showing the true U.S. positions. Information about those positions was also kept from Syria, which, although formally part of the coalition, was not entirely trusted.

The formal term of art for such a tactic is Denial and Deception, or D&D. *Denial* refers to depriving an opponent of accurate information; *deception* means feeding him false information. CIA training includes training in practicing as well as defending against deception. In addition to learning the history of military deception, intelligence analysts learn to be aware of their own prior assumptions by matching wits with a professional magician—who invariably proves to students that they too can indeed be fooled.

Self-Deception: The Need *Not* to Know

IN REAL LIFE, of course, deception plays out differently from the way it does in a magic show. Instead of a moment of "aha!" there is the gradual recognition of a disturbing possibility. And instead of the rueful appreciation of a well-executed trick, there is the unpleasant sensation of having been made a dupe.

People's egos and career concerns almost inevitably come into play, and those who have been duped resist admitting it as long as possible— and sometimes longer. As Admiral Hyman Rickover warned trenchantly, we should not love our opinions like our children. Still, the phenomenon is common enough, not only among everyday citizens but also among career bureaucrats of the U. S. government.

So the deceiver quickly finds an unlikely ally in the deceived. At a certain point—once self-deception has kicked in—the effort of concealment becomes almost superfluous.

The Israeli commission that investigated intelligence failures prior to the 1973 Yom Kippur War blamed those mistakes on what they called "the concept": the rigid prior "knowledge" on the part of key Israeli officials that prevented them from recognizing the preparations made by Egypt and Syria to launch a surprise attack on Israel, although those preparations should have been evident enough to an alert observer. The American term of art for the same phenomenon is "mind-set." As a retired CIA official explained, "One looks at an evolving situation not with wide open eyes, but with eyes that are too slanted to let one appreciate what is really happening—until it is too late. Then the [internal] cover-ups begin [emphasis added]."[53]

Self-deception has a characteristic path and momentum of its own: misconstruing early evidence; then actively defending against new information; and ultimately undermining further efforts at investigation. At this point, the most widely shared feeling among the deceived may indeed be the need *not* to know.

Deception in the September 11 Attacks?

DENIAL AND DECEPTION is an established field of study in military as well as intelligence circles, whose officers are thoroughly schooled in such historical cases of successful military deception. Five hours after the September 11 assaults, when Secretary Rumsfeld ordered his staff to focus on Iraq as well as al Qaeda, he, at least, must have done so with full knowledge of the principles of deception.

But what kind of information would have been available to U.S. authorities so soon after the attacks? Very likely, the bulk of the hard intelligence they possessed would have been "low-hanging fruit"—"information" they were *intended* to have.

By the afternoon of September 11, the CIA was already able to report that the names of at least two suspected al Qaeda operatives were on the passenger manifests of the hijacked airplanes. But al Qaeda members have access to false passports and other identity documents; the investigation would soon reveal how easily fraudulent identifications could be obtained in the United States. To get a Virginia identification card (and then a Virginia driver's license), the state required only that the applicant be vouched for by another resident of Virginia; seven of the nineteen hijackers had Virginia identification cards. The identities of the hijackers could easily have been hidden, in this carefully planned operation—and perhaps some were, as we'll see.

George Tenet, the director of the CIA, speculated later that the inclusion of the two "tainted" al Qaeda operatives (that is, operatives whose connection to al Qaeda was known to the United States) was a glitch in the terrorists' operation.[54] But this may have been an *intended* glitch. In 1993, when several culprits in the World Trade Center bombing were just as readily discovered, the "lucky break" served as a warning flag to the chief of the New York investigation, New York FBI Director Jim Fox: these arrests were entirely too easy.

In late June and early July of 2001, U.S. intelligence had intercepted a series of communications suggesting that al Qaeda was planning a major attack. U.S. analysts expected the assault to occur overseas, possibly around the Fourth of July. As the summer progressed and nothing happened, the assumption was that those plans had been disrupted or aborted.

Meanwhile, the September 11 conspirators had managed to maintain virtually complete operational security.

How was that feat possible, given that the flow of al Qaeda communications that summer had been so readily transparent? The most likely explanation is that alternative communications channels were available, and thus the intercepted communications may well have been from channels believed to be compromised. After September 11, accordingly, "some U.S. officials speculate[d] that the communications traffic was purposefully devised to throw analysts off the trail of the real operation."[55]

But if disinformation was part of the al Qaeda strategy, was there perhaps more than one dimension to that strategy? In addition to a calculated misdirection sending the United States to look for terrorists in one place rather than another—abroad rather than at home—the information may also have been calculated to direct the United States to look at one culprit rather than another: at al Qaeda, not Iraq.

In the days following the September 11 attacks, it was discovered that two important exchanges among bin Laden's lieutenants on September 10 had been intercepted by the National Security Agency (the Pentagon agency responsible for electronic eavesdropping). One said, "The big match is about to begin." The second said, "Tomorrow is zero hour."[56] Was that chatter also intended for American ears?

Who Carried Out the Hijacking?

FBI INVESTIGATORS WERE under tremendous pressure to produce immediate answers following the attacks. Just three days afterward, the FBI released the names of the nineteen hijackers (taken mainly from the airplane passenger manifest lists), along with whatever personal details they had managed to assemble, such as date of birth and place of residence. The public was asked to provide whatever information they had.

But the FBI could not know with certainty that the individuals it had publicly identified were in fact the men who had hijacked the planes. Might not some of the hijackers have used fraudulent or stolen identities when buying their tickets and for boarding the airplanes? John Martin, retired chief of the Justice Department's internal security section, cautioned, "This operation had tremendous security, and using false names would have been part of it. . . . The hijackers themselves may not have known the others' true names."[57]

And, as it turned out, five of those identified by the FBI were not in fact hijackers; the names were common Arabic names. Moreover, the FBI had not taken into account that in Saudi Arabia, the apparent homeland of fifteen of the nineteen hijackers, an individual uses three or even four names: his own name, his father's name, and a tribal name, sometimes also inserting the name of a favored ancestor between the second and third names.

The five individuals falsely identified as terrorists were quite understandably outraged; but the very fact of their being alive was sufficient demonstration that the FBI was mistaken and that they were in fact innocent. Subsequently, four families with sons with similar names stepped forward, acknowledging that the young men were missing; some had gone to fight in Chechnya and not been heard of recently.

Who was the fifth wrongly identified hijacker?

Airline manifests showed that Abdul Aziz al-Omari had boarded a flight to Boston along with Mohammed Atta, and that the two men then transferred to American Airlines Flight 11, which was soon to hit the North Tower of the World Trade Center in the first of the unimaginable events of that terrifying day.

Al-Omari had an engineering degree from Denver University in Colorado. His passport was stolen when his apartment was burgled in 1995, as he reported at the time. On the day the World Trade Center was hit, al-Omari was in fact at his desk in Riyadh, working at the Saudi telecommunications authority. It was never made clear just who the individual was who had obtained a Saudi passport and then a U.S. visa under his name.

A noted writer on intelligence affairs, Edward Jay Epstein, has coined the phrase "The Jeddah Ciphers" to refer to another aspect of the confusion over the hijackers' identities.[58] Thirteen of the hijackers had obtained visas from the U.S. consulate in Jeddah, which used to run an expedited application process known as Visa Express. The hijackers' applications had been filled out sloppily, and key pieces of information were missing, such as the name of the spouse of a hijacker (in fact, al-Omari) who claimed to be married. The fact that these flawed applications were approved indicates that the applicants were subject to no real scrutiny.[59]

It is possible that these identities are in fact accurate and, with the exception of al-Omari, that these were indeed the individuals who hijacked the airplanes. But it is equally possible that at least some of these identities were stolen: that the real individuals had previously perished in the no-man's-land where they had gone off to fight (whether in Afghanistan or in Chechnya), and that someone else had assumed their names. This would have been an easy way to disguise the participation in the plot of some individuals who were *not* Islamic militants but who had the skills necessary for its execution. It is unlikely, however, that we will ever know the facts of the case.

The Pilot: Hani Hanjour?

HANI HANJOUR IS SAID to be the individual who piloted American Airlines Flight 77 into the Pentagon. Unlike the other hijackers, Hanjour had visited the United States long before the attacks. In the mid-1990s, when Hanjour was working on his family's farm in Taif, he decided he wanted to study in the United States to become an airplane pilot. His brother, Abdul Rahman, eleven years older, ran an export business that brought him regularly to the United States; it was he who made arrangements for Hanjour's studies.

Hanjour is described by those who knew him at that time as very shy, introverted, and religious. Initially, in the spring of 1996, Hanjour stayed with friends of his brother, Susan and Adnan Khalil, in Miramar, Florida. They remembered him as socially inept, with poor English and bad hygiene. Hanjour stayed with the Khalils for a month before moving to California, where he took a course in intensive English. In September, he attended one brief (half-hour) class at the Sierra Academy of Aeronautics, but never returned. The vice president of Sierra speculated that he was intimidated by the school's two-year training program requirements, or by its $35,000 price tag, or both.[60]

The next month, Hanjour showed up in Arizona and enrolled at a flight school in Scottsdale, Arizona, called Cockpit Resource Management. During three months of instruction he proved a "weak student" who was "wasting our resources," according to CRM's owner, Duncan K. M. Hastie. Hanjour left, but returned for a few weeks in December 1997. Over the next three years he would call Hastie about twice a year, asking for more instruction. As Hastie recalled, "He wanted to be an airplane pilot. That was his stated goal. That's why I didn't allow him to come back. I thought, 'You're never going to make it.' "[61]

Hanjour somehow managed to obtain a pilot's license in April 1999. In February 2001, he appeared at Pan Am International Flight Academy in Scottsdale, Arizona, seeking certification to fly a commercial aircraft. His instructors made a serious effort to help him, but he was a poor student, and they ultimately told him he would not qualify for the advanced certificate. The Pan Am instructors judged that Hanjour would be a safety hazard at the controls of a commercial aircraft.[62]

About a month before the September 11 attacks, in the second week of August, Hanjour arrived in the Washington, D.C., area, still seeking flight lessons. At the Freeway Airport in Bowie, Maryland, he had three sessions in a single-engine plane, after which the school decided Hanjour was not ready to rent a plane by himself. Following the September 11 attacks, a former employee at Pan Am International told the *New York Times*, "I'm still to this day amazed that he could have flown [the plane] into the Pentagon. He could not fly at all."[63]

Was the hapless Hanjour the pilot of American Airlines Flight 77? If not, who was it that flew the plane with such accuracy? One possibility is that, of the five identified hijackers on that plane, one was traveling under a stolen name—someone with real flying experience, whose true identity it was important to conceal.

The Third Man

IN THE LATE AFTERNOON of September 8, just three days before the attacks, Mohammed Atta, the leader of the hijackers in the United

States, was seen at Shuckum's, a sports bar in Hollywood, Florida, in the company of two other men. One was Marwan al-Shehhi, Atta's friend and the presumed pilot of United Flight 175, which crashed into the South Tower of the World Trade Center. Al-Shehhi drank five screwdrivers made with a premium Russian vodka; Atta had cranberry juice and an order of hot wings, and played video games. A third companion, as yet unidentified, drank rum and Coke.[64] Who was the unidentified man?

The only fact that emerges clearly is that the "readily available evidence" of the hijackers' identities does not tell us as much as is commonly thought—and certainly does not address the question of whether any other party was involved, along with al Qaeda. We do know that at least one of the hijackers, and possibly several others, used a stolen identity. We know that one of the supposed pilots was incapable of flying a plane. In such a case, the phrase "all available evidence" is close to meaningless. We are wiser if we acknowledge that we simply do not know precisely who was on board those airplanes, or who might have helped to put them there.

The Handling of Terrorist Attacks in the 1990s

THE FEBRUARY 26, 1993, bombing of the World Trade Center was the occasion of a radical departure in America's understanding of terrorism. Prior to that attack, it had been assumed that major terrorist assaults on U.S. targets were state sponsored; the list of Middle Eastern states sponsoring terrorism included Iran, Iraq, Libya, and Syria (Sudan would soon be added). Starting with the World Trade Center bombing, however, a radically different understanding emerged. Terrorism was now thought to be carried out by "loose networks," of which al Qaeda became the most significant; and the assumption spread that these networks were *not* supported by states.[65]

In my book *Study of Revenge*,[66] which first appeared in October 2000, I disputed that thesis, arguing that the nature of terrorism had not changed. States, particularly Iraq, were still involved, but they were now taking innovative steps to hide their role. An important source for that book was Jim Fox, who as head of New York FBI had directed the investigation into the 1993 World Trade Center bombing. He believed that Iraq was behind the bombing and that it had worked with Islamic militants to conceal its hand.

This is not the place to review that argument. It is useful, however, to highlight what Fox believed to be elements of deception in that attack, because they resemble in some respects possible elements of deception in the September 11 attacks. One deception flag, for Fox, was the swiftness and ease of several arrests that followed the bombing. On March 4, just six days after the attack, a twenty-six-year-old Palestinian named Mohammed Salameh was detained by the FBI; having been left without an airplane ticket or money to buy one, he had actually gone back to the Jersey City Ryder rental agency to collect his deposit *on the van that had blown up with the bomb.* His arrest led to the detention of two associates, also Islamic militants. Thus, as in the case of the September 11 assaults, the most readily available information immediately after the 1993 bombing implicated Islamic militants.[67]

Fox's background was in counterintelligence. And his experience told him that these arrests were altogether too easy, particularly given the sophistication of the attack itself: a massive bomb, designed to topple one tower onto the other. The ease of the arrests suggested to Fox a conspiracy masterminded by another party, with Salameh and his friends intended to walk into the arms of U.S. authorities and take the blame.

There were of course others involved in the attack, as time and further investigative efforts would reveal. Abdul Rahman Yasin, an Iraqi-American born in the United States, had lived most of his life in Baghdad and returned to the United States in September 1992, six months before the bombing. The same day that Salameh was arrested, Yasin was picked up by New Jersey FBI in a sweep of sites associated with him. (Salameh had used Yasin's phone number on the Ryder rental application.) Yasin was quite helpful and cooperative, and the New Jersey FBI allowed him to leave their office that night. The next day Yasin left the country for Jordan, where he stopped at the Iraqi embassy in Amman before traveling to Baghdad, where he remained. (In the spring of 2002, he was interviewed in Baghdad by CBS's *60 Minutes*.)

New Jersey FBI considered Yasin a very useful confidential informant they had discovered themselves.[68] Jim Fox of New York FBI, however, believed that Yasin was a conspirator, and that he had probably been feeding misleading information to the FBI. In August 1993, the U.S. Attorney's office in New York decided the matter at least partly in support of Fox's view, and Yasin was indicted for his role in the plot; oddly, however, the U.S. government never (until 2003) made a public issue of Baghdad's harboring an indicted World Trade Center bomber.

As the investigation into the 1993 bombing proceeded, a far more complex picture of the assault emerged. The FBI learned that the mastermind was an individual who had entered the U.S. in September 1992 on an Iraqi passport in the name of Ramzi Yousef. He was known among the New York area militants as "Rashid, the Iraqi," but when he fled on the night of the bombing it was under yet another identity, a Pakistani passport issued in the name of Abdul Basit Karim.

Yousef was ultimately arrested in early 1995, as a result of a botched attempt to bomb a dozen U.S. airplanes in the Philippines. From what is known of Yousef's life in the Philippines, he does not appear to be an Islamic militant: he and his colleagues frequented nightclubs with their girlfriends, drank alcohol, and generally took part in Manila nightlife. One of Yousef's coconspirators in that plot, Khalid Shaikh Mohammed, fled the Philippines and remained a fugitive until March 2003. After they occurred, Mohammed was ultimately identified as the mastermind of the terrible attacks on September 11.

But who in fact are these men? Mohammed is said to be Yousef's maternal uncle, but there is reason to question the identities of both, as will be discussed in chapter 7. Are they Islamic militants or something else—another network, or state-sponsored agents?

Trial and Error

DURING THE 1990s, the United States treated terrorism primarily as a law enforcement issue, with the focus on the arrest and conviction of individual perpetrators. Law enforcement and counterintelligence are entirely different fields, with very different aims and analytic approaches; the nature of law enforcement, with its focus on the actions of individuals, makes it dangerously susceptible to systematic deception. And when the superficial appearance of events came to be accepted as the official U.S. account of the terrorist attack, a more far-reaching misunderstanding developed.

A prosecutor's job is very narrow. His goal is to secure a conviction, and perhaps a maximal penalty, for an individual indicted and arrested for a crime. The question of whether a state was involved in any given assault is not really relevant to that task; in any case, it is likely to be given very low priority. Gil Childers, lead prosecutor in the trial of Mohammed Salameh et al., explained the circumstances he faced as follows: the judge had set an early trial date in September, little more than six months after the World Trade Center bombing. When the trial began, Childers was still sorting through the evidence against each defendant—massive and complex as it was. Whether or not Iraq was involved in the attack was a question he had no time to consider.[69] Moreover, one could also suggest that the question of whether one or another defendant had actually been set up to be arrested was not only irrelevant but also potentially damaging to aspects of the prosecution's case.

The question of responsibility for major acts of terrorism cannot be viewed narrowly as a matter of law enforcement. Such an approach is inevitably distorting—and ineffectual: the September 11 attacks occurred in spite of an unprecedented series of terrorist arrests, trials, and convictions that began in 1993. Major acts of terrorism, particularly if they are carried out by foreigners, must be handled with due attention to overarching national security concerns, including possible state sponsorship. The objective has to be—as President Bush vowed—no more 9/11s.

U.S. policy on one important aspect of this issue has apparently shifted. Apart from Zacarias Moussaoui, who is to be tried in a U.S. federal court,[70] others involved in the September 11 attacks have been treated as enemy combatants.

Ramzi bin al-Shibh had repeatedly tried (and failed) to enter the United States in an apparent attempt to become a hijacker himself, and then sent money to the hijackers from Germany; Khalid Shaikh Mohammed is recognized as the mastermind of the attacks. These individuals were not, upon their detention, read their Miranda rights, flown back to the United States, and immediately given a lawyer in preparation for a criminal trial, as repeatedly happened with such arrests during the Clinton years. Bin al-Shibh and Mohammed have been kept abroad, to be interrogated to obtain information vital to rounding up other terrorists and helping to prevent another attack. In due course, a U.S. military tribunal will decide their fate.

Information Barriers and Blinders

IT IS IMPORTANT to understand how labeling terrorism a law enforcement issue affected the flow of information among the bureaucracies of the U. S. government. Under a law in effect until the fall of 2001, once a grand jury had been convened to investigate a terrorist attack, law enforcement officials involved in that investigation were precluded from sharing the information they gathered with the national security bureaucracies. That restriction was a post-Watergate reform; it was ended by the antiterrorism legislation passed following the September 11 assaults.

This meant that the CIA in 1993 was engaged in developing a pivotal assessment of the new anti-U.S. terrorism *without having access to any of the information gathered by the primary (FBI) investigators*, information that was far more relevant to understanding the World Trade Center bombing than the intelligence the CIA managed to obtain abroad. The lack of solid information was not apparently terribly troubling to the agency, and the theory of the new, stateless terrorism was readily embraced within the CIA, particularly by its Counter Terrorism Center (CTC).

The CTC in fact showed little initiative in obtaining those FBI materials that were legally available. By law, the results of the FBI investigation must be made available to legal defense teams. During a trial, both prosecution and defense may introduce into evidence any parts of the FBI investigation that help to make their case, thus entering much of the FBI investigation into the public record. Once the World Trade Center bombing trial began—and certainly when it ended, in March 1994—the CTC could have obtained the evidence from the trial, which consisted of thousands of pages of documents relating to the attack (phone records, passports, etc.). Any competent journalist involved in a major inquiry would investigate such a public record, but in fact no one at the CTC actually went to that trouble.

In December 1994, I briefed a handful of people from the intelligence community, including two members of the CTC, on the World Trade Center bombing, drawing on information from the trial as well as from interviews in New York. One of the CTC agents, who was responsible for following Islamic militants in Pakistan and Afghanistan, told me that he thought he had located Ramzi Yousef in the region, and that he had been unable to obtain Yousef's fingerprints from the FBI. He was delighted to learn that I could actually give him a copy of the prints that had been submitted as trial evidence; their very existence was evidently news to him.

The other official from the CTC who had been assigned to deal with the World Trade Center bombing simply sat silently through the presentation, staring at the ground. When I had finished, he sniffed that he would have wanted "better information." I understood subsequently that he had not previously seen the material I presented, let alone all the actual documents I had carefully reviewed. Gil Childers later expressed the opinion that I had done work that the U.S. government should have done.[71]

Nor did the situation improve with time, at least in regard to the critical 1993 bombing—critical, because it is considered to mark the start of the "new" terrorism. Before September 11, some senior officials in the newly elected Bush administration began to ask the CIA questions about various terrorist attacks, including that bombing. The phone records of Mohammed Salameh (introduced as evidence at the trial) show that he made forty-two calls to Iraq between June 10 and July 9, 1992, a crucial period in the early development of the conspiracy. The records were sent to the agency, with a request for an explanation of what they might mean. The agency replied that the FBI should be asked, as it was the FBI's information.

The claim, made by the CIA and others, that a new kind of "stateless" terrorism had come into being was based on a radically incomplete consideration of the available information. Moreover, it was developed under circumstances—with terrorist activity addressed mainly in the courtroom—in which the responsible officials were most likely to fall for a strategic deception.

Before long, the CIA had become unshakably attached to this radically erroneous understanding of terrorist activity. Over many years the agency ignored, and even suppressed, substantial evidence regarding Iraq's possible role in at least two major acts of terrorism against the United States: the 1993 bombing of the World Trade Center, and the 1995 plot against U.S. passenger aircraft. This pattern of self-deception would have critical implications for the agency's response to the attacks of September 11.

Chapter Three

BUREAUCRATIZING
THE INTELLIGENCE

I N T H E W E E K S after 9/11 there was a great deal of speculation
about Iraq's role in launching the attacks, some of it responding
to statements coming from Iraq itself. On September 12, Saddam
Hussein crowed, "The United States reaps the thorns that its
rulers have planted in the world." Alone among the world's heads of
state, Hussein was asserting that the United States had essentially gotten what it deserved. During the following week, he issued what Iraqi
television described as two "open letters" to the American people.

Saddam's "letters," read by the television announcer, reiterated
that America had brought on these attacks by its own actions, including
actions done to Iraq.

We say to the American peoples, what happened on September 11,
2001, should be compared to what their government and their armies

are doing in the world. . . . More than one and a half million Iraqis have died because of the blockade imposed by America and some Western countries, in addition to the tens of thousands who have died or were injured in the military action perpetrated by America. If you replay the images of the footage taken by the Western media themselves of this destruction, you will see that they are not different from the images of the two buildings hit by the Boeing airplanes.[72]

According to the Iraqi letter, there was a point to the September 11 attacks:

Americans should feel the pain they have inflicted on other peoples, so that when they suffer, they will find the right solution and the right path.[73]

As time went on, other information emerged to support the impression given by Saddam Hussein in these statements: that Iraq was linked to the attacks of September 11.

The Salman Pak Training Camp

FOLLOWING THE SEPTEMBER 11 assaults, two Iraqi defectors came forward to divulge that Iraqi intelligence had been training non-Iraqi Arab volunteers at Salman Pak, a sophisticated terrorism training camp located some twenty-five kilometers southeast of Baghdad. Most significantly, part of the Salman Pak operation included on-the-ground training in hijacking airplanes.

The two defectors appeared on a PBS *Frontline* investigation, "Gunning for Saddam." Jamal al-Qurairy had been a security officer at Salman Pak. Al-Qurairy reported that groups of non-Iraqi Arabs, Islamic militants, would come to train at the camp for approximately five months at a time. He saw one group in 1995 and another group of about forty men in 2000:

This basically was surprising because the fact that they are of different nationalities but they were mixed in the training. And the fact that this unit was under the direct supervision and control of the Iraqi Intelligence Service, which is highly unusual. . . . The other point is the fact that we don't have Ba'ath Party members in some of the countries that we have individuals being trained, like Saudi Arabia or Afghanistan. So I found that very peculiar. And the fact that the training was concentrated on a plane made it even stranger as far as I was concerned. The only time I saw them was when they were near the plane. I can't see them when they are somewhere else.[74]

Sabah Khodada, the other defector, had been a captain in the Iraqi army from 1982 to 1992 and later worked for the Division of Special Operations (Directorate M-21 of Iraqi intelligence). The DSO ran the terrorist training camp at Salman Pak.

The camp is huge. And the locations for the training are far from [where] anybody can see them from the outside. But even when we have visitors, even at the level of a minister, or even higher [the visitor will] be driven in the camp inside very specific type of a vehicle. They will sit on the backseat . . . in addition to the shaded windows, they will have to pull down curtains and they snap those curtains on the bottom, to make sure nobody can see anything outside this vehicle while they're driven around. . . . At the very highest level, they cannot see this training.[75]

Khodada taught recruits how to use machine guns, pistols, and other weapons, in what he called "typical infantry training." Other officers, from Iraqi intelligence, provided more unconventional instruction: hijacking airplanes, assassinations, sabotage, etc.

I saw them getting trained on this kind of situations where security will not allow you to get weapons into the plane—then what you need to do is to use all available methods and very advanced terrorizing method. . . .

These methods are used to terrorize the passengers and the crew of the plane. They are even trained how to use utensils for food, like forks and knives provided in the plane. . . . They are trained how to plant horror within the passengers by doing such actions. Even pens and pencils can be used for that purpose, they were trained. They can do it, and they can overcome any plane because they are very well physically trained, and they are very strong, and they can do it. They can overtake a plane in a very efficient manner. . . .

Training will include the way they would sit in the plane, how they enter the plane, provided they got the right documents from the top levels of Iraqi Intelligence, such as passports. . . . They will, for example, sit in two's, and they will assign who will sit to the right of the other guy, and who will sit to the other side. Two will sit in the front, two will sit in the back, and two will sit, for example, in the middle. They are trained to jump all at one time, and make a declaration that "We are going to take over the plane. And nobody [move], don't move, don't make any moves."

They will probably use a pencil or a pen, or even sunglasses or prescription glasses. Somebody will hold the crew members of the plane from their chins upward tightly, and you will pull it on his neck. He will think you are going to slaughter him and kill him. Including [sic] in this training is terrorizing by making very, very loud noises and screaming all over the plane. That will take over the planned horror, and will terrorize the plane, including the crew.[76]

Khodada also described a meeting with Saddam:

On January 1, 1996, we all met with Saddam personally. And he told us we have to take revenge from America. Our duty is to attack and hit American targets in the Gulf, in the Arab world, and all over the world. He said that openly. When you volunteer to become Saddam's fighter . . . they will tell you the purpose of your volunteer[ing] is to attack American targets and American interests, not only in Iraq, not only in the Gulf, [but] all over the world, including Europe and America.[77]

Khodada even sketched a map of the Salman Pak site for *Frontline*, showing an airplane parked in the southwest corner of the complex.[78]

After the *Frontline* show aired, a private company called Space Imaging, which operates the Ikonos civilian surveillance satellite, examined its satellite photo archives and discovered a photo of Salman Pak taken on April 25, 2000. The photo showed a solitary airplane, parked nowhere near a runway or an airport, in an area known to be controlled by Iraqi intelligence. The photo was "a close match," they reported, to the map of the facility sketched by Khodada. As *Aviation Week & Space Technology*, among others, observed, that point lent credence to the defector's story.[79]

It is necessary, of course, to be on one's guard regarding sources' reliability, and the accounts of defectors invariably raise questions about their unknowable motives. At the same time, it is self-defeating to raise the bar so high that the only admissible evidence would be an eyewitness report by (for example) a journalist—who cannot hope to be granted access. The corroboration provided by Space Imaging for what was *the* most crucial detail of Khodada's account certainly should have weighed against the tendency to dismiss any and all evidence provided by defectors.

Former CIA Director James Woolsey summed up the case in an interview for *The New Yorker:* "At Salman Pak we know there were Islamist terrorists training to hijack airplanes in groups of four or five with short knives. I mean, hello? If we had seen after December 7, 1941, a fake American battleship in a lake in northern Italy, and a group of Asian pilots training there, would we have said, 'Well, you can't prove that they were Japanese' "?[80]

Khodada's own sense of frustration was equally apparent:

I assure you, and I'm going to keep assuring you, that all these things are obvious. I don't know why you don't see it. When we were in Iraq, Saddam said all the time, even during the Gulf War, "We will take our revenge at the proper time." He kept telling the people, "Get ready for our revenge."

We saw people getting trained to hijack airplanes, to put explosives. How could anybody not think this is not done by Saddam? Even the grouping, those groups were divided into five to six people in the group. How about the training on planes? Some of these groups were taken and trained to drive airplanes at the School of Aviation, northern [sic] of Baghdad. . . . Everything coincides with what's happening.[81]

The official U.S. response, however, was cautious, verging on dismissive. "Although U.S. officials acknowledge terrorists were trained at Salman Pak, they say it is unlikely that these activities were related to the September 11 attacks," *Frontline* reported. Similarly, individual sources at the CIA would later dismiss the entire story. They began by separating the two sets of information, as if it were insignificant that the map Khodada had drawn of Salman Pak closely resembled the satellite photo from Space Imaging. Agency officials dismissed the defectors' statements as unreliable, on the a priori grounds that the defectors were in any case opposed to Saddam. And they suggested that the Iraqis might have been using the airplane just as the U.S. agencies would: for *counter*hijacking training.

That indeed was also the Iraqi claim, but it is difficult to fathom how any informed person could reach such a conclusion.[82] The CIA has a well-known tendency to ignore or dismiss information from "open" sources, preferring to rely on its own intelligence operation. (This appears to be the agency's particular version of the well-known bureaucratic response of dismissal: "Not Invented Here.") But the dismissal was part of a larger pattern, on the part of at least some agency officials, of systematically denying any evidence of an Iraqi connection with terrorist activity, even in those cases (as discussed below) involving evidence officially cleared by the agency itself.

Washington Post columnist Jim Hoagland must be given the last word on the controversy. "Imagine that Saddam Hussein has been offering terrorist training and other lethal support to Osama bin Laden's al Qaeda for years. You can't imagine that? Sign up over there. You can be a Middle East analyst for the Central Intelligence Agency."[83]

In the third week of the war against Iraq, a marine unit managed to secure Salman Pak, meeting little resistance, and indeed uncovered evidence of a terrorist training program. According to Central Command spokesman Brigadier General Vincent Brooks, "The nature of the work being done by some of those people we captured . . . give[s] us the impression that there is terrorist training that was conducted at Salman Pak."

> At a large intersection, on one corner there was a fire truck, and another corner was a large abandoned passenger plane, bleached by the sun, its tail broken off. The marines inferred it was used to practice hijacking. There was also a ravaged double-decker passenger bus, speedboats and green train cars. Storehouses were filled with gas masks.[84]

The Czech Connection

SOON AFTER THE ASSAULTS of September 11, Czech authorities reported that Mohammed Atta, the leader of the hijackers in America, had previously traveled to Prague—and that, on at least one occasion, he had met with an Iraqi intelligence agent there.

The Czechs had had good reason to watch the Iraqi embassy in Prague. In 1995, Radio Free Europe moved from Germany to the Czech Republic, at the invitation of Czech President Václav Havel. In October 1998, RFE began broadcasting to Iraq. But Czech officials grew worried about what Saddam's reaction to the broadcasts might be—and they soon learned they had good reason for concern. In late 1998, when Jabir Salim, a consul at the Iraqi embassy in Prague, defected to the British Secret Service, he revealed that he had been given $150,000 to recruit terrorists who would not be traceable to Iraq.[85] The objective was to bomb the RFE building, situated in the center of Prague along a heavily trafficked boulevard. In March 2003, Jiri Ruzek, director of the Czech Secret Service, affirmed in a BBC interview, "We have found out that it was decided to halt [the RFE] broadcasts to Iraq . . . and we have managed to obtain certain scenarios which were drawn up for this case. . . . One of the scenarios was also to carry out a terrorist attack."[86]

In a review conducted following September 11, Czech domestic intelligence (BIS) found that the first trip (of which they were aware) that Atta made to the Czech Republic occurred at the end of May 2000. On May 30, Atta flew from his home in Germany to Prague. Lacking a visa for the Czech Republic, however, he was turned back at the airport and returned to Germany. Back in Germany, Atta immediately obtained a Czech visa and returned to the Czech Republic, traveling by bus into the country on June 2. The very next day he was on his way to the United States, his first visit to this country. Apart from a few trips abroad, Atta was thereafter based in America, preparing the September 11 attacks.

This information is completely reliable, based as it is on Czech immigration records. Atta's twenty-four-hour stay in Prague was evidently a mission of the greatest importance, warranting two time-consuming attempts just days before his history-making journey to the United States. And this was in spite of the danger inherent in any border interview with officials. Those engaged in illicit activity, such as terrorism, normally seek to minimize the number of times they cross a border; it is considered bad "tradecraft" to do otherwise.

Such urgency suggests a specific purpose, some crucially important meeting connected with the purpose of his trip to the United States. By then, after all, Atta was completely caught up in a project so important that he was committed to die in its accomplishment sixteen months later.

The Czechs also reported that on April 8, 2001, almost a year later, Atta met with an Iraqi intelligence agent posted to the embassy in Prague named Ahmed Khalil Ibrahim Samir al-Ani. Having observed the meeting, the Czechs asked the Iraqi ambassador what the meeting had been about; they did not receive a satisfactory answer. On April 20, Hynek Kmonicek, then deputy foreign minister, declared al-Ani persona non grata, expelling him from the country.

These details were reported authoritatively in a press conference given on October 26, 2001, by the Czech Interior Minister Stanislav Gross, the official responsible for overseeing Czech domestic intelligence. Although the report of the April 8 meeting later became the subject of extended controversy (discussed below), the Czech officials most responsible for that investigation never changed their position. As late as June 2002, Kmonicek asserted, "The meeting took place."[87]

As with most intelligence reports, the basis of the Czech claim has not been made public and so cannot be independently assessed. Atta's car rental records do, however, seem to corroborate their account.[88] Nor is there any contradicting evidence, such as credit card records, that would demonstrate that Atta was in the United States (or anywhere else) at the time that the Czech authorities say he was in Prague. In June 2002, CIA Director George Tenet informed the congressional committees of inquiry that the agency "was still working to confirm or deny this allegation. It is possible that Atta traveled under an unknown alias."[89]

The stance of at least some CIA officials, however, was to firmly dismiss all information suggesting an Iraqi connection with the 9/11 terrorists, simply by disregarding the most obvious interpretation. They consistently set the bar of "proof" so high that no single piece of information could make the case, even while they steadfastly ignored the relationship among the various pieces of information.

Iraqi Press: Anticipating the Attacks

AN INTRIGUING ARTICLE appeared July 21, 2001, in an Iraqi paper, *Al-Nasriya*, published in the city on the Lower Euphrates of that name. (Like all Iraq's press, including local papers, *Al-Nasriya* was government controlled.) Titled "America: An Obsession Called Osama bin Laden," the short article praising bin Laden stated, "In this man's heart, you'll find an insistence, a strange determination that he will reach one day the tunnels of the White House and will bomb it with everything that is in it." Bin Laden, the article continued, "still thinks seriously, with the seriousness of the Bedouin of the desert, about the way *he will try to bomb the Pentagon after he destroys the White House.*"

Finally, it projected, "he will strike America *on the arm that is already hurting*" (emphasis added).

What might that last phrase refer to? In court testimony, former CIA director James Woolsey suggested that it quite possibly referred to the World Trade Center, still "hurting" from the strike eight years before.[90] Woolsey also noted the odd phrase that he "will curse the memory of Frank Sinatra every time he hears his song," and suggested that this was a reference to Sinatra's recording of "New York, New York." He noted too that the fourth hijacked plane that crashed in Pennsylvania was most probably headed for the White House. The *Al-Nasriya* article had thus alluded to two of the 9/11 targets, and may have also referred indirectly to the World Trade Center.

There were too many substantive points in the *Al-Nasriya* article, then, for it to be written off as coincidence. As Woolsey testified, the article's likely purpose was to establish a written record, to allow Saddam to claim credit for the attacks at some later date. Such a record had to be written obscurely and published in a relatively obscure source, in view of the expectation that a direct claim of responsibility would of course invite massive U.S. retaliation.

Such an indirect claim of responsibility appeared to be reinforced in the official Iraqi media on the anniversary of September 11. The website of the Iraq News Agency posted Saddam's two "open letters," and a number of Iraqi magazines—again, officially sanctioned—heralded the anniversary of the attacks. *Al-Iqtisadi* pronounced "September 11: God's Punishment." *Alif Ba* carried a bizarre picture of a dissolving skull against the backdrop of the burning towers, headlined, "September 11 Events Revealed the True Face of America."

The editors of the *Wall Street Journal* were so struck by these Iraqi magazine covers that they reprinted them in a long editorial—the first time the *Journal* had ever used color to print its editorial page.[91] An echo of these threatening images was discovered in the first week of the U.S. war against Iraq, in the form of a mural decorating the Iraqi military headquarters in Nasriya, depicting a plane crashing into a building complex resembling New York's Twin Towers.

The Administration and the Agency

JUST SIX DAYS after the attacks, Bush told his national security team, "I believe Iraq was involved; but I'm not going to strike them now."[92] Donald Rumsfeld, of course, had suspected Iraq's involvement from the day of the attacks. Vice President Dick Cheney had been authoritatively briefed by CIA Director George Tenet that there was "no evidence" of Iraq's involvement and initially endorsed that position, but his staff was convinced otherwise, and Cheney too soon came to understand that Iraq was probably involved.

The president decided first to attack the most obvious culprit, Osama bin Laden, making the reasonable judgment that the United States could not fight in Iraq and Afghanistan at the same time.

Bush nevertheless retained his early inclination to eliminate Saddam. On November 27, Bush met with Yemeni President Ali Abdullah Saleh in Washington. Saleh offered to mediate the American dispute with Iraq, citing an Arab proverb holding that if you put a cat into a cage, it may turn into a lion. Bush declined the offer, responding, "This cat has rabies. . . . The only way to cure the cat is to cut off its head."[93] Saleh was reportedly shocked by Bush's bluntness.

War was never Bush's preferred option for getting rid of Hussein, however: in fact, his first approach was to deal with Iraq through underground means. In early 2002, as the campaign in Afghanistan was winding down, the president signed an intelligence order directing the CIA to undertake a major covert program to topple Saddam.[94] Tenet gave the operation only a 10 to 20 percent chance of success. Nevertheless, even if no coup could be accomplished, the operation would prepare the way for military action by gathering intelligence and establishing contacts with individuals inside Iraq.

See No Evidence

WITH THE START of the U.S. military campaign in Afghanistan on October 7, 2001, attention shifted increasingly away from Iraq. The administration's public relations focus was to demonstrate the rightness of its campaign against bin Laden and the Taliban (particularly in the face of widespread doubts in the Muslim world regarding bin Laden's involvement in the attacks). The administration did not really begin to present the case against Iraq until the fall of 2002.

In the interim, the bureaucracies worked diligently to undermine whatever incriminating pieces of evidence had become public. The continuing saga of the Czech intelligence report is especially revealing.

In mid-December 2001, the U.S. intelligence officials who were inclined to dismiss the significance of the Czech report were nevertheless still willing to acknowledge that Atta had in fact met with an Iraqi intelligence official. According to a *New York Times* report,

"There was definitely one meeting," between Mr. Ani and Mr. Atta, an intelligence official in Washington said. "We don't know if it was significant. We certainly don't attribute to it the significance others attribute to it automatically. Just because there was a meeting doesn't mean it was connected to 9/11."[95]

In April 2002, when Vice President Dick Cheney flew to the Middle East to disclose America's intention to get rid of Saddam and to mobilize support, he mentioned the meeting between Atta and al-Ani. Within a few weeks, *Newsweek*'s Michael Isikoff published a story that the Czechs had recanted their claim about the meeting.[96] This report was immediately followed by a similar story by the *Washington Post*'s intelligence correspondent, Walter Pincus.[97] Apparently, neither *Newsweek* nor the *Post* had actually consulted a Czech source to verify the claim, which was sourced to unnamed U.S. officials.

Interior Minister Gross quickly responded through the Czech press. He said that he had asked the head of domestic intelligence, Jiri Ruzek, whether BIS had changed its view, and that Ruzek replied it had not. This direct rebuttal was reinforced by Jan Klas, the chairman of the parliamentary commission that oversaw the BIS, who added the caution, "I would take those press reports, even though carried by such a renowned paper as *Newsweek*, with a pinch of salt."[98]

But in spite of these authoritative rebuttals, the revisionist denials, once planted, never died. As Jim Woolsey noted, the U.S. denials were all anonymous leaks, whereas the Czechs who affirmed the story allowed their names to be used; Woolsey was inclined to credit the latter.

Like the Czech government, the Spanish government had become involved in the 9/11 investigation after it was discovered that Atta had made a visit to Spain before the attacks. A few weeks after 9/11, a Spanish diplomat complained personally to me that the CIA was not interested in hearing information suggesting an Iraqi link to the attack, and that that response was having a chilling effect on his own country's investigation.[99]

The pattern of officially discrediting evidence was not limited to the question of Atta's activities. In the fall of 2002, as war with Iraq approached, the administration did begin to refer publicly to contacts between Iraq and al Qaeda. That information had been subjected to a routine interagency review process in which the CIA—whose responsibility, after all, is intelligence—exercises a veto. The CIA's characteristic stance was selectively critical, almost to the point of absurdity.[100]

One analyst involved in the process gave the following example: Abu Zubaydah, a high-ranking al Qaeda prisoner captured in March 2002, told his interrogators that there was no formal agreement between al Qaeda and Iraqi intelligence because of the ideological hostility between them; but he went on to list numerous examples of informal cooperation between the two. Agency officials who rejected the idea of a link between Iraq and al Qaeda simply focused on the first part of the statement—and ignored the second part.[101]

Some of the evidence did survive this interagency laundering. The administration's case was first stated in some detail by Donald Rumsfeld (calling the evidence "bulletproof"), at a news briefing on September 26, 2002. The president reiterated the same points in an October 7 speech in Cincinnati. The case consisted of six points that had been hammered out in fierce interagency battles. Stripped of any detailed evidence, however, these general points tended to fall flat.

The same points were summarized in an October 7 letter from Tenet to Senator Bob Graham, chairman of the Intelligence Committee:

- Our understanding of the relationship between Iraq and al Qaeda is evolving and is based on sources of varying reliability. Some of the information we have received comes from detainees, including some of high rank.

- We have solid reporting of senior-level contacts between Iraq and al Qaeda going back a decade.

- Credible information indicates that Iraq and al Qaeda have discussed safe haven and reciprocal nonaggression.

- Since Operation Enduring Freedom, we have solid evidence of the presence in Iraq of al Qaeda members, including some that have been in Baghdad.

- We have credible reporting that al Qaeda leaders sought contacts in Iraq who could help them acquire WMD capabilities. The reporting also stated that Iraq has provided training to al Qaeda members in the areas of poisons and gases and making conventional bombs.

- Iraq's increasing support to extremist Palestinians coupled with growing indications of relationship with al Qaeda suggest that Baghdad's links to terrorists will increase, even absent U.S. military action.

Bureaucratizing the Intelligence

BUT IF THIS VERY general statement managed to survive the interagency debates, so did the pattern of clandestine bureaucratic denials. Whenever a senior official referred publicly to the existence of links between Iraq and al Qaeda, a flood of anonymous leaks would follow to discredit the claim—even though the specific material cited had in fact been "cleared" through the formal vetting process.

One had to sympathize with the frustration voiced by Secretary of Defense Donald Rumsfeld when, in early 2003, he flatly declined to reveal any specifics about an Iraq–al Qaeda link. "The last time I got into this subject," he complained, "I asked the agency [CIA] for a piece of paper as to what they had declassified with respect to that relationship. I read it here. For the next month, various senators and various press people were indicating that I had said something that the agency didn't believe. It was not true."[102] The president—and indeed Tenet himself—could have said the same. It became apparent that at least some intelligence officers were providing informal briefings to members of Congress and the media that contradicted the officially cleared intelligence.

Typical of the genre was a 2,400-word, page-one story that appeared in the *Wall Street Journal* in late October 2002. Its unnamed sources refer to "tantalizing hints" and "intriguing leads" concerning Iraq's involvement in terrorism, but in the last analysis it concluded that "there's no evidence of contact between al Qaeda and the Iraqis."[103] (The article's only named source debunking the administration's position was Kenneth Pollack, a former National Security Council staffer from the Clinton administration.) No mention was made of the fact that the administration's position had been thoroughly vetted in a formal interagency process.

When Secretary of State Colin Powell addressed the U.N. Security Council, he was determined to avoid that kind of "debunking," so he focused on what he considered the tightest, most concrete points. On

February 5, 2003, Powell—with Tenet sitting symbolically at his back—reported to the Security Council the U.S. findings regarding Iraq's involvement with al Qaeda. He added two simple points:

* Members of both organizations met repeatedly and have met at least eight times at very senior levels since the early 1990s. In 1996, bin Laden met with a senior Iraqi intelligence official in Khartoum and later met with the director of the Iraqi intelligence service.

* From the late 1990s until 2001, the Iraqi embassy in Pakistan played the role of liaison to the al Qaeda organization.

Powell went on, however, to include some additional material, apparently in line with the theory, favored by officials experienced in the bureaucratic trench wars, that institutional resistance is less when information is new. So Powell shared with the Security Council the story of one Abu Musab Zarqawi and his involvement with both al Qaeda and Baghdad.

A Jordanian-born Palestinian, Zarqawi had fought in the Afghan war, returning to Afghanistan in 2000 to oversee a terrorist training camp specializing in poisons (among other lethal arts). Following al Qaeda's expulsion from Afghanistan, Zarqawi helped establish a new poisons-and-explosives training center camp in northeastern Iraq.

In May 2002, Zarqawi traveled to Baghdad for medical treatment and remained there for two months. During that time, two dozen al Qaeda operatives converged on Baghdad and established their own base of operations there. As Powell explained, Zarqawi's network was behind a terrorist cell in Britain, which was known to possess the highly toxic agent ricin, and which appeared to be linked to another cell in France.

Even though Powell regarded this evidence also as particularly "hard," his presentation nevertheless precipitated a now-familiar flow of skeptical press stories. "Alleged Al Qaeda Ties Questioned," reported the *Washington Post*'s intelligence correspondent, again citing anonymous government sources.[104] When, a week later, Tenet testified before the Senate Armed Services Committee and pointed to Zarqawi as an example of the ties between Iraq and al Qaeda, the *Post* followed up with much the same story, again with anonymous sourcing.[105] And while the stories' headlines seemed to suggest substantive disagreement, most of the reported discussion revolved around issues of wording.

The anonymous demurrals, moreover, were now accompanied by an intimidating charge—that the administration was "politicizing" the intelligence. If the point of intelligence gathering is to get at the truth of an issue, however, it might be more accurate to say that an influential sector of the CIA was stubbornly *bureaucratizing* the intelligence— shaping the reporting and the investigation itself to serve interests defined not by administration policy, or broader U.S. national inter- ests, but by the narrowest definition of a bureaucratic "win." The aim was apparently to prevent embarrassment to the agency and/or to indi- vidual officers, which would imperil not only individual promotions but also the agency's position in the perennial interagency turf wars.

After all, the U.S. intelligence community—for whatever reason— had unquestionably made a blunder of historic proportions in its approach to international terrorism, as was becoming increasingly evi- dent as an unmistakable pattern of contacts began to emerge. Alongside the "loose network of terrorists" favored by the CIA, it was becoming clear that Iraq had been for many years playing an active part in the international terrorism industry.

Moreover, by focusing exclusively on the Islamist element of such major incidents as the 1993 World Trade Center bombing, the agency (as well as the FBI) had bungled the critical opportunity to investigate the shadowy, non-Islamist element that would go on to ever larger efforts, in 1995 and in 2001 (as we'll see in chapter 7).

When confronted with information that threatened to expose this calamitous error, the more bureaucratic players within the intelligence community simply dismissed it. They stoutly resisted all efforts to cor- rect the error of analysis, instead waging a campaign of media disinfor- mation to cast doubt on the motives of the revisionists.

Since September 11, it has become fashionable to speak about the need to "connect the dots"—that is, to draw reasonable inferences from limited available information. But in the increasingly public tug-of-war within the administration, each bit of information was systematically isolated, undercut, and reconfigured by anonymous CIA "sources" and their allies in the media. Even the most obvious connections were obscured, and the account that ultimately survived the intelligence policy meat grinder was, as we have seen, unconvincingly abstract. Quite possibly, even senior administration officials—including the president—may not have understood how strong the case against Iraq really was.

It is hardly surprising, in this context, that commentators abroad as well as in the United States would weigh the paucity of official information regarding Iraq's connection to terrorism and conclude that it disproved the existence of such a link. The effect was a growing movement to discredit the administration's Iraq policy and even to suggest unacknowledged—and presumably sinister—ulterior motives on the part of the administration or some of its officials.[106]

Chapter Four

THE NEW REGIME
IN IRAQ

O N FEBRUARY 26, 2003, on the brink of war in Iraq, President Bush presented his vision of a free and democratic postwar Iraq, in an address to the annual dinner of the American Enterprise Institute (AEI). The Republican think tank was a hospitable environment for the speech; many of those present had long called for the overthrow of Saddam Hussein's regime and its replacement by a constitutional government.

Two of the people attending the dinner (as was I) had long experience working on this issue within the U.S. government, and their candid response to the president's speech was discouraging: "It's not going to happen. They don't fire people."[107] While they certainly shared the president's goals, they believed that their own, ongoing efforts to implement these goals had been thwarted. In general, they felt outnumbered and outgunned by bureaucratic opposition in the CIA and State Department—and they felt strongly that the White House did not do enough to rein in the bureaucracies, to ensure that administration policies were carried out.

As of this writing it remains unclear what Iraq after Saddam will look like. A power vacuum exists, and Shi'a clerics are trying to fill it— including some coming from exile in Iran and enjoying Tehran's support, raising the specter of a strong theocratic influence in postwar Iraq. Another danger seems to be general lawlessness, with the prospect that no legitimate and effective authority capable of running the entire country will emerge.

Games Bureaucracies Play

THE U.S. BUREAUCRACIES have for decades resisted efforts to develop a liberal alternative for Iraq's governance, placing their bets instead on some post-Saddam version of the Ba'ath establishment. Even as the war with Iraq began, they continued to oppose efforts to bring democratic change in Iraq, some still failing to recognize that the brutal Ba'ath, widely despised within Iraq, cannot be remade as a viable political force.

The bureaucracies' preference for the Ba'ath—and their outright hostility to liberalism—is a very old story. This predilection in fact contributed to the unsatisfactory conclusion to the 1991 Gulf War, which ended when former President Bush called a cease-fire on February 28, 1991, with Saddam Hussein still in power. Bush had been led to believe that after such a massive military defeat, Saddam would be overthrown. The expectation at the CIA, and the State Department as well, was that some in the Ba'athist inner circle would launch a coup, producing a government that, while hardly democratic, would not rise to the level of brutal oppression achieved by Saddam.

As Bush explained to the British journalist David Frost five years later, "Everybody felt that Saddam Hussein could not stay in office. . . . I miscalculated."[108]

A Passion for Stability

IN THE VIEW of the previous Bush administration, a military coup would have the advantage of continuity, avoiding the messiness attendant on the fall of any dictatorial regime. The first Bush White House had a strong preference for "stability," as evidenced also in its approach to the imminent breakups in Yugoslavia and the Soviet Union, which it refused to acknowledge or prepare for until much water—and blood—had gone over the dam.

As Lawrence Kaplan and William Kristol have remarked, this stance reflected "a preference for order over liberty."[109] This was an administration that had hesitated to deal with the Russian reformer Boris Yeltsin, clinging instead to the Soviet Communist leader Mikhail Gorbachev. Bush himself famously advised the Ukranians not to break with the Soviet Union, in what *New York Times* columnist William Safire tellingly dubbed the "Chicken Kiev speech." The breakup of the Soviet Union, along with the collapse of most Communist regimes and the widespread discrediting of its antidemocratic ideology, constituted a tremendous U.S. victory, but rather than being of their own making it was one the first Bush administration had thrust upon it.

Apart from the Bush administration's general preference for the status quo, the promise of a coup in Baghdad seemed to offer distinct tactical advantages: Saddam would be removed without U.S. forces having to hunt him down or occupy the country. A National Security Council aide asserted, just days after the cease-fire, "our policy is to get rid of Saddam Hussein, not his regime."[110] Of course, this presumed it would be possible not only to carry out a coup in Iraq but also to promote some kinder, gentler Ba'athists.

The Iraqi National Accord

AFTER SADDAM INVADED Kuwait, the CIA, in coordination with Saudi intelligence, worked with a group of former Iraqi Ba'athists, many of whom had broken with Saddam over the years. They established a group called the Iraqi National Accord (INA), led by an Iraqi émigré named Ayad Allawi, who resided in London. Allawi's group claimed it could carry out a coup.

The INA included such figures as Salah Omar Ali al-Tikriti. Al-Tikriti had been a senior member of the Iraqi Ba'ath party in the 1960s. On July 17, 1968, the Ba'ath party staged a coup and seized power for the second time (having ruled Iraq briefly in 1963). In January 1969, six months later, the new regime publicly hanged fourteen people, eleven of them Jews. Al-Tikiriti was among the officials who harangued the crowd of some 200,000 workers and peasants, railing against Zionism and imperialism. The drama served to intimidate the middle class and help ensure that the Ba'ath would not be ousted a second time.

Al-Tikriti also had a history of breaking with the Iraqi regime only to restore former ties. He resigned as Iraq's U.N. ambassador in August 1982 and joined the opposition, after Iraqi forces fell on the defensive in the war with Iran and it began to look as if Iraq might lose the war. But he later reconciled with the government, and in August 1990 al-Tikriti headed the international division for Iraqi Airways freight services (based in London), essentially a political appointment made from Baghdad. Iraqi Freight Services Limited was among the businesses named as Iraqi-front companies by the United States Treasury Department, after Iraq invaded Kuwait.

Al-Tikriti maintained that his cousin Al Hakam al-Tikriti would join a coup against Saddam. Al Hakam headed the army's helicopter squadrons, and he was indeed on the list of plotters touted by Allawi and the Iraqi National Accord. There was nothing terribly secret about this information, which I was told while visiting London in January 1991. This struck me as an odd way of running a coup operation: didn't such open advertising put this highly placed military ally at great risk? Al Hakam in fact retained his position, and I retained my doubts about the Iraqi National Accord and their plans for a coup.

The story of the Accord was oddly reminiscent of events in the early days of the U.S.S.R. In the 1920s, the Soviets established an organization formally named the Monarchist Union of Central Russia, informally known as "the Trust." It purported to oppose the new Communist regime in Moscow and claimed to have recruited many disillusioned Soviet officials. The Trust provided a great deal of secret "information" to the exiles, who passed it on to Western intelligence agencies; it also helped the exiles run sabotage and assassination operations in the Soviet Union. By such means, the Soviet regime—working through the Trust—ultimately succeeded in neutralizing most anti-Communist exile groups in Europe, luring back to their deaths a number of their leaders while confounding six Western intelligence agencies with planted disinformation. (The Trust promoted, for example, a picture of dire Soviet economic weakness to create the impression that communism was failing: Russia was moving inevitably toward capitalism, and any outside effort to promote that goal would be superfluous.)[111] In the early 1990s, Jordanian intelligence, as well as other Iraqi opposition figures, warned that the INA was an operation of the same order as the Trust.[112]

The 1991 Cease-fire

ON MARCH 3, 1991, General Norman Schwarzkopf, commander of Centcom and head of the coalition forces, met with an Iraqi military delegation, headed by the deputy chief of staff, Lieutenant General Sultan Hashim Ahmad. (Ahmad served as Iraq's defense minister during the 2003 Iraq war.) The task of the two generals was to set the terms of a temporary cease-fire, which included issues such as the exchange of prisoners and establishing procedures for disentangling the two military forces.

The United States at that point controlled Iraq's skies and had imposed a ban on the flight of any and all Iraqi aircraft. While this was not an issue on the formal agenda, it was an important issue for Iraq to try to amend.

Accordingly, toward the end of the discussion (as reported in the declassified transcript), Ahmad explained to Schwarzkopf that "helicopter flights sometimes are needed to carry some of the officials, government officials . . . needed to be transported from one place to another, because the roads and bridges are out." Schwarzkopf told Ahmad how to mark helicopters to avoid their being shot down (emphasis added).

> **AHMAD:** This has nothing to do with the front line. This is inside Iraq.
>
> **SCHWARZKOPF:** As long as it is not over the part we are in, that is absolutely no problem. So we will let the helicopters and *that is a very important point, and I want to make sure that's recorded*, that military helicopters can fly over Iraq. Not fighters, not bombers.
>
> **AHMAD:** So you mean even the helicopters . . . armed in the Iraqi skies can fly, but not the fighters? Because the helicopters are the same, they transfer somebody . . . .
>
> **SCHWARZKOPF:** Yeah. I will instruct our air force not to shoot at any helicopters that are flying over the territory of Iraq where we are not located. If they must fly over the area we are located in, I *prefer* that they not be gunships, armed helos, and I would *prefer* that they have an orange tag on the side as an extra safety measure.
>
> **AHMAD:** Not to have any confusion, these will not come to this territory.

As the meeting ended, Schwarzkopf reiterated the salient points: "From our side," he began, "we will not attack any helicopters inside Iraq."

Why did Schwarzkopf allow the Iraqis to fly helicopters at all, let alone give permission for armed Iraqi helicopters to fly over U.S. troops? This was surely as imprudent as it was unnecessary. In a televised interview with David Frost on March 27, 1991, before the transcript of the talks had been declassified, Schwarzkopf recounted the exchange quite differently. He said he had been ordered "to dictate rather strong terms. . . . So when [the Iraqis] said to me, you know, 'We would like to fly helicopters,' I said not over our forces. 'Oh, no, no, definitely not over your forces, just over Iraq, because for the transportation of government officials.' That seemed like a reasonable request."

Is it possible that Schwarzkopf had allowed—indeed, encouraged—Iraq to fly its helicopters in the belief that Al Hakam al-Tikriti would help carry out a coup?[113] (Recall that Al Hakam, purportedly part of the INA, was the head of the army's helicopter squadrons.) No such coup materialized, in any case. How much of the anticipated military coup was disinformation, fed by Iraqi intelligence through the INA to the coalition?

At the time of Schwarzkopf and Ahmad's meeting at Safwan, popular uprisings in the southern Iraqi cities had just begun.[114] But, as it happened, the army helicopters would play a critical role—not in implementing an anti-Saddam coup, but in crushing what became an enormous rebellion against the defeated regime, encompassing fourteen of Iraq's eighteen provinces. Schwarzkopf's permission to fly helicopters could certainly have been revoked at this point, but as the uprisings continued and spread, Washington maintained a studied ambiguity about what it would do. On March 13 and 16, Bush warned Saddam that using helicopters against the Iraqi population constituted a violation of the provisional cease-fire. This rather minimal response provided at least a partial check on the regime's repression.

As the administration debated its response, it arrived at a chilling conclusion—that allowing Saddam to suppress the uprisings would in fact hasten his downfall. (The decision not to intervene was buttressed also by the administration's reluctance to become involved in an Iraqi "quagmire," as well as by suspicion regarding Iran's role in the rebellion.)

This bizarre conclusion was, in fact, the view of the most prominent Iraq experts in Washington. The *New York Times*, on March 21, 1991, cited one: " 'It is important to stabilize the situation in Iraq,' said Christine Moss Helms, an Iraq scholar who has advised the White House and Pentagon during the Persian Gulf crisis; 'Until the situation is stabilized, nobody is going to be able to focus on getting rid of Saddam Hussein.' "[115] Another prominent expert, who had also advised the White House and who worked for the Defense Department, told the *Washington Post* much the same:

> Experts on the region such as Phebe Marr of the National Defense University (a college for the Joint Chiefs of Staff) contend that the domestic chaos in Iraq will reduce the likelihood that the military can get rid of Saddam soon. "The rebellion is strengthening Saddam, not weakening him. . . . No military is going to overthrow him while they are fighting a rebellion."[116]

A senior U.S. official was quoted five days later, on March 29, after precisely that advice had been taken:

> Bush believes "Saddam will quash the rebellions and, after the dust settles, the Ba'ath military establishment and other elites will blame him for not only the death and destruction from the war, but the death and destruction from putting down the rebellion. They will emerge then and install a new leadership and will make the case [that] it is time for new leaders and a new beginning." . . .
> But this official expressed his own doubts. "There might not be a coup . . . and all these thousands and thousands will be dead while we looked on."[117]

Indeed, at a March 26 White House meeting, it had been decided to let Saddam Hussein crush the rebellions.[118] Later that day, the White House spokesman announced that the United States would not shoot down Iraqi helicopters. Saddam intensified the suppression of the uprisings, and the bloodbath that the unnamed senior official feared indeed came to pass. The perceived betrayal would haunt U.S. forces twelve years later, as they entered southern Iraq.[119]

The Communications Ban

WHILE THE CIA and the State Department favored cooperation with the INA, a ban also existed on any meetings between U.S. government officials and members of the Iraqi opposition. All such communications were to be conducted only through intelligence channels. In early March 1991, a midlevel Pentagon official named Paul Freeburg sought to hold a meeting with a Kurdish representative, after hearing him speak at the Brookings Institution. Zalmay Khalilzad, then head of the Policy Planning office in the Defense Department (and now White House envoy to the Iraqi opposition), agreed that it would be useful for Freeburg to meet with the Kurdish official, if only to learn about developments inside Iraq. Permission for the meeting was denied, however, by the State Department. April Glaspie, who had been U.S. ambassador to Iraq prior to Iraq's invasion of Kuwait, affirmed the ban, saying, "That's the correct thing. We can't talk to these people."

"I already have," Freeburg replied.

The former ambassador gasped, "You haven't!"

"I have."

"You must stop," was Glaspie's reply.[120]

Harry Rowan, a top aide to then-Undersecretary of Defense Paul Wolfowitz, learned of the communications ban when he sought to meet with Ahmad Chalabi, who would later head the Iraqi National Congress. Astonished, Rowan informed Wolfowitz, who began working to reverse the incomprehensible prohibition.[121] News of the ban was reported in the *Wall Street Journal* on the same day that the White House announced that the United States would not shoot down Iraqi helicopters.[122] The ban was lifted shortly thereafter.

The forces driving that ban, as it later became clear, were the CIA and the State Department's Bureau of Near Eastern Affairs. Both of these bureaucracies were committed to the notion that Saddam would (and should) be overthrown in an internal military coup. The prediction was mistaken. No coup occurred, either then or during the next twelve years.

The Military Coup Option

BUT THE AGENCIES' corporate mentality stayed the same. Twelve years later, as the United States again prepared for war with Iraq, the CIA was still working with Ayad Allawi and the INA.

The CIA was also working with a suspected war criminal, Nizar al-Khazraji. Al-Khazraji is a former chief of staff of the Iraqi army who defected in the mid-1990s and joined the INA. In 1999, he applied for asylum in Denmark. The Danish government rejected the request because of al-Khazraji's suspected involvement in the genocidal Anfal campaign against the Kurds in the late 1980s; nevertheless, they allowed al-Khazraji to live in the country. Then, in October 2001, al-Khazraji was placed under house arrest while Danish police investigated his possible role in war crimes. On March 17, 2003, while still technically under house arrest, he disappeared, and Danish authorities issued an international arrest warrant.[123] The Danish foreign minister also sent a letter of complaint to the U.S. ambassador in Copenhagen. Various reports put him in Saudi Arabia, and then either with Centcom in Qatar or in Kuwait.[124] U.S. intelligence, it appeared, had spirited him out of Denmark.

While the CIA had no problem working with a suspected war criminal like al-Khazraji—and an organization of dubious reliability like the INA—it did find it extremely difficult to work with Iraqi democrats. The Iraqi National Congress (INC) had long sought to overthrow Saddam through a popular insurgency and to establish a democratic, constitutional government in Iraq. But the INC came up against an insurmountable problem: the reluctance of the United States to accommodate such a program.

The INC had been created in 1992, after a coup failed to materialize and the popular uprising had been ruthlessly suppressed. Ahmad Chalabi, the driving force behind the INC's formation, was a wealthy Shi'ite businessman living in London. The Bush administration had informed the major Iraqi opposition groups that U.S. support would be contingent on their uniting into a single body. The INC was established as an umbrella organization incorporating both the established Kurdish and Shi'a groups, as well as independent elements. Even the INA was brought under the INC umbrella, and the INC began to receive U.S. funding through the CIA.

In 1993 the INC established itself in northern Iraq, newly liberated by the militias of the two main Kurdish parties, the KDP (Kurdish Democratic Party) and PUK (Patriotic Union of Kurdistan), under the protection of the U.S.-enforced no-fly zone established after the disastrous rout the United States had permitted in 1991. This was an area roughly the size of Austria. The INC ran a variety of media activities—newspaper, radio, and television—and developed a network of contacts with individuals inside Ba'athist-controlled Iraq. By the end of 1993, it began to make plans for action, but U.S. officials were unenthusiastic.[125]

Bill Clinton was now president. In the 1992 presidential campaign, he had taken the position that Bush should have gotten rid of Saddam during the war. Once in office, however, the Clinton administration was not prepared to commit much effort or resources to the goal of overthrowing Saddam, or take significant risks toward that end. Wary of allowing the INC to launch a campaign on the ground, which might involve the United States, the administration actually prohibited the organization from using any U.S. funds to buy weapons. Chalabi therefore spent some $8 million of his own money on arms for the INC.

Notwithstanding the earlier U.S. experience, the Clinton administration persuaded itself that Saddam could be overthrown through an internal military coup; this was the seemingly low-cost, risk-free way to get rid of Saddam. George Tenet, who handled intelligence matters at the White House before he became CIA director, was among those who believed a coup was still possible. Tenet acted in coordination with

National Security Adviser Anthony Lake, who maintained a generally timid approach to the country's national security problems. And together they let slip a genuine opportunity to bolster what could have been a successful action, sponsored by the INC, to overthrow Saddam.

In the spring of 1994, Steven Richter was named head of the CIA's Near Eastern Division.[126] Richter had headed the CIA station in Amman and had some involvement with Iraq policy in that post. He had recruited Mohammed Abdullah al-Shawami, an Iraqi Turkoman living in Jordan who had been a commander in Iraq's special forces. Tenet and Lake worked closely with Richter, completely bypassing the CIA director, James Woolsey, who would leave the agency in early 1995.

In June 1994, at Tenet's prompting, Richter called a meeting with leaders of the INA and several other former Iraqi officers. The CIA once again began to push for a military coup—at the expense of a popular insurgency. In late 1994, in a sort of bureaucratic coup, the Tenet-Richter alliance took control of the CIA's "Iraq Operations Group," which had been established under the previous administration to oversee Saddam's overthrow. The losers in this "coup" were the veterans who had worked out a long-term political program with the INC, and who had (in one agent's words) "kept the crazy ideas about silver-bullet coups away from the agency leadership."[127]

In March 1995, the INC launched a modest but successful offensive against the Iraqi army stationed in the north, opposite the Kurdish lines. Although effective on the ground, the move was stymied from Washington. On the eve of the attack, a former Iraqi general named Adnan Nuri (with whom the CIA had established a separate channel of communication) flew to Washington to warn that the INC was trying to draw the United States into conflict with Baghdad.[128] Anthony Lake sent a panicked message to the INC, warning that it was on its own. One of the two Kurdish groups pulled out of the offensive and then exploited the confused situation to attack its rival, leading the INC to call off its offensive.

General Najib al-Salhi was at that time commander of a mechanized Iraqi army brigade, across the line of confrontation from the INC. As al-Salhi explained after he defected four years later, the INC operations had a "strong effect" on the Iraqi army units there, who were in fact hoping that the INC offensive would continue. Al-Salhi had already coordinated plans with several other commanders, awaiting further deterioration in the situation. They planned to orchestrate a military revolt in place and declare themselves for the INC, but of course they abandoned the project once the INC broke off its operation.[129]

The INC's military action further soured its relations with the Clinton administration, which was now, in fact, pursuing its own plans for a coup. Those plans accelerated throughout 1995, as the following year's presidential election campaign approached; by July 1996, however, they ended in spectacular failure.[130] Predictably enough, the CIA-sponsored plot was penetrated; Saddam rounded up the conspirators, executing many of them, while Iraqi officials called the CIA station chief in Amman—using the CIA's own communications equipment—to tell the Americans to pack their bags and go home.[131]

Further disaster would occur the following month, at the start of the Labor Day weekend, when Saddam's Republican Guards attacked the INC headquarters in Irbil, in Kurdish-controlled Iraq. President Clinton was outside of Washington, campaigning. Three days after the attack, he ordered a cruise missile strike on insignificant air defense sites in southern Iraq; at the same time, he extended the southern air exclusion zone and proclaimed that U.S. interests lay in the south rather than in the north, where the Republican Guard attack had occurred. The operation was what Bush administration officials would later disparage as "pounding sand."

Blaming the Victim

UNTIL THAT POINT, some officials, including a few on the White House staff, were still prepared to fight to support the INC. After this debacle, however, their willingness to do so ended. To reverse it would have required a major effort, which the president was clearly unwilling to promote. Moreover, such an initiative would underline the fact that a major mistake had been made in not acting to prevent the Iraqi assault. The Clinton administration was very far from making such an acknowledgment: instead, they opted to blame the victim.

Following the Iraqi assault on Irbil, some six hundred Iraqi opposition members, mostly from the INC, were transferred from northern Iraq to the U.S. territory of Guam. There they were processed and screened for admission to the United States. FBI agents conducted the interrogations; with little background in Iraq and its politics, they operated at the direction of CIA agents located down the hall. Eight individuals were initially identified as threats to U.S. national security and were threatened with deportation to Iraq.

INS procedures allow the use of secret evidence. In these eight cases, classified information—information that could not be shown to them or their lawyers—was introduced as evidence of the danger posed by the detainees. After hearing the case, the immigration judge ordered that two of the men be given asylum, while six others were ordered subject to deportation.

Some illuminating details emerged from this episode, regarding one of the men released. Hashim Qadir Hawlery, a longtime member of a Kurdish party, had worked with the INC and then the INA. The INS's principal reason for suspecting Hawlery was that he would not admit membership in the "KLM." Hawlery, clearly puzzled, whispered to his lawyer during his hearing that KLM was a Dutch airline; was the INS asking about the airline? It turned out that the FBI agent who had reported Hawlery's involvement with the KLM understood the initials to stand for the "Kurdish Liberation Movement." While such a movement certainly exists, "Kurdish Liberation Movement" is not in fact the name of any organization. The translator at Guam had been extremely sloppy, summarizing the account Hawlery voluntarily gave of his long involvement with the Kurdish resistance as membership in the "KLM."[132] Once that point was clarified, the case against Hawlery evaporated.

The six others facing deportation had a bigger problem. How could they refute the charges, when they did not know what they were? An INC adviser, Francis Brooke, hit upon an idea: why not secure the assistance of James Woolsey? Woolsey was a lawyer; he was friendly; and as former CIA director, he would have the necessary clearances to see the secret information.

Woolsey agreed to take the case, pro bono. Even so, the INS refused to release the information to him. At first the INS suggested, preposterously, that Woolsey might share classified information with the clients (a criminal violation); then the INS asserted "no public purpose" would be served by providing him that information.

With a long career in national security, and as a very senior and highly respected former government official, Woolsey had connections. After Senators Trent Lott, Orrin Hatch, and Jesse Helms wrote a letter of complaint to Attorney General Janet Reno, the material was not only released but also declassified.

As the *New York Times* reported, the evidence proved "weak and unsubstantiated."[133] Some of the cases were ludicrous:

Safa al-Batat had almost died from a dose of thallium (rat poison), administered in an Iraqi assassination attempt. The FBI challenged his bona fides as a resistance fighter, suggesting that the poisoning might have occurred as a result of the "recreational" use of the substance. Al-Batat's lawyer, Niels Frenzen, suspected that the investigators had confused *thallium* with *valium*.

Ali Karim—a physician who had served as doctor to both the INC and the CIA officers based in northern Iraq—was accused of failing to provide his real family name, which was supposedly al Ufayli, in order to conceal his relationship to Arras Karim. Arras, effectively the INC's chief of intelligence, had taken refuge in Britain after the Iraqi assault on Irbil. The CIA's position was that Arras had ties to Iranian and Iraqi intelligence (a claim that was later disproved), and that Ali was trying to hide his ties to his unsavory cousin in order to gain entry into the United States.[134]

But "al Ufayli" was not the family's name. "Ufayli" is simply a term referring to a Shi'a Kurd, and both men were that. How U.S. authorities came to believe that "al Ufayli" was the doctor's last name and that he had concealed it was never explained. He had given his real name—Ali

Karim, which, in fact, suggested that he was related to Arras Karim. Nothing had been hidden.

All six men were eventually released and allowed to live in the United States in one status or another. It had required congressional intervention to contest the government's classified "evidence" against these men. Without that high-level effort, who can say how these cases would have been handled? And although all were eventually released, their extended detention risked sending a discouraging signal to other insurgents who might look to the United States for support, and with whom the United States might one day hope to work. Warren Marik, a former CIA officer, summed it up: "The lesson . . . is this: if the going gets tough, the friends of the U.S. could well end up in a U.S. jail."[135] In June 1997, *Washington Post* columnist Jim Hoagland summed up the case: "Iraq stands as the agency's most expensive and embarrassing flop since it was founded on July 26, 1947."

Further embarrassment, however, was yet to come.

The Revival of INC Fortunes

IN THE FALL of 1997, as Saddam began a series of challenges to the U.N. weapons inspectors, Congress began urging the Clinton administration to revitalize the INC and help it overthrow Saddam. Congress authorized the first appropriation in the spring of 1998, some $10 million. Half was earmarked to fund a new Radio Free Europe broadcasting program for Iraq; the other half was designated for "the democratic opposition *in* Iraq," with the expectation that a "significant portion" of that sum would go to the INC. Since the CIA had so mishandled the INC relationship, the money was to be dispersed through the State Department.

The Clinton White House was dead set against supporting an insurgency against Saddam. Nonetheless, the State Department—specifically the office of Near Eastern Affairs (NEA)—developed a plan for implementing the congressional legislation, which it called "Support for the

Democratic Opposition *of* Iraq." The choice of preposition—*in* vs. *of*—made all the difference.

The Meaning of *Of*

THERE EXISTED A LARGE Iraqi population in exile, much of it opposed to the regime. The money would be spent on promoting activities among this group of émigrés, rather than on developing a democratic opposition *in* Iraq.

NEA consistently resisted efforts by the INC to use the new funding to reestablish its presence in northern Iraq, while deriding the INC as an ineffectual exile group. NEA depicted the Iraqi opposition in the most negative terms possible. It claimed, for example, that the opposition was so hopeless that it consisted of not fewer than ninety-seven groups and even supplied Congress with a list. A considerable number of organizations on the list were unknown to any Iraq expert outside NEA; others were religious foundations, human rights organizations, and academic institutions, rather than political opposition groups.

Actually, there were few such groups of any significance. Iraqis in exile were, for the most part, a dispirited, unorganized lot, well aware that any political activity could bring retaliation by the regime against their families still living in Iraq. There were actually four or five major groups: the INC; the two Kurdish parties (the Kurdistan Democratic Party, headed by Massoud Barzani, and the Patriotic Union of Kurdistan, headed by Jalal Talabani); the Supreme Council of the Islamic Republic of Iraq (SCIRI, headed by an Iranian-based cleric, Mohammed Bakr al-Hakim); and the INA, if one wished to count it. Otherwise, there existed a number of small outfits (often amounting to a few men and a fax machine), and a sizable number of unaffiliated individuals.

NEA also discovered ingenious alternative uses for the money. Some money did find its way to the INC, but a good portion of it went to a variety of American establishments, as long as they could come up with a proposal linking their activity to Saddam's opponents. That activity need not have any specific aim (and preferably did not).

The preference was for workshops and seminars. The State Department supported a conflict management program for the Iraqi opposition, founded by Harvard University professor Roger Fisher, author of *Getting to Yes*.[136] Washington, D.C.'s Middle East Institute received over $250,000 to host "thematic conferences" on Iraq after Saddam. Quality Support, a firm in Springfield, Virginia, with no particular knowledge of Iraq, received $3.1 million to book hotel rooms, airline tickets, and conference halls for opposition meetings.[137]

With the crises over weapons inspections continuing, Congress was prompted to pass the Iraq Liberation Act in October 1998, providing for the drawdown of $97 million in Pentagon equipment. That legislation signaled the clear intent of Congress: it had a military component, and it aimed at liberating Iraq. The White House was first inclined to veto it but had a change of heart, with yet another crisis the following month. This time President Clinton called off a strike on Iraq at the last minute, after Baghdad faxed U.N. Secretary General Kofi Annan a note saying it would comply, more or less, with inspections. The White House now announced that it would implement the Iraq Liberation Act, and that its policy would shift to "regime change."

Neither the policy nor the regime in fact changed. By March 1999, Jim Hoagland—who followed Iraq more closely than any other journalist—was sharply criticizing Clinton's "virtual policy."[138]

A New Team

AFTER GEORGE W. BUSH became president in January 2001, a division soon emerged within the new administration. The State Department advocated continuing the existing policy on Iraq, with a modification of the sanctions—so-called smart sanctions—that were less restrictive on Iraq, thereby making them more palatable to the international community. (Only after the war did it become clear how correct Bush had been in calling the sanctions "Swiss cheese.") The Pentagon and the vice president's office believed Saddam should be overthrown and wanted the United States to support the INC more actively. But Iraq was not a high priority. The vice president was focused on energy policy, while the Pentagon leadership focused on "transformation," i.e., reshaping the armed services to fight mobile, information-age wars.

The attacks of September 11 changed almost everything—but not, however, the fundamental nature of the bureaucratic struggle over Iraq. The State Department (and CIA) continued to harass the INC, even though they had no viable alternative plan for postwar Iraq.

Even the most basic things were left undone: drawing up a provisional constitution for post-Saddam Iraq; developing an interim legal code; training a cadre of Iraqis for police functions. Virtually none of the measures to prepare for a post-Saddam Iraq envisaged in the Iraq Liberation Act of 1998 was ever implemented—not in the year and a half between September 11 and Iraq's liberation, and not in the period of nearly five years following the passage of the legislation.

Bureaucratic Horror Stories

I ASKED SEVERAL knowledgeable individuals what they found most astounding about how the U.S. government had dealt with the Iraqi National Congress. One insider pointed to the State Department's handling of its Office of Inspector General's (OIG) reports relating to the INC.

The Organization Smear

In 2001, the Inspector General's Office audited the Iraqi National Congress. It was a routine procedure, although those who requested the audit might have hoped it would help discredit the INC. The OIG found some problems with the INC's handling of State Department funds, and it recommended procedures for straightening them out. That is common enough, in part because government regulations are extremely complex and precise in their reporting and record-keeping requirements. The INC implemented the procedures, and a reaudit was performed the next year. At that point, the office of Near East Affairs actually urged the OIG to falsify its report. The *Wall Street Journal* obtained minutes of meetings between NEA and the OIG. "One redolent passage," the *Journal*'s editors observed, "dated May 17, 2002, says that, 'During the meeting Ms. [Yael] Lempert [NEA's Iraq desk officer] stated that NEA would appreciate any assistance the OIG could provide with NEA's desire to 'shut down the INC.' "[139]

Of course, as the *Journal* noted, NEA had no authority to "shut down the INC." The Inspector General's office not only gave the INC a clean bill of health—it also went so far as to criticize NEA for *its* handling of the INC grant. NEA had routinely underfunded projects; agreed to fund programs only over extremely short periods, so that long-term planning was virtually impossible; and back-funded, providing money only at the end of a grant period.[140] In short, NEA handled the funds in a way designed to hobble the effectiveness of the INC.

For any government office to seek to influence an inspector general's report is an extremely serious matter, implying politicization of government oversight procedures. No one has yet been held to account for this apparent attempt to use the OIG to further a covert political aim.

Even after the second audit and the INC's clean bill of health, NEA joined with antiwar congressmen in its crusade against the INC. Senator Patrick Leahy, a Democrat from Vermont who had voted against the war (and who, ironically, had been one of the recipients of an anthrax-laden letter), blocked the disbursement of over $600,000 to the INC. An aide to the senator cited the OIG investigation, claiming there had been "serious allegations" of the misappropriation of funds.[141] The audit report in fact expressed satisfaction with the INC, and Leahy was obliged to back down.

The Personal Smear

Another informed source cited the smear campaign against Ahmad Chalabi as the biggest stunner. Chalabi is a brilliant figure, a mathematician by training, with a Ph.D. (on the theory of knots) from the University of Chicago. Chalabi comes from an old, established Baghdad family, which held high office in Iraq before the 1958 overthrow of the Hashemite monarchy. Chalabi's grandfather was a government minister, as was his father on many occasions before becoming speaker of the Iraqi senate in the last years of the monarchy.

Chalabi had long opposed Saddam's regime. In the 1970s he had worked with the Kurds until their fight against Baghdad collapsed in 1975 when the shah of Iran and Saddam reached an agreement on dividing their riverine border, the Shatt al Arab. In the late 1970s, Chalabi founded the Petra Bank in Amman. In 1989, Jordan was closely aligned with Iraq.[142] In August 1989 the Jordanian government took over the bank, claiming Chalabi had mishandled funds.[143]

Notably, the seizure of the bank was carried out under secret martial law procedures. Martial law provisions had been established in Jordan following the 1967 Arab-Israeli war, but by 1989 they were rarely used. Chalabi fled Jordan to live in Britain. The bank's collapse followed, and in 1990 the Jordanian government issued a decree stating that anyone wishing to sue Petra Bank could do so only under martial law procedures, ensuring that matters related to its handling would largely remain under the control of the martial law administrators. It was not until 1992 that the Jordanian government got around to making any formal charges. A special security court, provided for under the post-1967 martial law procedures, was established on April 1, 1992. It held its first hearing on April 8, 1992. The next day, the court handed down a long judgment against Chalabi. As the *New York Sun* asked, "How was it possible for this court to thoroughly and fairly examine matters involving a complex international banking empire and issue a 223-page ruling all in the space of 24 hours?" And why was the matter handled in secret, in a security court, and not in public, in a regular court? Why was it suddenly taken up at that point? As the *Sun* observed, in a *60 Minutes* interview several months earlier, Chalabi had revealed documents detailing Jordan's involvement in helping Iraq purchase arms.

The Jordanian measures against Petra Bank led to a lawsuit between the Chalabi family and the Jordanian government in Hong Kong, regarding assets there. In 1993, the Hong Kong court, operating under British law, decided in favor of the Chalabi family, finding that Jordan's martial law takeover of the bank had been illegal.[144] Nonetheless, these charges, often touted by U.S. officials, would continue to dog Chalabi as he sought to mobilize support for Saddam's overthrow.

After the passage of the Iraq Liberation Act, the Clinton administration appointed a State Department official to the position of special representative for transition in Iraq. One of the first things he did was to impose a six-member leadership council on the INC, significantly reducing Chalabi's role. While acknowledging that the council was an unwieldy decision-making structure, the special representative explained that the United States did not want to make Chalabi look like an American puppet.[145]

Prior to the September 11 attacks, the campaign to thwart Chalabi's ascendance (some in Washington called it the "ABC campaign," for Anyone But Chalabi) was driven partly by U.S. officials who did not want to take any serious measures against Iraq; after September 11, it gained strength from the opposition to war. Other participants apparently believed that some sort of dictatorial regime was the only possible approach to governing Iraq. And, with time, the animus simply took on a life of its own.

The CIA developed a classified biography on Chalabi that was "full of lies."[146] It claimed that Chalabi was an embezzler (Petra Bank), an authoritarian personality who habitually traveled with a large retinue (which was demonstrably untrue).

The agency also maintained a dossier on Arras Karim, Chalabi's top intelligence aide (whose cousin had been detained by the INS, as discussed above, for allegedly hiding family ties). Ben Miller, a CIA analyst who was detailed to the White House to cover the Iraq desk, regularly showed administration officials a thick file on Karim purporting to demonstrate that he was an untrustworthy character with ties to Iranian and Iraqi intelligence.[147]

That was not true either. When the Defense Intelligence Agency (DIA) eventually took over an intelligence collection program run by the INC that the State Department had dragged its heels in implementing, it administered routine polygraphs to its INC contacts. The DIA checked out the CIA's allegations about Karim, and he passed with flying colors.

Know Thy Friends: The INC Contribution

STARTING IN JANUARY 2003, Chalabi and much of his staff began to reestablish themselves in Kurdish-controlled Iraq. A significant part of the INC Leadership Council imposed on Chalabi by the State Department, however, remained in London. The State Department insisted that any support it provided the INC must be used for activities approved by the entire Leadership Council, and a number of them wanted the money spent in London, where they were. Moreover, because Iraq was still formally under U.S. sanctions, an exemption from the Office of Foreign Assets Control (OFAC) was necessary to spend money there. Thus, as war loomed, the INC was unable to use any of its U.S. funding for activities in Iraqi Kurdistan. At that point, the CIA was virtually in charge of northern Iraq, and it saw to the enforcement of some other bizarre rules. The INC's intelligence cadres were not allowed to meet with the DIA officials who had also moved into northern Iraq; any information that the INC intelligence program gathered could be provided to the DIA only *outside* of Iraq.

The war began on March 19, with a U.S. strike on Baghdad, in an effort to hit Saddam. Five days later, on March 24, after much bureaucratic tugging and hauling, a Special Forces officer was sent to work with the INC, breaking the CIA stranglehold. The officer immediately reported back to Washington that he was stunned that the United States was not exploiting their capabilities.[148]

Chalabi had recognized that U.S. forces would need to have Iraqis alongside them, whether to help deal with Iraqi resistance, assist with police functions, or simply provide a liaison to the local population. As the Iraqi author Kanan Makiya explains, although the 1998 Iraq Liberation Act provided for the training of thousands of Iraqis, obstructionism from the State Department and CIA prevented any such training from taking place.[149] A minimal cadre of about a hundred Iraqis were belatedly given a quick training course in Hungary by the Pentagon at the end of 2002. Once in northern Iraq, Chalabi quickly began recruiting a "Free Iraq Force"—while still under OFAC restrictions.

As U.S. forces faced difficulties in southern Iraq in the war's early days, the Centcom commander, General Tommy Franks, asked for the participation of the Free Iraq Force (FIF). Another general at Centcom spoke to Chalabi shortly before he was to fly south and advised against Chalabi's making such a move. Chalabi then consulted a more senior Pentagon official, who gave the opposite advice. Chalabi, along with 700 FIF recruits, was flown to the southern city of Nasriyah on April 4.[150]

The bureaucracies opposed to the INC adhered to the view that a critical distinction existed between the exiles and those inside Iraq, and that those inside Iraq had *more* legitimacy. In fact, they looked to the remnants of the old regime, Ba'athists and tribal sheikhs, to help overthrow Saddam and to rebuild the country.

As it turned out, however, when Baghdad fell, there was nothing there. Authority in Iraq's cities collapsed as U.S. forces entered them. As Makiya explains, the institutions of the regime shattered like glass. The mistaken expectation had been that large sections of the institutions of the regime could be won over, at a sufficiently senior level, to maintain a command structure and the loyalty of its members; this simply did not happen.[151] In fact, as it turned out, there was only a single organized quasipolitical structure within the country: the Shi'a religious establishments. And Iran was quick to lend the harder-line elements among them support, including thousands of people trucked across the border into Iraq.[152]

The only real alternative to clerical dominance in Iraq, as it turns out, is a democratic, constitutional regime. If such a government materializes, it won't be because of anything the U.S. bureaucracies did directly to bring it about. If such a government does *not* emerge, the bureaucracies will consider their judgment vindicated: *we told you so.* But if that is indeed the result, many bitter Iraqis will continue to wonder whether timely U.S. support—including some serious capacity-building—might have led to a happier outcome.

Chapter Five

THE 1990S PEACE PROCESS AND THE UNDERLYING STRATEGIC MISCONCEPTION

Focus on Palestine

NO ISSUE IN THE MIDDLE East more consumed the attention of U.S. policy-makers, in the decade between the 1991 Gulf War and the 2001 terrorist attacks, than the Arab-Israeli "peace process."

On March 6, 1991, in his first major postwar address to the country, the first President Bush proclaimed before a joint session of Congress that "tonight in Iraq, Saddam walks amidst ruin"; he also promised that "for all that Saddam has done to his own people, to the Kuwaitis, and to the entire world, Saddam and those around him are accountable."

Within that same speech, Bush also affirmed: "We must do all that we can to close the gap between Israel and the Arab states and between Israelis and Palestinians."

A major Middle East peace conference was convened, under joint U.S.-Soviet auspices, in Madrid on October 30, 1991. The meeting, though, produced no real breakthrough. Notably, the PLO was not invited: Israeli Prime Minister Itzhak Shamir continued Israel's long-established policy of refusing to deal with the PLO; Yasser Arafat had openly backed Iraq during the Gulf War; oil-rich Arab states like Saudi Arabia and Kuwait had cut off its financial aid; and even Egypt, which had provided political support to the organization, no longer did so.

Arafat gained a new lease on life, however, through a deft and surprising move: he reached an agreement with Israel. Following elections in June 1992, Itzhak Rabin became prime minister, and his longstanding rival, Shimon Peres, became the nation's foreign minister. After clandestine negotiations in Oslo the following year (kept secret even from the United States), Israel concluded an understanding with Arafat. When the startling accord was presented to the United States, Washington readily endorsed it, and a carefully scripted signing ceremony was held on September 13, 1993, on the White House lawn. From then on, as senior Clinton administration Middle East adviser Martin Indyk explained, the focus of U.S. efforts in the Middle East became the "peace process." All other problems in the region were to be dealt with by "containing" them until the peace process had been completed.[153]

But of course the "peace process" never was completed. Today, amid daily violence in Israel and the Palestinian territories far more deadly than anything that preceded the Oslo accord, it may be difficult to recall the magnitude of the expectations surrounding that diplomatic effort—expectations that persisted, in one form or another, from the famous signing ceremony in September 1993 until the failure of the July 2000 Camp David summit and even beyond.

The Blind Eye

SUCH EXCESSIVELY OPTIMISTIC expectations were part of the rosy view of international politics that dominated the 1990s. At the same time they reflected, and contributed to, a broader intelligence failure regarding the Middle East in the same period.

The premise of the 1990s peace-process diplomacy was that a sharp line divided Islamic militants from such political entities as Syria and the PLO. The so-called secular entities were the "partners for peace." On the other side were the loose-cannon Islamic militants, "the enemies of peace." As Rabin asserted in late 1994,

> Even Syria and Lebanon, the governments there with which we negotiate are those who support peace. . . . The enemies of peace are the members of the movements and the organizations that belong to the ugly wave of extremism, fanaticism, fundamentalist terrorist Islamic movements, a wave that covers today most of the Arab and Islamic countries. They are the enemies of peace and in their lead is Iran.[154]

That analysis reflects the assumption that leaders such as Hafiz al-Assad and Yasser Arafat realized that they would have to comply with America's insistence on negotiations with Israel, given the predominant strength demonstrated by both the U.S. victory over Iraq in the Gulf War and the collapse of the Soviet Union (soon after the Madrid conference). Assad and Arafat were presumed to be too rational and calculating not to recognize their situation. International political realities had propelled them into seriously engaging in peace talks with Israel. (The possibility that the negotiations were not in fact serious, but merely a way of buying time, was unthinkable, too pessimistic for the prevailing worldview.) As a corollary, those parties who did not recognize and act upon the new political reality were simply irrational: religious fanatics—more precisely, Islamic militants.[155]

Yet this simple distinction is probably inapplicable in the context of the Islamic world, framed as it is by an essentially political religion in which "church" is not understood as separate from "state." Religious militants can and do collaborate with more secular figures. Moreover, the distinction blurs the critical historical divide within Islam, between Sunni and Shi'a, which itself plays a role in Middle East politics and terrorism.

In fact, each of the two camps described by Rabin was divided within itself, even as elements in each camp worked with elements in the other. For example, Syria and Iran were close allies, certainly until the death of Hafiz al-Assad in June 2000, and both countries were together involved in supporting Hizbollah terrorism.

Nevertheless, Israel chose to turn a blind eye toward the role of Syria, with whom it wished to reach a deal, preferring to blame Hizbollah terrorism entirely on Iran. Moreover, even though Palestinian Islamic Jihad was headquartered in Damascus, and the militant Islamic organization Hamas also maintained an office there, Israel did not make Syria's cessation of support for PIJ or Hamas terrorism a precondition of negotiations.

This point also pertains to the Palestinian Authority itself. Rabin believed that Arafat, unencumbered by human rights concerns, could stop the Palestinian terrorism of groups such as Hamas more effectively than Israel could. That confidence proved disastrously misplaced. Following its military incursions into the West Bank in the spring of 2002, Israel in fact found numerous documents linking the PA to terrorism, and demonstrating that the PA and Hamas cooperated tactically, even though they were rivals at a strategic level.[156] Once established in the West Bank and Gaza, the PA had actually developed its own terrorist organizations, including the al Aqsa Martyrs Brigade (an Islamic organization in many respects) and the Tanzim.

States and Militants

BUT THE NOTION that Islamic militancy was a single, unified movement—acting in opposition to the Arab entities with which Israel was pursuing peace—had a particular appeal to the peace camp in Israel. One former Israeli official saw in this radically formulated dichotomy a common bond between Israel and the Arabs:

> Islamic terrorism in the Middle East in the past two decades has not only been Israel's bitter lot. It also exists in Egypt. . . . Israel and President Mubarak's regime are in the same boat, since both organizations—the Islamic Group, which is fighting to bring down Mubarak's regime ("the infidel regime") and Hamas . . . spring from the same source: the Islamic revival movement.[157]

But just as the religious terrorist groups were less separate from the "secular" political entities than commonly supposed, they were also far less unified among themselves. To suggest that Hamas and the Islamic Group are essentially identical because their terrorism is motivated by Islamic extremism is no more reasonable than to maintain that Iraq and Syria were essentially the same (prior to March 2003), just because both are Ba'athist regimes. The primary political focus of Hamas is Israel; the main aim of the Islamic Group is to take power in Egypt.

The tendency to view the militant groups as one—as "the enemies of peace"—was the flip side of the insistence that the terrorists' Islamic radicalism fundamentally separated them from "secular" political authorities. It not only obscured the differences among them, but also reinforced the notion that they were not supported by other entities, such as Iraq, Syria, and the PA, which did not share their religious fanaticism. *The dominant tendency in the 1990s was thus to downplay the role of states in Middle Eastern terrorism,* and to emphasize instead the role of nonstate actors—above all, the Islamic militants.

This analysis should not be taken to dismiss the dangers posed by the militants. Their attacks on Israelis have taken a serious toll on the country and have stymied efforts to reach any agreement. Similarly, the spread of Sunni extremism, as promoted and funded by elements in Saudi Arabia and elsewhere, has had extremely negative consequences, and the measures being taken to block and roll back the expansion of that hateful ideology are certainly necessary. However, as happened in the 1990s, focusing too exclusively on Islamic terrorist groups and their ideology can blind policy-makers to the malfeasance of other actors in the region.

The thrust of the political and intellectual approach that dominated that decade was to turn a blind eye to the role of so-called secular entities like Syria, Iraq, and the PA in promoting terrorism. The Bush administration has taken a sharply different approach since the September 11 attacks, marked by the president's "Axis of Evil" speech, with its focus on the nexus between terrorist states and terrorist groups, irrespective of the ideologies they profess.

Another Aspect of a General Middle East Intelligence Failure?

AT THE TIME of the cease-fire to the 1991 Gulf War, there was a major debate about the wisdom of ending the war with Saddam in power. Yet those doubts did not last long; by the mid-1990s, the notion had taken hold that the United States had beaten Iraq decisively during that conflict. Maintaining sanctions on Iraq came to be seen as tantamount to victory in the war, as well as effectively neutralizing the Iraqi threat.[158] Saddam was regarded as yesterday's news, of little interest or significance.[159]

Moreover, after Iraq's presumed defeat in 1991, an apparently new problem emerged: Islamic militancy. The Soviet withdrawal from Afghanistan in 1989, together with the 1992 collapse of the Najibollah government there, caused the army of militants to fan out in search of new jihads. Some went to areas like Bosnia, where a Muslim insurgency against a non-Muslim ruling authority was being waged. Others returned home. Countries like Algeria and Egypt experienced a renewed wave of Islamic terrorism.

In the accepted intellectual construction, the threat of the early 1990s—Iraq and the Gulf War—was decisively defeated and finished when a new threat, that of Islamic militancy, emerged. The two threats are seen as separated in time and space.

But are these two phenomena in fact separate? In truth, the 1991 Gulf War did not really end until twelve years later, in 2003. In the intervening period, the conflict entered a new, less intense phase. The United States continued its part of the war: it maintained the economic siege of Iraq and enforced and expanded "no-fly zones" in the south and north. It even occasionally bombed the country, most seriously in December 1998. Nor did the conflict actually end for Iraq; instead it shifted to the arena of international diplomacy and to the single-minded pursuit of a military arsenal, focused, in fact, on the much-debated weapons of mass destruction.

If the Gulf War did *not* end with the 1991 cease-fire, then, but continued throughout the decade, it is reasonable to ask whether that war intersected with the problem of expanding Islamic militancy that emerged after the 1992 collapse of the Najibollah government. After all, these two developments occurred in the same space—the Sunni Muslim Middle East—and in the same time frame—the 1990s. In fact, although Iraq could not continue the war with the United States militarily, it was capable of carrying out major acts of terrorism—as it did, working with, and hiding behind, Islamic militants.

The Prevailing "Concept"

As we've seen, the term "concept" had been used to describe an intelligence phenomenon connected with the Arab-Israeli conflicts of the early 1970s. It was first used by the Agranat Commission, the official Israeli inquiry into the intelligence failures that led to the 1973 Yom Kippur War. "The concept" referred to the rigid and flawed view held by key Israeli officials that prevented them from recognizing the preparations being made by Egypt and Syria to attack Israel. As Joseph Kostiner of Tel Aviv University's Dayan Center for Middle Eastern Studies explained, the concept "is much more than a mistake."[160] It is an incorrect and misleading way of viewing information, based on false assumptions to which strong feelings may be attached, which results inevitably in wrong conclusions.

In 1973, key Israeli figures were acting under several unfounded and imprudent assumptions. They believed that Egypt would not go to war until it had an air force to counter Israel's, and that would not be before 1975. Furthermore, they believed that Syria would not go to war without Egypt. Therefore, the activities of Egypt and Syria as they readied to attack—though readily observed by Israel—were not seen for what they were: preparation for war. They were lost in the "noise" inherent in most intelligence analysis, dismissed because of the conviction that there could be no Arab assault before the mid-1970s.

This phenomenon—not seeing what is before one's eyes—occurs with regularity in history; from the U.S. failure to anticipate the Japanese strike at Pearl Harbor, to the Soviet failure to anticipate Hitler's invasion, to the failure of most U.S. and other officials to recognize that Iraq, with 100,000 troops poised on an unguarded strategic frontier, was about to invade Kuwait in July of 1990. At that key moment, rather than warn Saddam against attacking Kuwait, U.S. officials explicitly reassured him that the United States had no hostile intentions. The operative "concept" was that Saddam would not actually invade Kuwait—that his threats, and the concentration of Iraqi forces, related to an ongoing border dispute. Any strong U.S. warning to Iraq might be seen as provocative, making the situation worse, or so it was argued. As a senior Saudi official, reflecting back on that period, cautioned, "Saddam is capable of strategic deception."[161]

Because the conventional wisdom has so often been proved wrong, it is important at any such passage in history to question what "everybody knows"—especially with regard to the Middle East, a complex and unstable region that regularly serves up unpleasant surprises. And, given the unrealistic view of international politics that dominated the 1990s, including the exaggerated expectations surrounding the peace process, it is entirely appropriate to begin reconsidering events from that period.

Dividing the Coalition

THE TERM "GULF WAR COALITION" was given to the international alliance arrayed against Iraq during the 1991 war—an alliance that, importantly, included a bare majority of Arab states, headed by Egypt, Saudi Arabia, and Syria. Assembling that coalition in August 1990 was not a foregone conclusion. Had Egypt or Syria not backed the Saudis (who themselves required careful persuasion, in spite of their obvious vulnerability), an Arab majority for ousting Saddam from Kuwait probably would not have existed.[162]

Following the 1991 cease-fire, the Arab component of the coalition remained at first fairly robust. Many Arab states wanted to see Iraq's proscribed weapons programs destroyed. In August 1991, Riyadh allowed U.S. planes to be based in Saudi Arabia to support UNSCOM in its periodic confrontations with Baghdad; the following year, when the U.S. imposed a no-fly zone in southern Iraq, these Saudi-based planes were used to enforce it.

International interest in Iraq soon waned, however, and perception of the Iraqi threat grew ever dimmer. In late 1994, UNSCOM chairman Rolf Ekeus actually believed Iraq had largely complied with Resolution 687, the formal cease-fire, and that UNSCOM was close to completing its work of destroying Iraq's proscribed weapons. In January 1995, however, Israel provided detailed information about Iraq's import of large quantities of biological growth material, leading the weapons inspectors in their next report, in April 1995, to state for the first time that Iraq had an undeclared biological weapons program. The report had the effect of stopping the momentum that had been building to lift sanctions: suddenly there was an entirely new program for the inspectors to address.

For Saddam, the report may have signaled that sanctions would *never* be lifted, as envisaged in Resolution 687, because he was determined to retain Iraq's entire BW program. Saddam was not prepared, as he had been with Iraq's other weapons programs, to turn over part of it to UNSCOM and pretend that that was the whole of the program.[163] Iraq's problems were further compounded in August, when Hussein Kamil's defection precipitated stunning revelations about *all* of its proscribed weapons programs. The Clinton administration, paradoxically, regarded those revelations as a "godsend," or so one State Department official described them—because they made it easy to maintain Security Council support for sanctions, which had by now become the core of U.S. policy toward Iraq.[164] (The Arab members of the Gulf War coalition, however, reacted quite differently: Iraq's neighbors Saudi Arabia and Kuwait were alarmed, fearing what Saddam might do with that material someday.)

Saddam never did surrender those weapons programs. Rather, he adhered to a strategy of holding fast and waiting for the international community to lose interest once again. At the same time, Iraq actively worked to undermine the coalition. Saddam used oil sales and related contracts, allowed under Resolution 986 (oil for food), to win support from various parties.[165] And he also, I would argue, used force and intimidation to undermine the Arab part of the coalition.

The Crucial Case of Egypt

UNLIKE SAUDI ARABIA, Egypt was not directly threatened by Iraq. There was little reason for Egypt to remain a committed member of the anti-Iraq alliance, if there proved to be a serious price to pay for doing so.

Following the collapse of the Najibollah regime in Afghanistan, Egypt began to suffer an upsurge in Islamic violence, beginning in mid-1992. That year, fifty-five people (including civilians as well as security forces) died in Islamic terrorism in Egypt. The number peaked at 221 in 1993 and then began to decline slowly, as the Egyptian government "regained the initiative" in 1995 and 1996.[166] A last spectacular attack on tourists occurred in November 1997. Despite expectations, that assault marked the end of major Islamic terrorist violence in Egypt.

Islamic militants are widely regarded as a growing threat almost everywhere around the globe. Yet as determined as the militants are, they often face harsh and heavy-handed regimes, prepared to respond quite brutally, as in the case of the Egyptian government; and, as more recent press reports have noted, there has been a definite downturn in the use of violence by Egypt's Islamic extremists.[167] The noted Middle East scholar Fouad Ajami has remarked that the Arab governments are "entrenched regimes, which have mastered precious little save the art of staying in power."[168]

The capabilities of the Islamic militants also vary, no doubt, from place to place. The Armed Islamic Group in Algeria, for example, has been much more violent and persistent than Egypt's Islamic groups. Terrorism, like most complex human activity, requires skills and knowledge that are acquired through training.

One of the challenges to be posed to the conventional wisdom is the question of whether the Islamic violence that Egypt experienced—particularly between 1995 and 1997—was in fact what it is generally assumed to be. The 1997 attack on tourists in Luxor, in particular, reveals anomalies that raise questions about the prevailing "concept."

The November 17, 1997, Attack at Luxor

THE 1997 ATTACK at a major tourist site in southern Egypt, the temple at Luxor, killed fifty-eight foreign tourists. More tourists died on that one day, in that one attack, than were killed in the entire previous five years of Egypt's post-Afghanistan Islamic insurgency.[169]

The attack was a particularly hard blow to the Egyptian government, as the country is poor and tourism is its premier source of foreign exchange. Egypt's tourism minister described the aftermath of the Luxor attack as "the biggest crisis in the history of tourism in Egypt."[170] The assault set back Egypt's tourism industry for an entire year.

But the Luxor attack was a political as well as an economic disaster for Egypt. One Israeli expert on Egypt observed that it was "particularly shocking, not just for its sheer brutality, and the unprecedented number of casualties, but also because it came after a period of relative calm marked by a growing sense of stability."[171] An American journalist, one who had long lived in Egypt and studied its Islamic movements, asserted that Luxor was "a turning point, . . . because it portended a far more lethal agenda than any previously seen . . . [and] showed in embarrassing clarity how marginalized traditional leaders, including Mubarak, had become."[172]

The attack was unusually methodical. The six gunmen, dressed in plain black clothing, moved in pairs. They succeeded in catching a group of tourists in an area of the temple where "cramped terraces offered no route of escape," where the largest number were slain.[173] The rampage went on for some forty-five minutes before the gunmen, still unimpeded, finally commandeered a tourist bus and fled.

The gunmen were killed that day, though under circumstances that remain unclear. The Egyptian government announced that they were shot by police after a protracted gun battle. But the security forces in Luxor were not very capable, judging by the scale of the unchecked attack. The Egyptian security investigation conducted afterward raised questions about whether the handful of local security officials who pursued the attackers even possessed weapons with sufficient range to hit the gunmen, who died inside a deep cave.[174]

After Egyptian authorities found the individuals dead in the cave, they learned that one of them was an Egyptian militant who had been in Afghanistan; another they were unable to identify; and four were Egyptian students who were not Islamic militants at all. This was at odds with the prevailing "concept": that Egyptian militants acted exclusively on their own, without assistance from other parties. The apparent participation of (at least) four nonmilitants might have caused some reassessment of "the concept." But the response of observers outside the Egyptian government, at least, was to shoehorn the new evidence into the old concept. As the *New York Times* reported,

> What is unnerving about this, Western diplomats say, is that it suggests either that most of those who carried out the attack represented either an unknown splinter group or that they were persuaded to risk their lives on behalf of a militant organization with which they may have previously had little contact.[175]

The Luxor attack appeared to portend a new, more violent wave of Islamic terrorism in Egypt. Having carried out one spectacular assault, the militants were expected to follow up with others.

The other shoe never dropped, however. Once again, the "concept" was not questioned. When no further major attacks occurred, the assault at Luxor was simply deemed an anomaly, "an isolated outburst,"[176] presumably of the Egyptian militant movement.

After the Luxor attack, "everyone" assimilated it into their preexisting "concept." Yet Egyptian authorities were in a different position. They had to carry out a careful analysis of what had happened to ensure it would not happen again. Egypt had suffered an attack unprecedented in its virulence as well as its organizational effectiveness, implemented, at least in part, by terrorists who were not Islamic militants and who had no obvious motive for the attack, plus one man who remained unidentified. Given their mysterious deaths immediately after the attack, interrogation was impossible. A host of logical questions remained: *What else might have been involved? What was the motive?*

In the fall of 1997, around the time of the Luxor attack, Baghdad initiated a series of crises over UNSCOM that would have the effect of terminating U.N. weapons inspections a year later. With each succeeding crisis, the U.S. threatened to attack Iraq. The first crisis was defused by a Russian-engineered compromise on November 20.

The next crisis began in mid-January, two months after Luxor. Egypt played a prominent role in that confrontation, urging that it not be resolved by force—and it was not, for a variety of reasons, including opposition in the region.

Two months was sufficient time for the Egyptian security investigation to have recognized the anomalies in the Luxor attack. Egyptian officials fully understood Saddam's vengeful and vicious nature. Perhaps, like the Saudi official (noted below) who attributed the 1995 bombing in Riyadh to Iraq (in part because he considered the Saudi opposition incapable of such an attack), a similar thought had occurred to Egyptian authorities. What, after all, are the capabilities of Egypt's indigenous militant Islamic groups compared to the intelligence services of a terrorist state such as Iraq? Indeed, former *Wall Street Journal* reporter Richard Miniter confirmed in a private interview in April 2002 that at least some key Egyptian officials do in fact believe that Iraq was involved.[177]

Notably, there was no sequel to the Luxor attack, after Egypt moved toward Iraq's position in the second UNSCOM crisis.

The Attempt on Mubarak's Life

ON JUNE 26, 1995, Egyptian President Hosni Mubarak arrived in Addis Ababa, Ethiopia, to attend a summit of the Organization of African Unity. On his way in from the airport, Mubarak's motorcade was halted when a four-wheel-drive vehicle rammed the car carrying the Egyptian foreign minister, traveling just ahead of Mubarak's car. Several gunmen jumped out of the car and opened fire, while another vehicle carrying more gunmen maneuvered next to Mubarak's limousine, which took a fusillade of bullets.

As the *Washington Post* reported, "the attack bore the hallmarks of careful planning and organization."[178] Yet it did virtually no physical harm to any Egyptian official. Mubarak was riding in a heavily armored limousine with bulletproof glass, which the AK-47s did not succeed in penetrating. Ethiopian officials later discovered a bomb that never detonated, in a vehicle parked along the route the motorcade would have taken.

Two of the gunmen were killed in the attack, three more died in a shoot-out with Ethiopian authorities several days later, and one plotter escaped to Sudan. Egyptian authorities immediately denounced Sudan as being behind the attack, a conclusion the Ethiopians also reached several months later.[179] The United States accepted that conclusion and the following year persuaded the Security Council to impose sanctions on Sudan for its role in supporting terrorism.[180]

Thus, in the view of the U.S., Egyptian, and Ethiopian governments—a view implicitly endorsed by the Security Council—the attack on Mubarak was not simply the work of Egyptian militants acting on their own. It had been supported by a state, namely, the government of Sudan.

Questions, however, remain. Following the assault on Mubarak's motorcade, Ethiopian authorities found rocket-propelled grenade launchers in a safe house that had been used by the gunmen.[181] Why did the terrorists use AK-47s, which did no real damage, when they had RPGs? Was this assault something other than a serious attempt to kill Mubarak? Is that also why the bomb didn't go off? And if it was not an assassination attempt, what was it? The possibility that Iraq played a role in the drama is suggested by certain other elements of its staging.

Following the Gulf War, Baghdad established Khartoum as a major center for Iraq intelligence, under the command of Abd al Samad al-Ta'ish, a highly placed Iraqi intelligence agent who became Iraq's ambassador to Sudan in July 1991 and remained there until the summer of 1998. Iraq publicly defended Sudan against the Egyptian charge that Khartoum was behind the attack. Baghdad's official press blasted Cairo:

By fabricating premeditated charges against Sudan, the Egyptian ruler sought to show his willingness to serve his masters and highlight his role as a paid stooge who is ready to act on orders. This is the very role he has played against Iraq when he turned Egyptian territory into a bridgehead for the colonialist alliance troops during the 30-state aggression. This has also been manifested in his enthusiastically slavish endorsement of the Iraq sanctions.[182]

Babil, a newspaper owned by Saddam's son Uday, applauded the attack and explicitly threatened Mubarak. In a front-page editorial it asserted that it was "permissible" to shed Mubarak's blood "for what he did to Iraq." It also warned him to "wait until tomorrow . . . as it conceals more and more surprises from your victims," including Iraq, the Egyptians, and the Palestinians.[183]

Egypt ultimately concluded that Iraq was involved in the attack, working with Islamic Jihad, according to private reports by Ahmad Chalabi of the Iraqi National Congress and journalist Richard Miniter. Furthermore, they inferred that the attack was not really meant to kill Mubarak, based on the reasoning outlined above.[184]

Nevertheless, it does not appear that the Egyptians understood that at the time, or at least nothing in the public record suggests so. Cairo did not denounce Iraq; nor, on the other hand, did any apparent appeasement of Baghdad follow. In fact, when Hussein Kamil defected two months later, the Egyptians strongly backed the Saudis' concerns about the danger of Iraq's weapons.

The Bombing of the Egyptian Embassy in Islamabad

SEVERAL SIGNIFICANT TERRORIST attacks occurred in November of 1995. On November 13, 1995, the U.S. mission to the Saudi National Guard was bombed. This was the biggest bombing in Saudi Arabia up to that date, killing seven people (including five Americans). As a senior Saudi official privately affirmed, "Of course that was Iraq. That was a professional bomb. It was not made by a bunch of Saudis sitting in a tent in the middle of the desert."[185]

On the same day, an Egyptian diplomat at the World Trade Organization in Geneva was shot and killed.[186] An unknown group, the "International Justice Group," claimed responsibility.

Six days later, on November 19, 1995, the Egyptian embassy in Islamabad was bombed; fifteen people were killed. The "International Justice Group" again claimed responsibility, in a fax threatening to murder "the Pharoahs of Egypt"—referring to Mubarak and three other senior Egyptian officials.[187]

This was the first time any Egyptian embassy had been bombed, and once again it was assumed that Egyptian militants were solely responsible. The Gulf War, and Egypt's key role in the Arab coalition against Iraq, were not even considered as possible factors in the attack. Once again, observers took account of an anomaly by stretching the established "concept," as in this *Financial Times* analysis: "The fact that [the bombing] took place outside Egypt's borders appears to be part of a change in strategy by frustrated militants. Their campaign to topple the government by force has suffered badly at home."[188]

Attacking an embassy, however, is a far more ambitious, and far more difficult, venture than any other attack attributed to Egypt's Islamic militants—aside from the audacious 1995 assault on Mubarak. Was it really adequate to conclude simply that Egyptian militants, thwarted in their domestic operations, had now shifted their tactics beyond their national borders? The stunningly successful attack at Luxor two years later is in any case difficult to reconcile with that theory. And was there in fact no connection with the attack on the American facility in Saudi Arabia, just six days before, on the day of the assassination of the Egyptian diplomat posted to the World Trade Organization?

Fixated on the Islamic threat, observers failed to ask some basic questions. What are the actual capabilities of each Islamic group that is believed to be involved in each of these terrorist attacks? And what is the possible relationship among the events on the ground, and between the worlds of terrorism and politics?

The tendency was to perceive the Islamic militants as if they operated in a separate sphere, independent of such non-Islamic political entities as Iraq, and to assume that their terrorism was a phenomenon separate from other major developments in the Middle East (with the notable exception of the Palestinian cause).

Saddam's Concept

FOR SADDAM HUSSEIN, violence is an indispensable instrument that serves a wide range of purposes. As his foreign minister, Tariq Aziz, once told a delegation of Arab professors, "People do what you want, when you hurt them."[189]

Most probably, that was the point of the Luxor attack. If Egypt did not want to experience a sequel, it should show more sympathy for the suffering of the Iraqi people. Egypt did so—and that was the last significant act of Islamic terrorism directed against any Egyptian target. (Egyptian authorities had, in fact, successfully quashed the indigenous component of their post-Afghan Islamic terrorism some years before.)

None of this could be considered, let alone analyzed, at a time when the "peace process" was practically the sole U.S. preoccupation in the Middle East (and of many other countries). It wasn't just that such diplomacy consumed a great deal of time and attention; more to the point, it was premised, at least in its heyday, on false assumptions: the notion that the United States had decisively defeated Iraq in 1991, and the presumed existence of a sharp division between the so-called secular entities in the region and the Islamic militants. The Middle East is a lot more complicated than that.

Chapter Six

THE BATTLE OF
THE BELTWAY

The President and His Cabinet

PRESIDENT TRUMAN ONCE said of his successor, "He'll sit here and say do this, do that, and nothing will happen. Poor Ike—it won't be a bit like the army. He'll find it very frustrating."[190]

The "levers" of power in Washington operate rather like strings: they can be pulled, but they can't be pushed. Presidents can have great difficulty getting their entire cabinet on board for a given policy decision. The dramatic public difference of opinion over Iraq policy between Colin Powell at State and Donald Rumsfeld at Defense had its precedent in such dramas as the split between Shultz and Weinberger in the 1980s.

After a few attempts at pushing the strings of power, a president may become increasingly reluctant to give an order that he knows will not be executed. Major interagency disputes thus fail to be resolved, or they get resolved very late; no one will fold his cards until there has been an unambiguous presidential decision. The result is that the various bureaucracies continue on their own paths. Even after a clear decision has been made, sub-cabinet and sub-sub-cabinet officials may work to undermine it, while the overruled cabinet official may continue to emit public signals of his unhappiness with the policy.

In general, cabinet officials' public briefings, as well as diplomatic communications, may tend to reflect their own views rather than those of the president. When the president's policy is publicly presented by a cabinet officer, it may be in a perfunctory or unpersuasive manner. The president really needs to be his own best spokesman—a role that President Bush has clearly felt less than comfortable doing.

CIA: The Workings of Bureaucracy

AMONG ITS MAIN TASKS, the CIA gathers and analyzes information. Notably, there exists a bias *against* using or even recognizing information that is available in the public domain. The agency deals strictly with information that is classified, and therefore "intelligence."

The disdain for publicly available information arises, in part, because an enormous amount of secret information flows across the overloaded desks of CIA analysts. But this bias is also self-serving. The implicit claim is that the agency's information (to which only it has full access) is better than anyone else's, and therefore, so are the agency's conclusions. In fact, CIA analysts often respond to new (outside) information by saying simply, "We can't confirm it." Such an easy dismissal may simply be a matter of deflecting embarrassment after encountering information the analyst should already have had. It can also, however, be a pernicious way of dismissing information that the analyst (and his boss) don't want to hear. "We can't confirm it" sends the unwelcome bit of news down the rabbit hole.[191]

In general, agency management is inclined to develop good ties with whatever administration holds the White House at the time. The Clinton White House showed a general reluctance to hear bad news on the national security front on a range of issues, including Iraq and terrorism, a reluctance that had, in the words of one former CIA official, "a palpable influence." The theory of a new kind of terrorism that did not involve states was strongly promoted by the Clinton White House; the agency not only bought into that theory, but promoted it too. One member of the Senate Intelligence Committee offered this account of what had transpired over the past decade: the White House "put the kibosh" on the investigation of New York FBI into Iraq's role in the 1993 World Trade Center bombing, and then brought in intelligence to support its position.[192]

One leading opponent of the case against Iraq in this period was Paul Pillar, the deputy head of the CIA's Counter Terrorism Center for much of the 1990s. Pillar was later appointed to his current position as the CIA's national intelligence officer for the Middle East, in which capacity he also evaluated intelligence related to the war with Iraq.

In April 2001, Pillar published a book on terrorism strongly endorsing the view that state-sponsored terrorism has declined drastically and that the terrorist attacks that began with the Trade Center bombing are predominantly the work of "nonstate organizations," or even "individuals and tiny protogroups."[193]

Nothing in the book anticipates the horror of the attacks that would be launched just five months later. Rather, Pillar refers to terrorism as "a problem managed, never solved"[194]—a phrase that would seem more appropriate to a discussion of automobile fatalities than to state-sponsored terror. While we can do our best to minimize the damage, he suggests, it is a problem so diffuse in its causes and sources that, in the end, we simply have to live with it.

Pillar accordingly took strong issue with Bush's policies in the war on terrorism, and particularly with the positions expressed in the president's 2002 State of the Union Address. According to Pillar, Bush should not have said that "Iraq could give weapons of mass destruction to terrorists because there is no evidence of this occurring in the past." There was "no evidence," he also asserted, "that Iraq had sponsored terrorism since the 1993 assassination attempt on former president George H. W. Bush."[195]

What are the implications for someone in Pillar's position, if he is wrong? What if Iraq proves to have been involved both in the 1993 Trade Center bombing and in the September 11 strikes? One clear implication is that a massive intelligence failure had occurred. A deeper implication would be that a fundamental intelligence error had become the dominant theory during the intervening seven years, such that the U.S. mishandling of the first attack in fact contributed to the second.

Pillar, and others who produced such analyses and theories, obviously have a strong interest in maintaining the record as it currently stands. Indeed, shortly after the September 11 attacks, a former CIA official asserted, "You can go to war on the WMD, but not on the terrorism."[196] Although the argument that Iraq was involved in the September 11 attacks would certainly have made a more compelling case for war, he did not even want to see the issue pursued: retired officials generally tend to reflect the perspectives of the agencies they once worked for.

In the end, that approach prevailed. In view of the bureaucratic opposition to linking Iraq to the September 11 attacks, and even to al Qaeda more generally, the administration based its case for war principally on Iraq's retention of proscribed weapons.

As the country's premier foreign intelligence gathering and analysis organization, the CIA plays a leading role in formulating the official U.S. understanding of national security issues, including foreign terrorism. It is the authoritative judge of the quality and meaning of information that it obtains, and it can exercise a veto over the interpretation of intelligence by other, competing national security agencies. (The FBI is of course part of the Justice Department, and although it participates in terrorism investigations, it is not involved in the interagency national security process.) Other players tend to be relegated to a decidedly secondary position in the information process—including the president himself and his cabinet officials (and sometimes even the director of the CIA).[197]

When, for whatever reasons, the agency decides to leave key stones unturned, the inevitable result is policy-making in an information vacuum—with potentially enormous damage to national security interests and to broader national interests as well.

The Information Bottleneck

A BUREAUCRACY IS a self-contained and self-serving organization. Although it forms part of a larger organizational structure—usually a government—its day-to-day activities are shaped by the needs of the organization itself, or more often, of a smaller subset or division within the bureaucratic agency. Max Weber, the grandfather of modern political sociology, was probably the first to point to the importance of the control of *channels of information* in managing a bureaucracy. Thus, a key resource of any bureaucracy is information, which it harvests and protects like money in the bank.

As such, the CIA is the quintessential bureaucracy: as a clandestine information agency, the CIA's mission closely parallels the bureaucratic imperative to harvest and protect information.

In the case of the CIA, the control of information is so zealously guarded that its release, even to authorized government officials, is a matter of bureaucratic strategy, tailored to the benefit of the agency itself or even of a particular agency division. This is a reality well understood by the CIA's clientele in other agencies within the government, who make a point of cultivating working relationships with key agency officials—much as media representatives, for example, cultivate their government sources.

In effect, there are three broad thresholds to be crossed in the effort to obtain classified information: obtaining the official security clearances; demonstrating an official "need to know"; and, finally, having unofficial access—a personal relationship with someone in a position to provide the information.

Entrenched

POLICY ASSESSMENTS at the highest administrative levels are not reached without some blood on the floor. Even when policy debates don't make it to the pages of the national press, the struggle to define the administration's worldview may be a battle of epic proportions, with winners and losers afterward clearly defined. Once in place, therefore, a policy orientation becomes virtually impossible to dislodge by any weight of evidence or argument, other than by replacing key players.

For the CIA, moreover, revising an assessment is at least as unpalatable as sharing its trove of information. Whether or not international terrorism has an "address," it's a known fact that every government policy determination does. A particular analysis or position paper is usually closely identified with a particular individual, at a particular "desk," within a particular division of the agency.

Moreover, certain institutional features make the CIA more difficult for the administration to control than other agencies. As in the case of the military services, the CIA has its own self-contained personnel system. Promotion is handled separately from the ordinary civil service system and is to a large extent impervious to performance reviews by "civilian" officials. And, in contrast to the military, CIA culture does not enshrine the principle of subordination to civilian command, which is a bedrock principle of the U.S. armed services that is inculcated at all the military academies. The independence of its personnel system, together with the secrecy of its budget (which is unpublished) and the power to classify information, may place key levers of the CIA's governance beyond the administration's grasp.

Having committed itself to the position that state sponsorship of terrorism was not relevant to the new wave of anti-U.S. attacks, the CIA would utilize a range of bureaucratic tactics to protect that position. One such tactic is bureaucratic inertia—the policy "string" that cannot be pushed. Little or no agency resources, apparently, were devoted to testing the new theory of stateless terrorism by pursuing potentially troublesome leads; more disturbing, all evidence or questions presented by outsiders was systematically discredited.

This was certainly so during the Clinton years, when the agency was presenting a view that the White House had actively elicited. It was so too in the early months of the Bush administration, when a handful of senior administration officials sought to revisit that theory. And it remained so after the September 11 attacks, when it became, if anything, even more difficult for individuals to change that now-received wisdom. Indeed, as we've seen in chapter 3, at least some agency officials mounted their own campaign of disinformation, by providing misleading briefings to media and even in interagency discussions within the government.

This, in short, was why media commentators could continually intone that the government had found "no evidence" of a connection between Iraq and terrorist organizations, reflecting certain good-faith—but utterly mistaken—assumptions: that such a critical investigation would naturally have commanded the highest level of effort and resources within the agency—and that the off-the-record statements of government officials could be relied on. In fact, not only the CIA but also the Defense Department's intelligence office was in possession of significant evidence and suggestive leads that pointed directly to Iraqi involvement in anti-U.S. terrorism.

Bureaucracy and the Public Interest

As a rule, very few of the individual officials within any agency give sustained attention to questions of mission or overall policy. Even at the highest levels of the bureaucracy, the key "policy" goal tends to be narrowly defined in terms of positioning the agency as an effective player within the administration. For midlevel staffers, the key issue is maintaining "credibility" for their own administrative division. The term "credibility" is understood here in the Beltway sense, which refers not to accuracy or reliability but merely to having "access" to important higher-ups, i.e., being a credible bureaucratic player. With access, the division can expect to be notified of important intra-agency meetings; can have its requests responded to in timely fashion; and may even manage to play a role in the drafting of crucial policy documents. Such visible indicators of access are important tokens in the bureaucracy board game; they allow a division to maximize its influence, funding, and areas of responsibility. Without access, a division sinks into irrelevance and virtual invisibility in the intra-agency contest over "turf." Bureaucratic cultures in fact tend to distrust individuals who profess excessive concern for larger policy goals, while they accept and endorse an almost obsessive regard for self-serving matters of promotion, pay levels, and "face time."

The Bureaucratic Imperative

THE NARROW FOCUS of bureaucrats is actually an aspect of their professional (as opposed to political) orientation. A couple of phrases, widely used in Washington's bureaucratic circles, reinforce this narrow scope of interest. The approving term "team player" encapsulates the ethos of loyalty to the bureaucratic agency, especially vis-à-vis competing agencies. The phrase "that's above my pay scale" bespeaks an individual's unwillingness to discuss even important policy issues, beyond whatever details he or she has been "tasked" to address. In general, bureaucratic ethics tend to echo that classic statement of parochial loyalty: "What's good for General Motors [or State, or Defense, or CIA] is good for America."

One analyst involved in the post-September 11 effort to examine the intelligence for links between Iraq and al Qaeda complained that individuals in the agency refused to acknowledge the significance of what was before their eyes, precisely because it tended to expose their prior serious error. "The primary concern of these people," he complained, "is their careers—whether they make GS-14 or not."[198]

Another figure involved in that effort explained that a handful of analysts—who had strongly supported the position that Iraq was not involved in terrorism—dismiss virtually all evidence linking Iraq to al Qaeda or to the September 11 attacks as "fragmentary and inconsequential." At the same time, the same people insist that the information is sensitive and has to be kept classified. Thus, the administration could issue no public report about Iraq's involvement in terrorism (although a classified draft exists) owing, essentially, to obstructionism by the CIA. On the same day that CIA Director George Tenet was presenting certain valuable and highly classified information to Congress on the issue, the agency released a report dismissing the possibility of a link between secular Iraq and the religious Osama bin Laden.[199]

Senator Fred Thompson, who served on the Senate Intelligence Committee, was asked on the eve of his departure from Washington what were the three or four most important things that needed to be rectified regarding the U.S. national security apparatus. "I would start with the intelligence community," Thompson replied. "I would get some people whose judgment I trusted—and not all of them former this, that or the other. . . . I would require some accountability that I don't think that we have had, and do a thorough review of what was necessary and how we can make the transition that we haven't yet made from a Cold War apparatus to the world we live in today. . . . It all begins with intelligence."[200]

George W. Bush has proved to be astonishingly steadfast in pursuit of his policies (even bullheaded, depending on one's point of view). Whether he will prove equal to the challenge of governing the CIA, however, will be as crucial in defining his presidency as the war against Iraq itself.

The Shadow Administration:
Washington "Think Tanks"

As SOMEONE WHO had followed closely the evidence both of Iraqi intentions and capabilities and of Iraq's prior involvement in terrorism, I found it increasingly difficult, through the late 1990s, to share the complacency of much of official Washington regarding Iraq.

When I once had occasion to press a senior regional expert from a prominent Washington think tank on this issue, his candid reply was far from reassuring.

Where, I asked him, would responsibility lie if Saddam Hussein did something terrible—some crime he could only perpetrate because he had been left in power after the Gulf War? What if Iraq developed a nuclear weapon and used it? What if Saddam succeeded in carrying out a major biological terrorist attack? Who would bear the responsibility for those deaths?

He did not disagree with my assessment of the dangers; he just did not appear to give much thought to them. "The times are very cynical, and everyone must do what he must do for his career," was his reply.[201]

That discussion occurred in late November 1998. This was just two weeks after Clinton had announced his support for the Iraq Liberation Act and began calling for regime change in Iraq.[202] It was a radical about-face for the administration, and now the echelons of foreign policy mavens and team players began executing their own pivot turns.

By the time of our conversation, then, this particular analyst had developed a sudden new interest in patching things up with me (my own views were by then well known to anyone who cared to listen). This he conveyed in classic Washington style, by passing on the policy gossip from a dinner hosted by "Madeleine" (that is, Secretary of State Albright). Iraq had been the topic of discussion, and everyone present (he assured me) had supported the goal of overthrowing Saddam. But his blow-by-blow account of the dinner went on to recount the chorus of caveats that various participants had raised: we had to be cautious, proceed slowly, take care not to rush into anything.

It quickly became clear that no one was, in fact, talking seriously about overthrowing Saddam, and he understood that as well as I did.[203] Hence my very pointed question about individual responsibility—and his candid answer about "careers."

Middle East Policy Officials and Experts

AT THAT POINT, a mere handful of people constituted the Iraq expertise resident in Washington. (Since then, many more have polished up their knowledge of the subject.) President Clinton had been reluctant from the first to address the problems posed by Saddam Hussein. By the time of the conversation recounted above, Clinton had been in office for nearly six years, and most people had trimmed their sails accordingly.[204] Those in the administration who had at first favored an activist posture had scaled their expectations and recommendations downward; a very few who disagreed with the policy had actually left.

In the spring of 1996, for example, an official working in the office of the secretary of state took advantage of a shared transatlantic flight to raise the question of Iraq policy with a senior figure in the White House responsible for Middle East issues. The State Department official was concerned about the unconventional weapons that had been revealed after Hussein Kamil defected. Much like the think tank expert cited above, the White House official did not try to deny the obvious dangers. Following some exchange, he simply challenged, "Would you like to tell the president in an election year that we might have more of a problem with Iraq than we thought?" Having thus disposed of the matter, he returned to the book he had been reading.[205]

This was in fact a standard Washington approach to a standard difficulty. In essence it is a form of self-censorship, anticipating (and reinforcing) the "political constraints" on policy. It is never easy to tell the boss news he won't want to hear, especially when it concerns a serious policy issue that needs to be dealt with. To anticipate the "political constraints" is considered politically savvy; to push against them is considered naive.

The worried State Department official soon left government; the White House official stayed on.

During this period, the State Department's Office of Northern Gulf Affairs issued a classified internal analysis of its Iraq policy, pronouncing it an "unqualified success."[206] As time passed, less and less internal dissent was expressed with the policy of "containing" Iraq, as flawed as it was ultimately shown to be, most dramatically by the revelations following Kamil's defection.

The Art of Writing a Book

HERB MEYER, a longtime aide to Bill Casey, director of the CIA under Ronald Reagan, famously remarked that in Washington it never hurt to be fashionably wrong; what was lethal was to be correct ahead of one's time. In a similar spirit, the late Bill Geimer, who worked with Dick Cheney and Donald Rumsfeld in the Ford administration, once commented that people usually came to Washington with an idealistic spirit, but then they began to see "what the system rewards."[207] The Byzantine twists of Iraq policy provided more than one example of the political realities that Meyer's and Geimer's remarks referred to.

In general, the views of Iraq experts outside government mirrored those of their counterparts in the administration. By the summer of 1998, the debate between the president and the Congress over Iraq policy had grown particularly contentious, driven by Saddam's repeated challenges to the weapons inspections, and the administration's failure to develop a meaningful response to them. At that point, the prestigious Washington Institute for Near East Policy (WINEP) published a collection of papers on the subject, titled *Iraq Strategy Review: Options for U.S. Policy.*[208]

The WINEP volume presented five policy choices for dealing with Saddam. The options included: two versions of containment ("broad" and "narrow"—two very similar outlines essentially representing the administration's policy); deterrence (removing the constraints on Iraq and relying on the threat of retaliation to thwart Saddam's ambitions); providing support to the Iraqi opposition; and, last, launching a war to overthrow Saddam.

An unusual set of essentially artificial and self-imposed constraints governed the construction of this volume. A number of factors were *not* to be considered, including the nature of the threat posed by the Saddam regime. The editor, Patrick Clawson, ruled out that question in his introduction: "This study is not the place to analyze how great is the Saddam threat."[209] But shouldn't a study of U.S. policy toward Iraq begin with exactly that—a considered estimate of how serious a threat we face? Both historic experience and contemporary polls consistently show that the American public is (sensibly enough) far more willing to accept sacrifices if they believe important national security objectives are involved.

Even stranger, the author of each chapter of the *Iraq Strategy Review* had been instructed to act as the advocate—as if performing on a debate team—for his assigned policy option. Each author was to "[present] the best case for the respective policy, regardless of his own opinion."[210] The result was a series of highly abstract, speculative, and even self-evident essays. The deterrence chapter, for example, observed that deterrence might be a "realistic means of dealing with Iraq," given the flagging interest in the international community in dealing with Saddam—except for the fact that it might not work, if Saddam could not be effectively deterred.[211] The chapter on a possible invasion of Iraq stated that, while it would solve the problem definitively, the policy "would entail significant costs and run some very serious risks."[212]

None of this was news, of course, and almost the whole of the volume was equally bland. The book is nevertheless worth discussing here because of one anomalous detail. Every option, as it turned out, had some advantages—save one, which happened to be the option favored by the U.S. Congress: providing material support to the Iraqi opposition, specifically the Iraqi National Congress (INC).

That chapter, written by Kenneth Pollack of the Washington Institute and Daniel Byman of the Rand Corporation, stated flatly that supporting the INC would be a disaster: "a risky strategy that will not pay off for years, if ever."[213]

While still in draft form, the manuscript was circulated for comment. One senior national security figure advised against printing the monograph at all, deeming it worthless. Another suggested that the editor find someone sympathetic to the INC to write that chapter, so it would have the same quality as the others. This suggestion was adopted, and a chapter on supporting the INC was indeed solicited from a sympathetic individual. Nevertheless, when WINEP's *Iraq Strategy Review* appeared, the original chapter savaging the INC remained. Clawson himself used the new favorable chapter on the subject as the basis for an appendix to the book, reaching conclusions diametrically opposite to the chapter's original position. Support for the INC, he wrote, "is a risky strategy that could lead to the slaughter of opposition forces and a grave setback to U.S. interests in the region; the favorable draft had concluded, "A victory for the INC might well be the most promising development in the Middle East in 50 years."[214]

But this was par for the course among the Iraq experts. It is what "the system" rewarded. One person who wrote an article endorsing "containment" explained that he did not really believe his prescriptions were adequate to deal with the threat posed by Saddam, who he thought should be removed. When I asked him, "Why didn't you write that?" he replied that public support did not exist for ousting Saddam.[215] But public opinion is malleable; why, one might ask, publish any policy analysis whatsoever if not to provide the substantive background for a properly informed public debate?

Assessing the public mood, surely, is not the job of an Iraq analyst, who is supposed to explain the problem and present, as accurately as possible, the viable options that exist to deal with it. Mustering public support for a necessary course of action, then, should be left to those responsible for shaping public opinion—our political leaders.

The Art of Adjusting Positions

IRAQ STRATEGY REVIEW in fact marked one step in a more extensive campaign to delegitimize the option of supporting the Iraqi opposition. Pollack and Byman revised their chapter attacking the INC, adding a third author, Gideon Rose, a former intern at the Clinton White House who was now deputy director of national security affairs at the private, nonprofit Council on Foreign Relations (CFR). The resulting piece appeared as "The Rollback Fantasy" in the January/February 1999 issue of *Foreign Affairs*, the publication of the CFR.

"The Rollback Fantasy" sought to refute what it described as "one of the hottest foreign policy ideas in Washington today"—the notion that the United States should arm, train, and otherwise support the Iraqi opposition in overthrowing (or "rolling back") Saddam. If by a "hot" idea, the authors were suggesting that the position they were attacking was a popular one, the statement was highly misleading. Those who were calling for an overthrow of the Saddam regime, in one form or another—some of whom would go on to senior positions in the Bush administration—were at that point clearly incurring a career risk by taking issue with President Clinton's policy (and with the bureaucracies that supported it). It was not Pollack et al. who were going out on a limb; it was those who insisted that it was necessary for the United States to take on a task of evident difficulty—i.e., overthrowing Saddam Hussein.

Much as in the case of the WINEP volume, the authors of "The Rollback Fantasy" did not directly address the question of the threat posed by Saddam's regime. The argument rested wholly on the difficulty of the proposed remedies, including the objection that it would be impossible to mobilize public support for "rollback" "without an obvious goad other than U.S. frustration." The implicit assumption was that the threat posed by Saddam was not really very serious, and the conclusion was that the United States "really has only one option left—the much maligned existing policy of containment."[216]

It is surely too cynical (even for Washington) to suggest that *Foreign Affairs* may sometimes be read as a collection of job applications. Nevertheless, Kenneth Pollack was subsequently contacted by the White House and interviewed by National Security Director Sandy Berger, who hired him to handle the Iraq portfolio.[217] Pollack stayed in that position through the rest of Clinton's term, during which Iraq remained very much on the back burner. Nothing whatsoever was done to restore weapons inspections; and, while the administration pretended to accommodate congressional pressure to support the INC, it worked consistently to undermine and constrain the organization.

When, in early 1999, the White House conducted an internal review of Iraq policy, one National Security Council staffer summarized the effort this way: "the whole point was to get Iraq to disappear off the radar screen." Whatever talk there was of aiding the Iraqi opposition and changing the regime was "purely for public consumption."[218] As it turned out, Iraq—and national security in general—was scarcely an issue in the campaign.

By March 2002 the political landscape had shifted beyond recognition. Not only was there a new party and a new president in the White House, but American public opinion had been fairly wrenched from its moorings by the attacks of September 11. One indicator of this tectonic shift was a new Pollack article, again in *Foreign Affairs*—this one titled "Next Stop Baghdad?" The article appeared soon after President Bush's "Axis of Evil" speech, in which the president highlighted Iraq as the next objective in the war on terrorism. And Pollack's new article actually echoed that determination.

Now senior fellow and deputy director for national security studies at CFR, Pollack endorsed the necessity of removing Saddam: "The strategic logic for invasion is compelling." Nevertheless, Pollack claimed, the reasons "have little to do with the events of September 11," even though that was what had precipitated the change in Bush's own position. Instead, Pollack attempted to take a long-term perspective that might somehow bridge the gap between his new position and his previous support of the opposite policy of halfhearted containment.

Pollack begins by saying, "The hawks are wrong to think the problem is desperately urgent or connected to terrorism," and then goes on to borrow a page from the "hawks'" playbook—even while distorting their position: "but they are right to see the prospect of a nuclear-armed Saddam as so worrisome that it requires drastic action." This one-liner said nothing about Iraq's biological and chemical weapons, or its links to terrorists—issues that claimed far more urgent attention after September 11.

In fact, the concern about Iraqi nuclear weapons was only one of the very serious reasons for war, and it loomed somewhere in the future. The danger posed by biological terrorism was grave, and it existed in the here and now; this was precisely the "imminent threat" that was repeatedly stressed by the president and others in the lead-up to the war.

The problem for Kenneth Pollack (and others) was simply that *once the danger of Iraqi terrorist activity was admitted, the inescapable implication followed that the Clinton administration—including Pollack himself— had consciously turned a blind eye to a major threat to the country.* By stressing the prospect that Saddam might acquire a nuclear bomb, Pollack could point with alarm to this future threat, while continuing to dismiss the more imminent dangers that others, whom he derided, had warned of for several years.

Thus, in March 2002, Pollack argued that the policy of containment had been "a sensible approach to a situation in which there were few attractive options. It served its purposes well and far longer than most thought possible." But now it no longer worked: "containment has started to unravel."

This position, however, implied that the United States should long ago have taken serious steps to get rid of Saddam Hussein. Containment had worked "longer" than expected, but now—as indeed expected—it was no longer effective. In other words, it had always been the makeshift that its opponents had alleged. And now that it had unraveled, a new president had the task of mobilizing support for the inevitable confrontation.

Shouldn't the United States have addressed the problem back in 1995, when Hussein Kamil defected and the extent of Iraq's arsenal was revealed? The shock of learning about Iraq's illegally retained stockpiles of unconventional weapons would have made it far easier to mobilize international support for effective action against Saddam then. In 2003, a full eight years later, the international community had, apparently, become accustomed to Iraq's retention of those weapons. There's a quaintly named principle in law—acquiescence and estoppel—that speaks to Pollack's disingenuous change of tack, as well as to the irresponsibility of many others: if you don't object to something in a timely fashion you have implicitly accepted it.

Having about-faced to become an advocate for Saddam's ouster, Pollack nevertheless continued to attack those he insisted on calling the "hawks." He endeavored to position himself midway between the "doves," who showed too much faith in weapons inspections, and the "hawks," who (as he, remarkably, alleged) had "repackaged their ideas to fit the times."

The Revisionist Case for War

THE FOREIGN AFFAIRS article prompted a book contract, and six months later The Threatening Storm appeared. It constituted Pollack's argument for war. Because Pollack had worked for the CIA, as well as the NSC, the book was cleared for publication with both offices before publication.

If to err is human, to acknowledge error is statesmanlike. Dick Cheney, as secretary of defense, supported the decision not to oust Saddam in 1991, but after the September 11 attacks he remarked memorably that it was rare in history to be able to correct a mistake like that. Pollack, however, seems incapable of really adopting that perspective.

Significant Distortions

THOUGH THE *THREATENING STORM* is in many respects authoritative and comprehensive—even magisterial—at several key points its record of the past decade of Iraq policy is slightly twisted, to make that record seem far more defensible than it really was.

One example is Pollack's account of the Clinton administration's embarrassingly casual response to Iraq's 1996 attack on the Iraqi National Congress (discussed in chapter 4). Pollack claims that Secretary of Defense William Perry traveled to the Middle East to gain support for a strike, but was rebuffed.[219] The administration had favored a more robust response, Pollack claims, but was thwarted by others.

In fact, not only was Perry in Washington during the entire time, but the president also continued his scheduled activities, out on the campaign trail. Columnist Jim Hoagland called attention to the fact that Clinton did not return to Washington to hold a face-to-face meeting on the crisis, and that he gave the impression of being only partially engaged—that he had simply checked off (in Hoagland's words) the "least ambitious, least risky option box on a decision list prepared by [NSC Adviser Anthony] Lake."[220]

Another example is Pollack's treatment of Iraq's own revelations regarding its weapons programs, particularly after the 1995 defection of Hussein Kamil. We learned that Iraq had produced anthrax and botulinum in far greater quantities than it had previously admitted, and in weaponized forms, and we had hints also of research on smallpox. Nor was there evidence that any of this material had been destroyed as claimed. Pollack's assessment is that this information "hurt Saddam by displaying to the entire world the perfidy of his regime and its determination to flout the will of the Security Council."[221] But the more important finding, surely, was the revelation that Saddam was extremely dangerous—a point that Pollack (and others) had ignored for years.

Another misrepresentation involves U.N. Security Council Resolution 986, which provided for the U.N.-supervised sale of Iraqi oil. Pollack describes as "a major concession" the announcement by Iraq, in January 1996, that it was willing to implement the resolution.²²² In fact, the resolution provided Saddam a significant lifeline. Not only did it help relieve serious economic pressures on the regime, but it also became a vehicle for Iraq to award contracts and gain international political support. It was less an Iraqi "concession" than a significant U.S. defeat, as Paul Wolfowitz noted at the time.

The Weaker Argument for War

THE PRACTICAL CONSEQUENCE of Pollack's inability to admit error is that the rationale for war, as presented in this seemingly authoritative volume, is made to appear unnecessarily weak. The *casus belli* is reduced to Iraq's nuclear program, and anyone who thinks that there are other compelling (and more immediate) threats is wrong. In Pollack's book, the hawks are described as having "an almost obsessive fixation on getting rid of Saddam's regime," even though other, more generous, commentators would note at the time that the "hawks" had been right all along. Pollack's book amounts to an attempt to endorse President Bush's policy while providing an alternative, and ultimately unconvincing, rationale for it.

In the first sentence of the book, Pollack assures us (and himself): "As best we can tell, Iraq was not involved in the terrorist attacks of September 11, 2001. American intelligence officials have repeatedly affirmed that they can't connect Baghdad to the attacks despite Herculean labors to do so."²²³ So begins the revisionist statement of the reasons for war.

The Threatening Storm takes pains to characterize Saddam as not a great current threat, but rather a future danger. This allows Pollack to defend his past record while assuming a prominent, if belated, position in the prowar camp.

In a section titled "The Threat," Pollack suggests that Iraq retains only a "residual biological warfare program" and that "under present circumstances, Saddam's ability to employ his WMD is fairly circumscribed." A major threat will not exist "until [Saddam] develops a nuclear weapon—or proves that he can effectively employ advanced biological agents to kill massive numbers of people."[224] Yet there was every reason to believe that Iraq was capable of doing just that. The idea that Saddam had to "prove" such a capability to U.S. analysts before he was deemed a threat is bizarre.

Pollack seems to contradict himself in another section of the book, where he argues that restoring weapons inspections would not substitute for war. There he explains that by the mid-1990s defectors like Kamil and Khidhir Hamza (a senior Iraqi nuclear scientist) had already established that Baghdad's nuclear program was "bigger than it had ever been."[225] Nothing—not the Gulf War, inspections, or sanctions—had stopped that program. Given that Pollack felt Iraq's nuclear program was uniquely dangerous, why did he wait so many years to raise the alarm?

The *New York Times* called *The Threatening Storm* the most influential book of the season—and it probably was. It undoubtedly caused some readers to support the war who would not otherwise have done so.

But the book fundamentally distorted our understanding of our own recent history. Based as it was on only partial truth, the book presented the weakest argument for going to war, one that would fail to persuade many of the world's governments—not to mention international public opinion. Had the war gone badly (including the widely predicted casualties from Iraqi biological or chemical terrorism), this line of argument, which sidestepped the fundamental issue of Iraqi-sponsored terrorism, would have looked even weaker.

Washington's Tame Experts

THE OVERWHELMING MAJORITY of Washington's Iraq experts were content to endorse the Clinton administration's passive posture toward Iraq, ignoring the dangers that Saddam posed. This was the line to take in order to secure the right speaking engagements, journal publications, and dinner invitations, as well as, above all, official "access"—the privileged and up-to-date information from administration officials that is the chief currency of any pundit.

Pundits who behaved otherwise would sit out in the cold. The number of individuals willing to do that, for the sake of a policy argument, could be counted on the fingers of one hand.

The Middle East is a large and difficult region, with a range of problems that can be hard to understand. It is an area of undeniable importance to the United States: major international crises erupt there with dismaying regularity. Indeed, America's last two major wars were fought there.

In a critical sense, however, the Middle East is not given great importance in Washington. A background in the Middle East is unlikely to win one a post as secretary of state or NSC adviser, for example, as might a background in Russia or China. The study of the Middle East tends not to attract the country's best and brightest (and I am no exception). Moreover, American interest in the Middle East is focused rather narrowly on Arab-Israeli issues. The study of Iraq can easily end up subordinated to those more general concerns; in fact, it constitutes a backwater even within the historically marginalized field of Middle East studies.

This discouraging background may have something to do with the dismal performance of the experts in this field in the 1990s. After all, it had been known for seven years that Iraq possessed a major biological weapons program, which it took extensive steps to keep hidden. Equally widely known was the fanatical hatred of Saddam Hussein for the United States. The overwhelming majority of experts on Iraqi affairs, both in and out of government, were either silent or openly disparaging of the evident threat posed by such a combination.

Those who provided the intellectual substance for the critique of Clinton's "containment" policy—the critique that after September 11 became the rationale for war—were generally not the Iraq experts but rather a handful of strategic thinkers. These were individuals who were willing to take up an issue that put them at odds with the Clinton administration, because they believed a major danger to the country existed. These thinkers were a dedicated minority; and their views would never have become policy, if it had not been for President Bush himself.

Chapter Seven

KNOW THE ENEMY

WE ARE AT WAR with al Qaeda," CIA Director George Tenet warned in an internal memo after the simultaneous bombing of two U.S. embassies on August 7, 1998. Three years later, when the terrorist war came so lethally to U.S. soil, every American could appreciate that assessment. But America had never faced an enemy quite like this—one with quasimilitary capabilities, whose physical aspects are so elusive.

Al Qaeda's amorphous quality makes this enemy appear especially threatening. "Jihadists," we are told, "can be everywhere and anywhere."[226] The United States may have eliminated al Qaeda's base in Afghanistan, but the organization may well have regrouped elsewhere. We don't even know if it matters whether its political leaders—Osama bin Laden, or Ayman al Zawahiri (the head of Egyptian Islamic Jihad)— are dead or alive. According to one widely held view, this is an enemy that may not be defeated in our lifetime no matter what policies we adopt; nor is Cold War–style deterrence likely to carry much weight against so diffuse a target.[227] If this view is correct, for the foreseeable future we will remain vulnerable to an unforeseeable sequel to September 11, an attack that will emerge apparently from nowhere to kill thousands of Americans in one deadly stroke.

This view of al Qaeda, currently widely accepted, is actually an elaboration of a novel conception of the nature of terrorism that emerged over the course of the 1990s. We had previously assumed that major terrorist attacks against the United States were invariably state sponsored; they received logistic support and direction from hostile governments. Punishment—and deterrence—were therefore possible, at least in principle. This new theory, on the other hand, holds that today's breed of terrorism does not involve states but is rather the work of elusive terrorist "networks."

The 1993 bombing of the World Trade Center, intended to topple one tower onto the other, was the first instance of this shadowy "new terrorism," masterminded by the equally shadowy explosives expert Ramzi Yousef. Al Qaeda's terrorism, from this point of view, is at bottom a larger, more complex, and more sophisticated form of a phenomenon that began with the World Trade Center bombing and came full circle with the strikes on September 11.

In the period since then, however, U.S. officials have learned a great deal more about al Qaeda. Above all, the focus on bin Laden appears to have been somewhat misplaced. He was not in fact the operational mastermind of al Qaeda's terrorism but rather a sort of inspirational figurehead, not only bankrolling the operation but also articulating the radical Islamic worldview, brimming with hatred and resentment of America, which has proved so powerfully attractive to alienated Muslim youth.

The capture and interrogation of Abu Zubaydah, a high-ranking al Qaeda operative who was seized in March 2002, provided the first insights that led to this revised assessment. Only then did U.S. officials start to learn that the operational mastermind of al Qaeda's terrorism was not bin Laden but the man known as Khalid Shaikh Mohammed.

U.S. authorities had first become aware of Mohammed when he participated with Ramzi Yousef in a 1995 plot to bomb a dozen American jumbo jets operating out of the Philippines (a plot that backfired, mercifully, when Yousef accidentally started a fire while mixing explosives). Yousef was arrested a month later, but Mohammed successfully fled the Philippines and remained a fugitive. For a long time, his importance was not really appreciated.

As it turns out, Mohammed joined al Qaeda in 1997. He soon became the head of the group's military committee, and then he reportedly engineered not only the 1998 embassy bombings, but also the assault on the U.S.S. *Cole* in October 2000, in addition to the September 11 attacks.

Mohammed was arrested on March 1, 2003, in a private house in Rawalpindi, a city that is home to Pakistan's military and intelligence elite, located just outside the capital city of Islamabad.

The Baluch Terrorists

WITH THE REVELATION of the key role played by Mohammed in al Qaeda's terrorist operations, a new element had to be factored into the picture of "loose networks" of Islamist terrorists. Mohammed was not merely Ramzi Yousef's coconspirator in the 1995 plot against American jetliners; the two in fact reportedly have a long-standing connection. Both have been identified as Pakistani Baluch, born and raised in Kuwait. Mohammed, moreover, is supposedly a relative of Yousef. They are part of a larger circle that includes Abdul Hakim Murad, who was arrested and convicted with Yousef for the 1995 plane bombing plot. Murad, another Pakistani Baluch, is said to be Yousef's childhood friend. U.S. officials have since identified three more members of this circle as major al Qaeda figures and relatives of Yousef and Mohammed. Needless to say they too are Pakistani Baluch.

In short, the current understanding of U.S. officials, developed in the investigation of al Qaeda since September 11, is that a tight-knit group, essentially a family, lies at the core of the major Islamic terrorist attacks that America has suffered over the past decade.

Why?

THE ORDINARY AMERICAN'S acquaintance with Middle Eastern politics, having expanded to include first al Qaeda and then the Taliban, was about to expand further, in the direction of Baluchistan.

Most Americans are unfamiliar with the Baluch, indeed unaware of their existence. In fact, the United States has virtually nothing to do with them, in either the public or the private realm. During the trial of Yousef and Murad, the judge offered to provide the Baluch terrorists an Arabic translator (unnecessary, as both men speak fluent English). Murad's response was telling. He quipped to his lawyer, "Why not a Baluch translator?"—emphasizing his own primary ethnic identity: Baluch, rather than Arab.

The Baluch are a Sunni Muslim people living on both sides of the border between eastern Iran and western Pakistan. After World War II, when India was partitioned, the Baluch pressed in vain for a state of their own. Like the Kurds, the Baluch are a distinct people with a distinct language and inhabiting a specific territory, but lacking the ultimate political expression of those qualities, i.e., a separate state.

Much of Baluch territory is extremely rough and inhospitable desert, controlled by neither Iran nor Pakistan, and notorious as a smuggling route for opium from Afghanistan (among other clandestine activities).

The Baluch are generally considered as tough as their terrain. They have long been in a state of violent opposition to the Shi'a government in Tehran. Following Iran's 1979 Islamic revolution, and the drastic intensification of Shi'a rule introduced by the Ayatollah Khomeini, Baluch opposition to the Iranian government also intensified. In the mid-1970s, the Baluch also fought the Pakistani government. But while Pakistan's Baluch are now reconciled with their government, the Iranian Baluch remain in opposition to theirs.

What, we might ask, does all this have to do with Americans, or even with the U.S. government? Why should Baluch be involved in such monstrous attacks against this country? After all, on the famous Middle Eastern principle that "the enemy of my enemy is my friend," the Baluch might plausibly have looked to the United States for support against the hated ayatollahs.

Indeed, prior to 1993, there is no record whatsoever of Baluch attacks on U.S. targets. Even today, not a single Baluch group appears on the State Department's official list of terrorist organizations. So what would explain this extraordinary years-long vendetta?

Iraq and the Baluch

ALTHOUGH THE BALUCH have no apparent reason for assaulting Americans in the murderous terrorist attacks they have planned and/or executed over the past decade, some elements among the Baluch did in fact cooperate closely with a particular regional military power that was fiercely antagonistic to the United States.

General Wafiq Samarrai headed Iraqi military intelligence during the Iran-Iraq war (from 1980 to 1988) and during Iraq's invasion of Kuwait. (Saddam removed Samarrai from that position in June 1991, apparently doubting his loyalties, and shifted him to the palace, where he could be more closely watched.) In late 1994, Samarrai defected to the Iraqi opposition.

According to Samarrai, Iraqi intelligence has deep and well-established contacts with the Baluch on both sides of the Pakistan-Iran border. Iraq used the Baluch against Iran during the Iran-Iraq war, and Iraqi military intelligence in fact maintained an office in the Arab emirate of Dubai, where it ran Baluch spies into Iran.[228] Iraq also supported the Pakistani Baluch in their revolt. In early 1973, Pakistani authorities discovered in the residence of the Iraqi military attaché in Islamabad a huge cache of weapons intended for the Baluch—some 300 Soviet submachine guns, plus 48,000 rounds of ammunition.

The subject of the Baluch connection is a sensitive one in what were once Iraq's governing circles. In August 1995, after Hussein Kamil defected to Jordan, I obtained his phone number and called him in Amman. He denied that Iraq had been involved in the 1993 World Trade Center bombing. When I asked him about Iraq's ties to the Baluch, he replied blandly that Iraq had friendly ties with many people. But when it became clear that I was specifically interested in the Baluch, Kamil politely but firmly ended the conversation.[229]

A Terrorist "Family"

APART FROM THE PALESTINIAN community, many of whom were barred from returning to Kuwait after its 1991 liberation, most foreigners working in Kuwait have not been especially active in radical movements. Foreign workers in Kuwait make a great deal of money compared to what they would have made had they remained at home. Workers from third world countries often support not only their immediate family, but also an extended family in their native country. To become involved in disapproved political activity is to risk deportation by the Kuwaiti government, as I was told by a Kuwaiti official who himself had doubts about the terrorists' identities.[230]

Nevertheless, Mohammed, Yousef, and Murad are all said to have been born and raised in Kuwait. Mohammed is supposed to be Yousef's maternal uncle, and Murad is supposed to be Yousef's childhood friend. U.S. intelligence now also says that three other major al Qaeda figures are Pakistani Baluch, from the same small circle. Two are older relatives, brothers of Ramzi Yousef: Abd al Munim Yousef and Abd al Karim Yousef. The third is said to be a younger cousin, Ali Abdul Aziz.

Notably, U.S. officials believe that Abd al Munim and Abd al Karim are skillful enough to replace Mohammed in directing al Qaeda's terrorism.[231]

Thus instead of a loose network of radical Muslim terrorists, we now have the picture of *a single family* located at the center of almost all the major terrorist assaults against American targets over the past decade, starting with the bombing of the World Trade Center in 1993—an attack undertaken with no evident source of outside funding or training—and culminating in the September 11 strikes. Scarcely mentioned is the existence of intelligence ties between the Baluch and Iraq, though an insider such as General Samarrai has insisted that they are serious and longstanding.

The notion that one family lies behind this unprecedented campaign of increasingly spectacular terrorism is difficult to credit. It is without any precedent. No terrorist organization has had a family at its heart, and there has never been a string of major terrorist attacks directed by a wayward family, such as Yousef et al.

The Kuwait Files

THE IDENTITIES OF ALL these individuals—Ramzi Yousef; Yousef's uncle Khalid Shaikh Mohammed; Yousef's two brothers, Abd al Munim and Abd al Karim; and Yousef's childhood friend, Abdul Hakim Murad—are all based on documents from Kuwait. (That may be true also for Yousef's cousin, Ali Abdul Aziz.) And these documents all come from *files that predate Kuwait's liberation.*

But, of course, nothing in Kuwait's files from that time can be assumed to be reliable. Iraq occupied the country from August 2, 1990, until its liberation on February 28, 1991. During that time, Iraqi intelligence had ample opportunity to tamper with Kuwait's files, if it so chose.

It is a standard practice of Soviet-style intelligence agencies to develop a false identity, or "legend," for agents involved in "wet" or illegal operations. The purpose, of course, is to avoid retaliation for an act of aggression by preventing it from being traced back to the sponsor.

There exists an alternative explanation to the theory that these Baluch terrorists represent a single, uniquely violent (and—from a certain perspective—an unusually talented) family: that is, these people are elements of Iraq's Baluch network who were given legends by the Iraqi *mukhabarrat* (intelligence) during Iraq's occupation of Kuwait. The Baluch network was actively used by Iraq throughout the Iran-Iraq war; it would still have been available two years later, when Iraq invaded Kuwait.

At that time, 95,000 Pakistanis lived in Kuwait. Shortly after the invasion, Iraqi forces seized some two dozen Pakistani nationals and held them hostage.[232] This was, of course, a very violent period, and there has been no real accounting of what happened to third world nationals then. Legends could easily have been developed for Iraqi intelligence agents, using the Kuwaiti Interior Ministry files of individuals who died in that period. Indeed, it would not have been beyond the Iraqis to have killed people for that purpose; or, they could have made up entire files.

Who Is Khalid Shaikh Mohammed?

THERE REALLY WAS an individual named Khalid Shaikh Mohammed, born to Pakistani parents in Kuwait on April 24, 1965. He grew up in Kuwait, attended high school there, and graduated in 1983. In January 1984 he traveled to the United States to enroll at Chowan College in Murfreesboro, North Carolina, a small Baptist school that had begun aggressively recruiting foreign students to boost its enrollment. After one semester at Chowan, Mohammed transferred to North Carolina Agricultural and Technical State University (A&T), a historically black college in Greensboro. He graduated in December 1986, with a bachelor of science in mechanical engineering.

Is the September 11 terrorist mastermind, now in U.S. custody, the same person as the individual described above? Or did the real Khalid Shaikh Mohammed die, and was his identity then assumed by a terrorist agent? At the time of the terrorist's arrest, Mohammed would have been only thirty-seven years old—but the arrest photo, with its grizzled side-burns and heavy jowls, suggests an older man.

That, however, is a subjective judgment. Yet it would be easy enough to investigate the question much more thoroughly and reliably.

Three sets of information exist regarding Mohammed: (1) informa-tion from U.S. and Kuwaiti sources from the 1980s, before Iraq's inva-sion of Kuwait. (This would include U.S. immigration records and college documents, as well as information to be obtained from individ-uals who might remember Mohammed.) (2) Documents from Kuwait. (3) Information since the liberation of Kuwait (including evidence from the terrorist's arrest and interrogation; from the interrogation of other al Qaeda prisoners, and from the investigation into the 1995 plane bombing plot).

The Kuwaiti documents should be scrutinized for internal consis-tency, and for any irregularities that would suggest the file was doctored.

The information about Mohammed from the 1980s should be com-pared with the information about him that has emerged since Kuwait's liberation. The terrorist may prove to be taller (or shorter) than the stu-dent. His U.S. interrogators might ask him what he remembers about the American colleges he is supposed to have attended. If he cannot recall anything about them—especially personal information, like the classes he took or some of the teachers he had—that would be a signifi-cant indicator that he is not who he purports to be.

There may be individuals who remember Mohammed from his time in America, who would be able to say whether the terrorist is really the student or not. There may also be individuals in Kuwait who would remember him from before Iraq's invasion. (This sort of statement always has to be carefully vetted, possibly by polygraph, particularly in the context of a high-profile investigation.)

There do appear to be some individuals who have a genuine memory of Mohammed. Professor Gaith Faile heads the science department of Chowan College and recalls Mohammed as "a B-type student" who "wasn't unusually radical. I didn't notice anything different about him."[233] Mohammed al Bulooshi, a fellow Baluch from Kuwait, studied with Mohammed at Chowan. He states, "We lived in one building, had breakfast, lunch and dinner together, us and thirty Arab students. We all became quite close." Al Bulooshi also said that Mohammed "was so quiet, there was no indication that he was involved in [religious extremism]. I would never have thought in a million years that he could be involved in these terrorist things."[234] These and other acquaintances should be allowed to meet with Mohammed, to try to provide an authoritative answer to the question as to whether the terrorist is really the same person as the student or not.

Who Is Ramzi Yousef?

ALONG THESE LINES, there is a file in Kuwait, related to Ramzi Yousef, that is highly significant. Yousef entered the United States on September 1, 1992, on an Iraqi passport in the name of Ramzi Ahmed Yousef. He fled on the night of the World Trade Center bombing using a Pakistani passport in the name of Abdul Basit Karim.[235]

There really was an individual named Abdul Basit Karim, born on April 28, 1968, in Kuwait to Pakistani parents. He attended high school in Fehaheel—an old fishing village south of Kuwait City, and the same town where Mohammed went to school, possibly at the same school. (Directly across the highway from Fehaheel is the town of al-Ahmadi, a major center of Kuwait's oil industry, where Murad claims to have been raised.) After graduating from high school, Karim studied in Britain at the Swansea Institute in Wales. In June 1989, he returned to Kuwait with a degree in electronic engineering. He obtained a job in Kuwait's Planning Ministry and appears to have been living in Kuwait when Iraq invaded a year later.

In the course of the investigation into the 1993 bombing, the Kuwaitis quickly recognized that their official file on Karim was incomplete. There should have been copies of the front pages of his passport in the file, including—significantly—his picture and signature in the file, but they are missing

The Kuwaitis attributed that gap to the Iraqi occupation. They did not recognize, however, that the entire file had been corrupted, and that information had also been inserted into Karim's file. Most significantly, the file contains the notation that Karim and his family left Kuwait on August 26, 1990, traveling from Kuwait to Iraq and crossing from Iraq to Iran at Salamcheh, on their way to Pakistani Baluchistan.

But a traveler does not provide authorities with his entire itinerary when he crosses a border. He just explains where he came from and where he is going directly. Moreover, ten hundreds of thousands of people were fleeing Kuwait and Iraq then. It's difficult to imagine that any bureaucrat was carefully recording their travel plans. Indeed, there was no Kuwaiti government then; there was an Iraqi army of occupation. Iraq had to have put that information into Karim's file.[236]

Finally, Ramzi Yousef's fingerprints are in Karim's file. But every person's fingerprints are unique. There are only two possible explanations for this: either Yousef is really Karim, or the fingerprint cards were switched, the original card (with Karim's prints) removed and replaced with one bearing Yousef's prints.

Yousef Is Not Karim

IN 1996, I VISITED the Swansea Institute to meet with two of Karim's teachers. They had a clear memory of him. Karim had been a quiet, pleasant, hardworking young man. They did not think that the student they knew was the same man who had emerged in New York a mere three years after his graduation from Swansea as the master terrorist known as Ramzi Yousef. They were fairly certain of that, although to be absolutely 100 percent sure, they felt they would have to meet with Yousef in prison.

Most compelling is the difference in height. Yousef is six feet tall, according to his arrest card. Karim, according to his teachers, was at most five eight, as is also confirmed by an available document.[237] (This point is discussed in much greater detail in *Study of Revenge*.)[238]

Four inches is a significant difference in height. If Yousef is six feet tall, but Karim was at most five eight, then they are two different people. That can mean only that the fingerprint cards were switched in Karim's file, which was otherwise tampered with. The evident purpose was to create a legend—a fictive identity for Yousef. And the only party that could have reasonably done so is Iraq, while it occupied Kuwait.

Following the 9/11 attacks, moreover, Professor Ken Reid (Swansea's deputy principal) told the BBC that he was "personally convinced" that Ramzi Yousef "is not our former student." "I am personally convinced," he said, "that our former student is no longer alive."[239] (Reid was familiar with the view of Karim's teachers that his personality was entirely different from that of the terrorist Yousef, as well as the physical differences between them.)

David Rose, a reporter for the British paper *The Observer*, discussed the issue with a spokesman for MI-5 (British domestic intelligence). The spokesman maintained that there was one piece of information that showed that Yousef and Karim were in fact the same person, but that this evidence was classified and he could not share it; at the same time, he expressed open hostility to U.S. officials who suspected Baghdad was involved in the September 11 attacks. Another source later explained that the British (or some British officials) claimed that latent fingerprints retrieved from material that Karim had left behind at Swansea matched Yousef's fingerprints.

But why was that bit of information so sensitive that it could not be revealed to Rose? Perhaps because it was not true? A British paper later quoted another MI-5 source as saying, "The two sets of fingerprints were entirely different."[240]

After speaking with the MI-5 spokesman, Rose then called the

Swansea Institute and was told that Karim's teachers had been instructed by British authorities not to talk to anyone about the subject. Nevertheless, Rose was assured, "We stand by what we told Jim Woolsey and Laurie Mylroie"— that is, that they did not believe that Yousef was the person they had taught. (Woolsey had visited Swansea in early 2001 and was told the same thing I was told.)[241]

Indeed, British police investigated Karim some years ago. They produced a report (a copy of which was sent to U.S. officials) suggesting that Karim is *not*, in fact, Yousef.[242] That is one reason that the first four U.S. indictments of Yousef (issued between August 1993 and September 1994) include the charge: "Ramzi Ahmed Yousef obtained a Pakistani passport in the name 'Abdul Basit' that was procured by means of a false claim and statement, and otherwise procured by fraud and unlawfully obtained."

That charge, of course, implies that Yousef is one person and Karim another; one cannot really obtain one's own passport fraudulently.

Ramzi Yousef has been tried and convicted twice in a New York courthouse, once for the plot to bomb U.S. airplanes and once for the 1993 World Trade Center bombing. Judge Kevin Duffy heard both trials. At the end of the proceedings, when Judge Duffy sentenced Yousef to life plus 240 years, he stated, "We don't even know what your real name is."[243] The judge was absolutely correct. "Ramzi Yousef" is an alias, and "Abdul Basit Karim" is a concocted legend.

The identities of the two terrorist "masterminds"—Yousef and Khalid Shaikh Mohammed—cannot be taken at face value. If it can be shown, through a straightforward investigation, that the terrorist arrested in Pakistan is not the same person as the individual born Khalid Shaikh Mohammed in Kuwait, that would be a clear indication that Kuwait's file on Mohammed had been corrupted. Indeed, if the terrorist is not the real Mohammed yet his fingerprints are nonetheless in Kuwait's file on Mohammed—just as Yousef's prints are in Karim's file— that would indicate beyond any doubt that the fingerprint cards had been switched, and the file doctored to create a legend for the terrorist.

That demonstration would be tantamount to proof that the September 11 mastermind is an Iraqi intelligence agent—for the only party that could reasonably have tampered with those files was Iraq, during its occupation of Kuwait.

Al Qaeda and Iraqi Intelligence

MOHAMMED, YOUSEF, AND MURAD did not fit the profile of Islamic militants in 1995, when they conspired to bomb a dozen U.S. airliners in the Philippines. As the *Los Angeles Times* reported, "In Manila, the trio acted like anything but Islamic terrorists. All had local girlfriends. They hung out at karaoke bars and strip clubs."[244]

Although Yousef and Murad were captured soon after the failure of that plot, Mohammed managed to escape to the small Persian Gulf sheikhdom of Qatar, where he found employment as a mechanical engineer in the country's Water Department. In January 1996, the CIA tracked him to Qatar.[245] U.S. authorities were concerned that if they asked the government to turn Mohammed over, someone there might tip him off. They considered a military operation to grab him but decided that would be too difficult. Indeed, when they asked Qatar to extradite Mohammed, their fears were realized: he was alerted and fled.

In May 1996, the Sudanese government, under strong U.S. pressure, expelled bin Laden to Afghanistan; in 1997 Khalid Shaikh Mohammed joined him there, unknown to U.S. authorities. As one U.S. intelligence official explained after Mohammed's capture, "It wasn't until recently that any of us even realized he was part of al Qaeda. . . . The big problem nailing him down is that the informants we relied on, especially before 9/11, were mujaheddin. They'd been in Afghanistan, in Sudan, back in Afghanistan. *Khalid was never a part of any of that* [emphasis added]."[246]

Washington Post columnist Jim Hoagland posed an important question: "How did al Qaeda, within two or three years, go from obscurity to becoming super-terrorists capable of blowing up U.S. embassies, warships, and skyscrapers with astonishing precision?" He went on to raise the question addressed in this chapter: how did a group of Baluch who grew up in Kuwait acquire such remarkable skills as terrorist master-minds, and why would they devote their lives to killing Americans? Hoagland then hinted at a possible answer. "Could al Qaeda have been the target of a takeover operation by an intelligence service with good legend-manufacturing skills and a great, burning desire for revenge on the United States?"[247]

Indeed, the Baluch crew began their mega-terrorist attacks against America long before al Qaeda did—*and bin Laden has not been indicted for any of Yousef's terrorism.* Contacts between Iraqi intelligence and al Qaeda began in the early 1990s, when bin Laden was still in Sudan, according to U.S. officials.

Did the involvement of Iraqi intelligence with al Qaeda intensify significantly after bin Laden relocated to Afghanistan? Is that why al Qaeda's first major attack—the embassy bombings—occurred two years later? And did al Qaeda in fact come to serve as a front for Iraqi intelli-gence, with Iraqi agents such as Mohammed serving in key positions?

Sitting on a Smoking Gun

A NUMBER OF THE RESPONSIBLE U.S. authorities have long under-stood the significance of Ramzi Yousef's identity: Yousef is not Karim; Karim's file in Kuwait was tampered with to create a legend for Yousef; and that constitutes the decisive evidence that Yousef is an Iraqi intelli-gence agent. In late 1994, Jim Fox (recently retired from the Bureau) passed this analysis on to the New York FBI. He and I had discussed this issue, and he agreed that Karim's file in Kuwait, when properly under-stood, constituted the key information tying Iraq to the World Trade Center bombing. After he told his former colleagues of this, Fox remarked to me that they now understood they had the smoking gun—the only question was what they would do with it.[248]

The answer? They sat on it, as Fox anticipated they might. In Washington, the Clinton White House did not want to hear that Iraq was involved. At that point, it believed that its strike on *mukhabarrat* (Iraqi intelligence) headquarters the year before—which the White House linked publicly *only* to Saddam's attempt to kill former president Bush—would, in fact, deter Saddam from *all* future acts of terrorism. Even if the New York FBI was correct in its suspicions that Iraq was also behind the Trade Center bombing, that was beside the point. The strike on *mukhabarrat* headquarters a few months after that bombing had taken care of the problem, in the minds of the most senior White House officials.[249]

In another part of Washington, FBI headquarters thought that Fox, while director of the New York office, had not provided enough evidence to support his belief that Iraq was involved. (This probably entailed some degree of deference to the White House.) The CIA, without access to the results of the FBI investigation, was not in a position to reach any independent conclusion. It too accepted the theory that no state was involved in the Trade Center bombing. These perspectives quickly became ingrained bureaucratic positions.

In New York, a somewhat different problem emerged. The terrorism trials created a situation in which prosecutors, who naturally begin with a lack of interest in the issue of state sponsorship, became actively hostile to pursuing the question. Their job, after all, is to bring to trial and obtain convictions of individual perpetrators. The question of state sponsorship is supposed to be handled in Washington. Moreover, to speculate about the involvement of states in any particular terrorist attack might have implications for the trials: it might not affect convictions, but it might well affect the sentences meted out, if it were understood that a state sponsor had engineered a complex intelligence operation and that a significant number of those brought to trial were merely low-ranking members of the conspiracies. Thus, the response of the U.S. Attorney's office in New York to the key question of whether or not Ramzi Yousef was Abdul Basit Karim was, "It doesn't matter what we call him, we just try a body."[250]

Everyone involved behaved according to the well-established practices of bureaucratic organizations; and because the question of state
sponsorship was never properly addressed, the result, quite arguably,
was the September 11 attacks. Even after that rude awakening, the
bureaucratic opposition to pursuing the question of Iraq's role in terrorism only intensified, for the most part. And that has had serious
implications for the investigation of those attacks.

The question of Yousef's identity, of course, touches only on the two
plots in which he was involved. It does not relate directly to the September 11 assaults. But the ferocious bureaucratic opposition to examining
Yousef's identity has successfully deterred an official investigation into
the identity of Khalid Shaikh Mohammed.[251]

The bureaucratic resistance is, in fact, so intense that probably only
the president could rein it in, and that with some difficulty. The actual
investigation, however, would not be so difficult. In addition to the suggestions about Mohammed's identity, above, other steps could be taken
to pursue the question of the identities of the Baluch terrorists:

* Obtain the British report on Abdul Basit Karim that suggests he is not
  Ramzi Yousef.

* Bring those who knew Karim personally, such as Karim's teachers at
  Swansea, to visit Yousef in prison, so they can pronounce with 100 percent certainty if he was their student or not.

* Do DNA tests of Yousef and Mohammed. That could establish, scientif-
  ically, whether or not they are related.

* Talk to Abdul Hakim Murad, who is currently serving a life sentence in
  a U.S. prison for the plot to bomb planes in the Philippines. His terrorism did not result in the deaths of any Americans, and he may well
  know the story of these identities. Prosecutors routinely reach deals
  with lesser suspects to get the bigger fish. The country has a compelling
  national security interest in understanding this terrorism, including

the possibility of actually proving Iraq's involvement. If Murad can provide that proof, then perhaps he should be offered a reduced sentence.

* Obtain the Kuwaiti files on all the major terrorists who are supposed to have been born and raised there. Examine them for inconsistencies that might suggest that they have been tampered with.

No doubt, others could come up with many other suggestions.

A Civics Lesson

IF THE READER has difficulty imagining such a perverse state of U.S. national security intelligence, I sympathize. I would have great difficulty believing the story myself, if I had not experienced it. As someone who very much appreciates being born in this country and living here, I, like many others, want to think well of its leadership and institutions. But leadership does not happen automatically.

A serious problem emerged in the 1990s regarding this country's handling of terrorism and of Iraq. These are difficult issues in any case, but in that decade there was a striking absence of presidential leadership. It is futile to expect government agencies and bureaucracies to assume a leadership role in the absence of clear presidential direction. The simple fact is that the national security bureaucracies are subject to the same array of inefficiencies and perverse incentives as other agencies of government—with the added problem that most of their activities are, by definition, shielded from public scrutiny.

Chapter Eight

WAS OPERATION IRAQI FREEDOM LEGAL?

Robert F. Turner

S THIS IS BEING WRITTEN, although there appears to be broad agreement that Operation Iraqi Freedom was a necessary, wise, and just use of military force, there is still a widespread view that it was unlawful under the U.N. Charter. Indeed, the U.N. secretary general has made that assertion,[252] and the president of the American Society of International Law estimated that 80 percent of international lawyers agreed that the intervention was unlawful. In view of the seriousness of this charge, the issue merits attention in any consideration of the problem of Iraq.

Before addressing the legal merits of the issue, it might be useful to note that there are occasions when violating international law may be justified. In an 1810 letter to Maryland newspaper editor John B. Colvin, Thomas Jefferson reasoned that observing the law was important, but it was not the *highest* duty of a nation. "The laws of necessity, of self preservation, of saving our country when in danger, are of higher obligation. To lose our country by a scrupulous adherence to written law, would be to lose the law itself . . . thus absurdly sacrificing the end to the means."[253]

When John F. Kennedy threatened to use armed force to prevent the Soviet Union from delivering nuclear-armed ballistic missiles to Cuba in 1962, he almost certainly violated international law. Neither Cuba nor the Soviet Union had used or threatened to use force against America, the Security Council had not authorized the threat of force, and the United States at the time had nuclear missiles in Turkey aimed at the Soviet Union. Yet, most of the world understood that this was a prudent measure given the character of the Castro regime.

A common theme in writings by many international lawyers today is that operations like the 1999 NATO intervention in Kosovo and Operation Iraqi Freedom are illegal under the Charter, but they are also probably justifiable in moral and policy terms because of their humanitarian benefits.

In reality, the legal case for Operation Iraqi Freedom is much stronger than most critics realize. Moreover, to the extent that it may arguably have been contrary to current law, it may contribute in the long run to the progressive development of customary legal rules to make them compatible with twenty-first-century values.

International law is a dynamic institution, formed in part by formal international agreements like the U.N. Charter, but equally by state practice eventually accepted as creating legal rules. Circumstances and values change, and new technology may require decisions on issues that previously were of little import. Throughout most of human history, for example, issues such as who owned the fish in the sea or the land beneath the sea had no relevance. There were fish enough for all, and the inaccessible ocean bottom had no apparent value. During the twentieth century, however, highly efficient harvesting technologies threatened stocks of migratory fish, and it became feasible to extract valuable resources—such as oil—from the ocean floor. Issues of legal ownership then became important. When President Truman declared U.S. jurisdiction over the offshore continental shelf in 1945, the proclamation was widely accepted and began the process of changing the legal regime governing the law of the sea. Thirteen years later, national jurisdiction over the continental shelf was codified in a U.N. treaty on the law of the sea.

In a similar way, Operation Iraqi Freedom may contribute to clarifying and perhaps broadening what is generally referred to as *jus ad bellum*, or the international law governing the initiation of coercion in international relations.

The History of *Jus ad Bellum*

THROUGHOUT MOST OF THE HISTORY of the nation-state system, the supreme entity has been the sovereign state. Rules of law governing state behavior depended entirely upon the consent of those states, and the lack of effective international enforcement mechanisms required states to resort to "self-help" measures to protect their interests. War was permissible not only to redress grievances, but also to conquer territory or commit other acts of blatant international aggression.

As the Permanent Court of International Justice confirmed in its 1927 *Lotus* case, international law is a permissive regime, and restrictions upon the sovereignty of states "are not to be presumed" in the absence of a clear legal rule regulating their conduct in a given area. With the consent of all parties, disputes may be submitted to international tribunals, arbitral panels, mediation, or other means of third-party dispute resolution. Consistent with their other legal obligations (including the modern prohibition against the aggressive use of armed force), states may also seek to redress their grievances by measures of self-help (e.g., a reciprocal breach in response to a material breach of a treaty obligation by another state), and other members of the world community can assist in pressuring wrongdoers to behave by what is often called "horizontal enforcement" of the law.

Jus ad Bellum in the Twentieth Century

THE HORRORS OF WORLD WAR I led in 1919 to the establishment of the League of Nations, and in 1928 the Pact of Paris (also known as the Kellogg-Briand Treaty) outlawed resorting to war as an instrument of national policy. This, it was hoped, would end all nondefensive uses of armed force.

Unfortunately, although the League was the vision of President Woodrow Wilson, the U.S. Senate refused to consent to the ratification of the covenant that would have made the United States a member. A more fundamental problem was that neither the League of Nations nor the Kellogg-Briand Treaty address—much less resolved—the issue of enforcement.

When Japan invaded Manchuria in 1931, the League of Nations debated and issued a report condemning the act. Japan withdrew from the League, and nothing else was done. Nor did the United States have the will to try to enforce the treaty initiated by Secretary of State Frank Kellogg and his French counterpart. Secretary of State Henry Stimson limited the American response to a threat "not to recognize" Japan's territorial gains achieved by conquest.

In 1935, Italy invaded Ethiopia. Once again, the League of Nations debated and passed a resolution condemning the aggression, but nothing serious was done to enforce international law. The lesson was apparently not lost on Adolf Hitler. As the brilliant Yale historian Donald Kagan has observed: "The democracies seemed weak, indecisive, and cowardly, and their failure and inaction gave courage to their enemies."[254] When Hitler threatened to invade Czechoslovakia's Sudetenland at the 1938 Munich Conference, France and Great Britain assured him they would not intervene—in the vain and ultimately tragic belief that his aggression would end there, and that appeasement would keep them at peace.

The United Nations

IN THE FINAL months of World War II, world leaders gathered in San Francisco to establish the United Nations. Although it is widely assumed that the goal of the United Nations was to unite countries in response to future acts of international aggression, the new organization's primary purpose was actually more proactive. The great Chinese military thinker Sun Tzu, writing 2,500 years ago, observed that the "acme of skill" is not to win one hundred victories in one hundred battles, but to "subdue the enemy without fighting."[255] Consistent with this wisdom, the new United Nations was premised upon what might accurately be described as a "preemptive" approach. Article 1 begins:

> The Purposes of the United Nations are: (1) To maintain international peace and security, and to that end: to take effective collective measures for the prevention and *removal* [my emphasis] of threats to the peace, and for the suppression of acts of aggression.

Actually responding to "acts of aggression" was thus framed as a fallback to the strategy of preventing aggression by *removing* "threats to the peace" before aggression can occur. Through this lens, then, it seems clear that in the debate over the war in Iraq, France and Russia breached that fundamental undertaking of the Charter, as after a dozen years of failed political and economic sanctions they proved unwilling to approve "effective" collective measures to remove a regime the Security Council had unanimously determined to be a "threat to the peace."

The basic prohibition against the use of force was contained in Article 2(4) of the Charter, which provided:

All Members shall refrain in their international relations from the threat or use of force against the territorial integrity or political independence of any state, or in any other manner inconsistent with the Purposes of the United Nations.

Although commentators often referred to "just-war" theory in assessing American threats to use force to remove Saddam Hussein from power, the law of the Charter differs significantly from that of the more traditional approach. The framers of the Charter had personally lived through two world wars, and they placed greater emphasis on preserving "peace" than upon achieving "justice." Whereas just-war theory would permit some wars to promote more just societies, or even to propagate the Christian faith, the Charter basically limits resort to force (absent authorization of the Security Council) to situations where defensive force is necessary to preserve human life.

This time, the world organization was to have teeth. A Security Council was established with power to enforce the U.N. Charter's prohibition against aggression. Article 25 of the Charter obligated all U.N. members to carry out decisions of the Security Council, and Chapter VII of the Charter authorized the Council to take a variety of measures—including authorizing member states to use armed force against an offending state—under the heading "Actions with Respect to Threats to the Peace, Breaches of the Peace, and Acts of Aggression."

Security Council Action on Iraq (1990–2003)

THE EASIEST WAY TO JUSTIFY Operation Iraqi Freedom would be to find formal authorization from the U.N. Security Council, as occurred when the Council in 1990 authorized Operation Desert Storm. Short of that, the Council may have made factual determinations that strengthen other theories that the operation was lawful. Finally, a review of Security Council action may reveal a pattern of behavior that suggests the Security Council clearly lacked the will to carry out its responsibilities under the Charter.

Even prior to Iraq's 1990 invasion of Kuwait, the U.N. Security Council had found it necessary to pass no fewer than fifteen separate resolutions dealing with Iraq—most of them related to Iraq's 1980 invasion of neighboring Iran and the use of illegal chemical weapons during that conflict. When Iraq invaded Kuwait on August 2, 1990,[256] the Security Council responded the following day with Resolution 660. Acting under Chapter VII, Articles 39 and 40, the Council decreed "that Iraq withdraw immediately and unconditionally all its forces to the positions in which they were located on 1 August 1990."

As an aside, this is a fine example of the careless draftsmanship that characterizes some Security Council resolutions. Why on earth demand that Iraqi forces be kept in "the positions in which they were located on 1 August," when they were aggressively poised for invasion on the border of Kuwait? Surely it would have been preferable to give Iraq the option of returning these forces to their barracks, permitting them to go on furlough, or even demobilizing some of them. In this instance the consequences were not serious. Similarly careless phraseology in Resolution 687, however, has been interpreted as imposing no conditions on Iraq in return for the 1991 cease-fire beyond voicing an insincere "promise" to obey the law—with no requirement of actual compliance.

Four days later, on August 6, 1990, the Council acted again. Resolution 661, passed pursuant to Chapter VII, imposed an embargo on the sale or transfer of weapons and virtually everything else to or from Iraq, but it specifically did not affect "supplies intended strictly for medical purposes, and, in humanitarian circumstances, foodstuffs." This was modified from time to time, but the Security Council has always permitted the exporting to Iraq of humanitarian supplies, and in 1995 it authorized the sale of oil by Iraq for the limited purpose of funding the supply of food, medicines, and other humanitarian supplies needed by the Iraqi people.[257]

In this regard, it might be useful to point out that in the 1990s Saddam Hussein initiated a game of "chicken" with the world community with respect to humanitarian aid. He correctly gambled that the world community cared far more than he did about the welfare of innocent Iraqis, so he refused to make full use of the opportunity to alleviate the humanitarian crisis through the oil-for-food program. Indeed, U.N. experts have reported that a substantial part of the food and medicine that was received under this program was stored in warehouses rather than distributed to needy Iraqis, and Saddam reportedly exported some of it illegally for personal financial gain. By refusing to address the (totally unnecessary, and unintended by the United Nations) human suffering of the Iraqi people, Saddam Hussein was taking terrorism to a new level—essentially threatening to slaughter his own civilians if the world community did not give in to his demands and permit him to develop illegal weapons of mass destruction. In propaganda terms, the maneuver was highly successful, since the international sanctions—and the United States—were widely blamed for the resulting deprivations.

Saddam Hussein ignored the Security Council's demands and proceeded with the rape of Kuwait. On November 29, 1990, again acting under Chapter VII, the Security Council passed Resolution 678, which gave Iraq "one final opportunity" to comply with Resolution 660 and, if Iraq had not complied by January 15, 1991, authorized member states to use "all necessary means" to implement earlier resolutions "and to restore international peace and security in the area." This final clause obviously expanded the authorization from simply expelling Iraqi military forces from Kuwait to a broader authority that might arguably have permitted the removal of Saddam Hussein from power.

Some legal scholars who argue that Operation Iraqi Freedom was unlawful clearly misunderstood the full scope of Resolution 678. For example, Professor Mary Ellen O'Connell (writing in a publication of the American Society of International Law) argued that "resolution 678 never authorized the use of force to forcibly change Iraq's government."[258] This contention appears to contradict the statement made in the immediately preceding paragraph in her own article, where she wrote: "Resolution 678 allowed the use of 'all necessary means,' including, presumably, taking the defense of Kuwait to Baghdad and ending the regime of Saddam Hussein."[259] If the only way to restore "peace and security in the area" was to remove from power a repeat offender who refused to change his ways, that would seem fully consistent with the authority granted by the Security Council.

Unfortunately, when the United States Congress in January 1991 granted President Bush the constitutional authority[260] to use armed force "pursuant" to Resolution 678, it narrowed the authority to that of implementing only Security Council Resolutions 660 through 677, which did not include the authorization to "restore peace" provided in Resolution 678. That was necessary in order to get sufficient Democratic votes to pass Senate Joint Resolution 2. Even with the narrowed language, the resolution was opposed by more than four out of five Senate Democrats and could have been defeated by a shift of just six votes.

Saddam continued to ignore the Security Council, and on January 16, 1991, the U.S.-led coalition launched Operation Desert Storm, shocking many observers by expelling Iraqi forces from Kuwait and decimating Saddam's much-touted Revolutionary Guard in six short weeks. On February 27, Iraq informed the Security Council by letter that it would comply with all Security Council resolutions. As the world watched images of fleeing Iraqi forces being cut down at will by American air power, President George H. W. Bush—following the advice of Joint Chiefs of Staff Chairman General Colin Powell—announced that the coalition commanded by General Norman Schwarzkopf had ceased combat operations.

On March 2, in Resolution 686, the Security Council reaffirmed Resolution 678 and other prior resolutions and underlined "the importance of Iraq taking the necessary measures which would permit a definitive end to the hostilities." The following day, acting again under Chapter VII, the Security Council approved Resolution 687, the resolution governing the cease-fire, by a vote of 12–1–2 (with Cuba the dissenter, and two abstentions). The cease-fire resolution included the following provision:

> Iraq shall unconditionally accept the destruction, removal, or rendering harmless, under international supervision, of:
> (a) All chemical and biological weapons and all stocks of agents

and all related subsystems and components and all research, development, support and manufacturing facilities;

    (b) All ballistic missiles with a range greater than 150 kilometres and related major parts, and repair and production facilities.

Paragraph 9 required that Iraq yield possession of all of its weapons of mass destruction to a U.N. "Special Commission," which would also oversee the destruction of prohibited ballistic missiles in Iraq. Paragraph 32 required Iraq "to inform the Security Council that it will not commit or support any act of international terrorism or allow any organization directed towards commission of such acts to operate within its territory and to condemn unequivocally and renounce all acts, methods and practices of terrorism." As a Security Council decision under Chapter VII of the Charter, this immediately became a binding legal obligation on Iraq. Paragraph 33 of Resolution 687 declared that "upon official notification by Iraq to the Secretary General and to the Security Council of its acceptance of the provisions above," a "formal cease-fire" would enter into effect between Iraq and the U.N. coalition that had implemented Resolution 678.

Article 2(2) of the U.N. Charter imposes an obligation of "good faith" on all members in connection with fulfilling their Charter obligations, and the demanded "notification" was obviously but a symbol for the underlying bargain that, in return for the cease-fire, Iraq would carry out the obligations it had accepted in good faith. Sadly, that assumption proved misguided. Thus began a futile charade in which the Security Council passed Chapter VII resolutions denouncing Iraq's failure to comply, followed by further violations by Saddam Hussein, to which the Security Council responded merely by passing new resolutions. By the late 1990s, whatever credibility the world community had derived from the success of Operation Desert Storm had largely been frittered away by the Security Council's unwillingness to "take effective collective measures" as envisioned by the Charter.

As early as August 15, 1991, for example, Resolution 707 noted "with grave concern" Iraq's continued violation of the terms of Resolution

687 and declared under Chapter VII that Iraq was in "material breach" of the cease-fire resolution, which "provided the conditions essential to the restoration of peace and security in the region." Once again, it demanded that Iraq:

> provide full, final and complete disclosure, as required by resolution 687 (1991), of all aspects of its programmes to develop weapons of mass destruction and ballistic missiles with a range greater than 150 kilometres, and of all holdings of such weapons, their components and production facilities and locations, as well as all other nuclear programmes, including any which it claims are for purposes not related to nuclear-weapons-usable material, without further delay.

When Iraq had not complied by October 2, the Council passed Resolution 778, again "condemning" under Chapter VII Iraq's continued failure to comply with its obligations. An interesting resolution was passed on October 15, 1994, after Iraq had moved military units toward its border with Kuwait. Security Council Resolution 949 explicitly "recalled" and "reaffirmed" previous resolutions on Iraq, "in particular paragraph 2 of resolution 678 (1990)," which, it will be recalled, had authorized member states "to use all necessary means"—a clear authorization to use military force—"to restore international peace and security in the area."

In 1996 the Council passed Resolution 1060, "deploring" Iraq's continued violations and again "demanding" immediate compliance. It too was ignored by Saddam. This went on painfully, year after year, until on March 2, 1998, the Security Council had had enough and expressed its determination "to ensure full compliance by Iraq without conditions or restrictions with all its obligations" under previous resolutions. And to make sure that *this* time Saddam would take them seriously, the Security Council threatened that "any further violations" would be followed by the "severest consequences" for Iraq.

Saddam was apparently less than intimidated. A few months later, on August 5, 1998, he announced that Iraq would no longer allow U.N. weapons inspections (though monitoring continued for a few more months). The "severest consequences" that the Security Council could agree upon consisted of passing Resolution 1194, "condemning" Iraq's decision to cease all cooperation and declaring it to be "a totally unacceptable contravention" of Iraq's legal obligations. A clearly annoyed Security Council once again "demanded" that Iraq "rescind" its decision and "cooperate fully" with the United Nations. But Saddam Hussein had long ago stopped taking the threats and blustering of the U.N. Security Council seriously. Perhaps he had been secretly assured that one of his allies on the Council would veto any meaningful effort to uphold the Charter; or perhaps—like Hitler sixty years earlier, who assured his generals that he had seen the British and French leaders at Munich, and they were "little worms"²⁶¹ who lacked the will to resist him—he had concluded that his adversaries would not seriously challenge him. In any event, having by now approved more than a dozen Chapter VII resolutions in as many years denouncing Iraqi violations of its orders, recognizing that Iraq constituted a threat to the peace, and issuing renewed ultimatums ordering Iraq to clean up its act, by 1998 the Security Council had achieved a level of irrelevance as the "primary organ" of the world community for the maintenance of international peace and security rivaling that of the League of Nations more than six decades earlier.

On October 31, 1998, Iraq announced that it would also terminate UNSCOM monitoring; five days later, the Security Council (to no one's surprise) passed Resolution 1205 noting "with alarm" the Iraqi decision and expressing, yet again, its determination "to ensure immediate and full compliance by Iraq without conditions or restrictions with its obligations under resolution 687" and other relevant resolutions (by then there were evidently too many to list). And, apparently convinced that its previous approach had been too tough, the Council now hinted that if Iraq would just promise once again "to fulfill all its obligations" the Council might quickly bring an end to its 1990 economic embargo.

Although the Security Council had years earlier authorized the importation into Iraq of foodstuffs, medical equipment and supplies, and other "humanitarian" relief needs, Saddam Hussein had continued to hold a significant portion of the supplies sent to Iraq in warehouses, reserved for his personal use, to reward the party faithful, or to be sold illegally at a profit. So on December 17, 1999, acting again under Chapter VII, the Security Council passed Resolution 1284, which called upon Iraq "to take all steps to ensure the timely and equitable distribution of all humanitarian goods, in particular medical supplies, and to remove and avoid delays at its warehouses." This was given the same careful attention Saddam had given to past Security Council resolutions, and the humanitarian situation deteriorated still further.

In November 2002, in response to pressure from the United States and Great Britain, the Security Council approved Resolution 1441—once again acting under Chapter VII and thus again implicitly recognizing that Saddam's regime remained a "threat to the peace." Two pages of preamble "recalled" and "deplored" various acts of Iraqi noncompliance with prior Council resolutions—specifically, "recalling" that "resolution 678 (1990) authorized Member States to use all necessary means . . . to restore international peace and security in the area," and deploring that the government of Iraq had failed to comply with "its commitments pursuant to resolution 687 (1991) with regard to terrorism" and its commitment "to end repression of its civilian population and to provide access by international humanitarian organizations to all those in need of assistance in Iraq."

The Council now, once again, formally found Iraq to be "in material breach" of the cease-fire resolution. Acting again under Chapter VII, the Council decided "to afford Iraq, by this resolution, a *final opportunity* [my emphasis] to comply with its disarmament obligations under relevant resolutions of the Council." And, as if referring to previous unenforced threats would strengthen rather than weaken the resolution's effect, the Council recalled "that the Council has repeatedly warned Iraq that it will face serious consequences as a result of its continued violations of its obligations."

At the end of January 2003, chief U.N. inspector Hans Blix told Security Council members: "Iraq appears not to have come to a genuine acceptance, not even today, of the disarmament which was demanded of it and which it needs to carry out to win the confidence of the world and to live in peace." When the United States and Great Britain demanded that the Security Council authorize the use of force, France and Russia nevertheless promised to veto any such resolution. At that point it became apparent that the Security Council lacked the will to "take effective collective measures" to deal seriously with the problem, and the Security Council essentially became irrelevant to the task of trying to uphold the rule of law and implement the primary purpose of the Charter. If anything was going to be done to enforce the Security Council resolutions and protect the world community and the people of Iraq, the United States and Great Britain would have to accomplish it, acting outside the Security Council.

On March 20, 2003, the United States and Great Britain each reported to the Security Council that they were using armed force against Iraq—signaling the start of Operation Iraqi Freedom. The legal justifications given were somewhat different: the British focused upon the need to enforce the resolutions of the Security Council, while the United States argued that Iraq's flagrant and material breach of Security Council Resolution 687 for more than a decade had the effect of terminating the cease-fire agreement and leaving Resolution 678—authorizing the use of force against Iraq to restore peace and security to the area—in force.

Professor O'Connell dismisses the American argument on the theory that

> [Security Council] resolutions are not treaties and do not automatically terminate upon material breach. . . . They are not agreements among equals reached through negotiations, aimed at achieving consensus and binding on all parties alike if they give their consent. Council resolutions . . . are mandates imposed on certain states that must be respected, whether those states consent or not.[262]

In theory, she is certainly correct. But the cease-fire provision of Resolution 687 was in fact worded as if it were an international agreement with Iraq. Whereas Chapter VII resolutions of the Security Council are legally binding upon all states, Iraq's record of totally ignoring them may have led some on the Security Council to assume that a requirement that Iraq "accept" the Security Council's terms might increase the likelihood that this time Iraq would obey the law. Paragraph 33 of Resolution 687 provided that the Security Council:

> Declares that, upon official notification by Iraq to the Secretary-General and to the Security Council of its acceptance of the provisions above, a formal cease-fire is effective between Iraq and Kuwait and the Member States cooperating with Kuwait in accordance with resolution 678.

There is, however, a more fundamental problem with the American argument.[263] Although not a party to the 1969 Vienna Convention on the Law of Treaties, the State Department had acknowledged that its substantive provisions do reflect customary international law and are thus binding upon the United States. While, pursuant to Article 3, the Vienna Convention applied only to treaties made "between states," its basic principles may have a broader scope. Article 60 deals with terminating or suspending treaties because of a material breach, and provides that in the case of a bilateral treaty—that is to say, a treaty with only two parties—a material breach by one entitles the other to terminate or suspend the treaty. But if the "agreement" upon which the cease-fire in Iraq was based is viewed as "bilateral," it is between Iraq and the U.N. Security Council, and presumably neither the United States nor Great Britain can elect on behalf of the Council to declare the 1991 agreement terminated. It is important to understand that a material breach does not, ipso facto, terminate the underlying agreement; it merely creates a right in the other party or parties to declare the treaty terminated.

If one elected instead to view the cease-fire as a multilateral agreement between Iraq and the individual states who were members of the Security Council when the agreement was reached, it would be governed by the principles set forth in Article 60(2) of the Vienna Convention,

which empowers "the other parties by unanimous agreement to suspend the operation of the treaty in whole or in part or to terminate
it. . . ." This theory would require not merely a new resolution of the
Security Council (requiring the concurrence of all five permanent
members), but also a unanimous decision of either those states who
were on the council or their current successors in interest.[264] Neither
theory would permit the United States and/or the United Kingdom to
terminate the agreement, despite the fact that Iraq's material breach
has been affirmed by various Security Council resolutions over more
than a decade.

On the other hand, one might argue that a more reasonable and less
legalistic approach is warranted in this case, and that it is obviously clear
that the cease-fire agreement was intended to be predicated upon Iraq's
fulfillment of various legal obligations—including certain key measures of
disarmament under international supervision. The Vienna Convention
on the Law of Treaties generally favors a textual approach to interpreting
international agreements, but context may be considered when a textual
interpretation "leads to a result which is manifestly absurd or unreasonable." It is not reasonable to suppose that the Security Council did not
intend for Iraq to fulfill the obligations it had assumed as part of its "consideration" for the cease-fire—obligations which, under the Charter, did
not require the specific consent of Iraq, since by ratifying the Charter it
had already consented to carry out the decisions of the Security Council.

It is also absolutely clear that Iraq materially breached those agreements and refused legally binding demands by the Security Council to
comply for more than a decade. It is also clear that by 2003 the Security
Council lacked the will to fulfill its Charter responsibility to enforce the
law against Iraq. When France and Russia announced that they would veto
any resolution authorizing the use of force, they essentially removed the
Security Council as a meaningful player in the struggle for peace in Iraq.

Under Article 24 of the Charter, the Security Council has only "primary responsibility" for the maintenance of international peace and
security, and under Article 51 individual states have the right to use
force defensively "*until the Security Council has taken measures necessary*

to maintain international peace and security" [emphasis added]. Examining the situation in Iraq in light of the totality of the circumstances—including Saddam's long history of unprovoked aggression against at least four neighboring states, his repeated use of weapons of mass destruction against neighbors and his own people, and repeated Chapter VII findings by the Security Council that he remains a "threat to the peace" (a finding implicit in every Chapter VII resolution)—it seems silly to say that France or Russia can claim the right to immunize from effective defensive action an obvious and recognized threat to world peace. Such an interpretation of the Charter would seem to fall into the "manifestly absurd" category discussed above.

So whether or not one accepts the American argument that military force against Iraq remains authorized by Resolution 678, the lawfulness of Operation Iraqi Freedom ought to be ascertained in the context of Saddam Hussein's past behavior, the factual determinations often unanimously made by the Security Council, and the applicable law—including the law of individual and collective self-defense and the doctrine of "humanitarian intervention" (both of which will be discussed below).

Iraqi Support for International Terrorism

In ADDITION TO ITS NUMEROUS RESOLUTIONS directed specifically at Saddam Hussein's Iraq (some of which also mentioned the issue of terrorism), the Security Council has repeatedly denounced international terrorism and authorized the use of armed force in self-defense against countries that sponsor terrorism. Such resolutions predate the September 11 attacks on the United States. For example, on October 18, 1999, Resolution 1269 condemned "all acts of terrorism" and "reaffirmed" that "the suppression of acts of international terrorism, including those in which States are involved, is an essential contribution to the maintenance of international peace and security."

The very first words in Article 1 of the U.N. Charter are, "The Purposes of the United Nations are: (1). To maintain international peace and security." The Security Council has declared that the "suppression of acts of international terrorism, including those in which States are involved, is an essential contribution" to that goal. It is thus difficult to argue that the effort to remove from power a significant supporter, funder, and facilitator of international terrorism is contrary to the purposes of the Charter.

One day after the September 11, 2001, terrorist attacks in the United States, the Security Council unanimously passed Resolution 1368, expressing its determination "to combat *by all means*"—language arguably even stronger than the phrase "by all necessary means" used in Resolution 678 in 1990 to authorize the use of military force—"threats to international peace and security caused by terrorist acts." It also recognized "the inherent right of individual or collective self-defense in accordance with the Charter," *presumably to emphasize that the United States and its supporters had an independent right to use armed force against the perpetrators of those attacks.* The Council also reaffirmed that "any act of international terrorism" was "a threat to international peace and security."

Two weeks later, on September 28, the Security Council invoked Chapter VII in unanimously passing Resolution 1373 deciding that "all States shall . . . prevent and suppress the financing of terrorist acts." One of the facts that does not seem to be in dispute is that—both before and after the passage of this resolution—the Iraqi regime of Saddam Hussein provided money and various other types of support for international terrorism. (That a much stronger case can be made, pointing to Iraq's direct sponsorship of terrorism, should be clear from evidence presented in chapters 2, 3, and 7 of this book.)

Reaffirming "the need to combat by all means . . . threats to international peace and security caused by terrorist acts," Resolution 1373 also—in binding language under Chapter VII—prohibited states from "providing any form of support, active or passive, to entities or persons involved in terrorist acts," from giving "safe haven to those who finance, plan, support, or commit terrorist acts," and from permitting "the movement of terrorists or terrorist groups" through their territory.

As has been demonstrated, Iraq violated all of these legal constraints. Moreover, the fact that Saddam's Iraq violated its international legal obligations with respect to terrorism was a specific finding of Security Council Resolution 1441, approved in November 2002.

Finally, if it is true that Saddam Hussein's regime was engaged in an ongoing campaign of terrorism against the United States—including the 1993 effort to assassinate former President Bush in Kuwait—probable Iraqi involvement in the first World Trade Center attack in February 1993 and its continued harboring of one of the suspected terrorists, as well as increasingly clear Iraqi cooperation with Osama bin Laden and al Qaeda in their campaign of terror against Americans—then the United States and its supporters have another independent basis for using force in self-defense, a principle that has been recently affirmed by the Security Council.

The Demand for "Regime Change"

PARTICULARLY OFFENSIVE TO INTERNATIONAL LAWYERS both in the United States and around the world was the American demand that, if Saddam Hussein continued to flagrantly violate his international legal obligations and force became once again necessary to uphold the Charter, a "regime change" would be part of the process. There was no legal basis, lawyers asserted, for using force to bring about a regime change.

This argument appears to slight the case of World War II, which imposed regime change in Germany, Italy, and Japan (though that was not the primary justification for waging that war). Moreover, the theory that it is legally permissible in exceptional circumstances to use force to effect a change of regime dates back centuries and can be found in the writings of some of the most respected writers on the subject.

Franciscus de Vitoria, for example, writing in his 1532 treatise *On the Law of War*, acknowledged:

It is undeniable that there may sometimes arise sufficient and lawful causes for effecting a *change of prince* or for seizing a sovereignty; . . . especially when security and peace cannot otherwise be had of the enemy and *grave danger* from them would threaten the State if this were not done.

That, of course, was written long before the advent of weapons of mass destruction. Vitoria could have had no concept of the "grave danger" posed by a repeat offender like Saddam Hussein, in possession of nuclear and biological weapons and convinced that the world community lacked the will to resist his unlawful acts. And Vitoria clearly viewed the use of force to effect a regime change in this circumstance as *defensive* rather than aggressive in character.

We may also consider whether the operation violated Article 2(4) of the Charter. Did it impermissibly interfere with the "territorial integrity" or "political independence" of Iraq, or of any other country? Was it "inconsistent with the Purposes of the United Nations"? The answer to these questions would appear to be no. When the dust has settled, Iraq will presumably completely control every square foot of territory it held under Saddam Hussein. And with respect to legitimate governing authority, the sovereignty of Iraq will almost certainly have been *enhanced,* not diminished, by the intervention. The overwhelmingly dominant view today is that sovereignty resides in the *people* of a country, and it is wrong for such authority to be seized by military force—whether by a foreign conqueror or a domestic tyrant. There is similarly no indication that Iraqi "political independence" will be in any way diminished: to the contrary, the intervention will presumably contribute substantially to the self-determination of the Iraqi people.

The Security Council debates over Haiti or Somalia (discussed below) strengthen the argument that the Charter itself permits collective intervention to replace Saddam's dictatorial rule with a government of, by, and for the people of Iraq. In the case of Somalia, indeed, the U.N. supported intervention, while the United States was criticized for not acting quickly enough to help end the suffering. Finally, the dramatic growth of international human rights law since 1945 may well have implicitly amended the Charter so as to permit the use of armed force by a state not only to protect the lives of its own people and other innocent victims of aggression from the wrongful use of force, but also to protect the lives of the Iraqi people themselves. In both cases, the balance being weighed is between the harm done to human life by resort to arms on the one hand, and the human destruction and suffering inflicted by a state on its own people in the absence of outside intervention on the other.

Individual and Collective Self-Defense Under the Charter

ONE OF MANY misunderstandings about the United Nations is the widespread belief that only the Security Council may authorize the use of military force in international relations. In reality, Article 24 confers upon the Security Council only the "primary responsibility" for the maintenance of international peace. Article 51 explicitly confirms that "nothing in the present Charter shall impair the inherent right of individual or collective self-defence if an armed attack occurs against a Member of the United Nations." Some scholars seek to read this as an exceptionally narrow right, but the committee that drafted Article 2(4) in San Francisco announced that "the use of arms in legitimate self-defense remains admitted and unimpaired" by the Charter.

Article 31 of the Vienna Convention on the Law of Treaties provides that "a treaty shall be interpreted in good faith in accordance with the ordinary meaning to be given to the terms of the treaty in their context and *in the light of its object and purpose.*" The first "purpose" set forth in the U.N. Charter is "to maintain international peace" by taking "effective collective measures for the prevention and removal of threats to the peace." The Security Council is the preferred and "primary" instrument for achieving this purpose, but it is not given exclusive authority.

Nor, for that matter, has the Security Council itself applied a narrow, literal interpretation to the language of the Charter. When in 1950 North Korea invaded South Korea, the Security Council immediately called upon U.N. members to respond collectively to the aggression, despite the fact that the "armed attack" had not been "against a Member of the United Nations." (Neither North nor South Korea were admitted to the United Nations until 1991.)

The right of individual states to use force defensively was an essential provision for the United States and many other states during the drafting of the Charter. This was in part precisely because Article 27 vests each of the five permanent members of the Security Council (China, France, Great Britain, the United States, and now Russia) with a veto over substantive decisions of that body.

Senator Arthur Vandenberg (R-Mich.), a member of the U.S. delegation to San Francisco, told the Senate:

> If the omission [of the right of collective self-defense, by which Member States could assist each other without Security Council authorization] had not been rectified there would have been no Charter. It was rectified, finally, after infinite travail, by agreement upon Article 51 of the Charter. Nothing in the Charter is of greater immediate importance and nothing in the Charter is of equal potential importance.[265]

Addressing the Inter-American Bar Association in 1949, Senator Vandenberg explained that the realization that Security Council action could be blocked by any of five permanent members made it imperative that the Charter permit states to defend one another (and, of course, themselves) when the Council is blocked from effective action. "If the Security Council fails to act—or is stopped from acting, for example, by a veto—Article 51 continues to confound aggression. The United Nations is thus saved from final impotence. So is righteous peace."

Whether the United States had a legal right under international law to use force against Iraq at the time of Operation Iraqi Freedom is dependent upon specific facts. If Saddam Hussein's government played a significant role in orchestrating, implementing, or merely financing the September 11 attacks, or in more general terms was a major facilitator of al Qaeda, the right to act against it in self-defense would seem clear—particularly in view of the robust rhetorical response to those attacks on the part of the Security Council. Alternatively, if Iraq had been engaged in a series of attacks on the United States—such as trying to assassinate former President Bush, involvement in the first World Trade Center bombing in February 1993, the 2001 anthrax letters, etc.— that would also justify necessary and proportional measures of self-defense. Similarly, an ongoing campaign of terrorism or other forms of armed attacks against another country might give that country a right of self-defense and thus empower it to authorize the United States to assist in its collective self-defense.

It is important to understand that the legal rationale for acts of self-defense is not retribution or revenge, but only to prevent the further loss of life. Thus, the United States could not now take measures in defensive response to acts carried out by Iraq in 1991 in Kuwait. However, if Iraq were indeed continuing to hold Kuwaiti citizens hostage in Iraqi prisons, this would be relevant to the equation, in balancing the threat against the defensive response.

One can also argue that Iraqi attacks on American and British aircraft engaged in enforcing the "no-fly zones" in northern and southern Iraq created a right to respond with armed force in self-defense. This point has been acknowledged even by strong critics of Operation Iraqi Freedom.[266]

Anticipatory Self-Defense

THE PRECISE CONTENT OF THE LAW of self-defense at the time when the Charter was written is in some areas unclear. Particularly problematic was the issue of whether a country could respond once it became clear that a neighbor was about to attack or whether it would have to absorb the first strike. Many scholars recognized the moral arguments for permitting defensive actions when the evidence of an imminent attack was overwhelming—especially if the aggressor was a repeat offender—but at the same time recognized that giving formal legal sanction to such a doctrine could also provide cover for blatant aggression. In 1939 Nazi Germany alleged that its invasion of Poland was a defensive response to a Polish attack on Germany, and in 1950 North Korea similarly tried to mask its aggression against South Korea with false allegations that it had been attacked first. The risk of abuse of a doctrine of anticipatory self-defense is even greater, since it would permit the use of force without even having to allege the other state fired a single shot.

Nevertheless, particularly with respect to an adversary like Saddam Hussein, who has a long history of committing unlawful aggression and violating the most fundamental rules of international law, the case for anticipatory self-defense is a compelling one. The most respected international law scholar at the time the U.S. Constitution was written was Emerich de Vattel, whose 1758 treatise *The Law of Nations* was widely read and quoted by the Constitution's framers. Consider this excerpt from Book III of that classic study:

> [T]here cannot exist a doubt, that, if that formidable potentate certainly entertains designs of oppression and conquest . . . the other states have a right to anticipate him. . . . This right of nations is still more evident against a sovereign, who, from a habitual propensity to take up arms without reasons, or even so much as plausible pretexts, is continually disturbing the public tranquility.

While modern scholars are divided on this point, the stronger view seems to be that there was indeed an established legal right to use force in anticipatory self-defense when the Charter was written, but that the circumstances had to be exceptional for such a claim to be viewed as legitimate. In a major law review article on "Anticipatory Collective Self-Defense in the Charter Era" published in 1998, Professor George K. Walker concluded (emphasis added):

Thus, in 1945, when the Charter provided, through article 51, for an inherent right of individual and collective self-defense in the context of the contemporary Act of Chapultepec, the right that the Charter negotiators intended as inherent included a right of anticipatory collective self-defense. . . . [T]he terms of prior agreements, negotiated before and after 1945, and state practice, show that it would be appropriate, as a matter of international law, *to include anticipatory self-defense as a response option until the Council acts pursuant to article 51.*[267]

The fifty-eight years since the Charter was written have seen changes that tend to strengthen the case for recognizing a right of anticipatory self-defense—not the least of which is the proliferation of weapons of mass destruction. It was once possible to contend that a potential victim of imminent aggression should be required to wait until the first enemy tank had crossed the border before launching a defense; but such a determination becomes more problematic when the first clear evidence of aggression might be a nuclear or biological attack that could claim tens or even hundreds of thousands of lives. The demonstrated ability of modern aggressors to coordinate simultaneous attacks—as exhibited in the August 1998 attacks on American embassies in both Kenya and Tanzania, and the September 11 coordinated attacks on both World Trade Center towers and the Pentagon—tips the scales of justice still further in favor of permitting anticipatory self-defense in exceptional circumstances.

The case for preemptive action against Saddam Hussein is particularly strong. He not only holds a unique status among world leaders as a "repeat offender"—having been guilty of massive acts of international aggression against Iran in 1980 and Kuwait in 1990, and of lesser acts of flagrant aggression against Saudi Arabia and Israel in 1991—but he has also repeatedly demonstrated a willingness to use weapons of mass destruction against both his neighbors and his own people.

Most important, perhaps, the legal case for anticipatory self-defense is strengthened by the fact that the U.N. Security Council has repeatedly made the factual determination that Saddam's regime was a "threat to the peace," and that Saddam was in flagrant and material breach of numerous binding Security Council resolutions for more than a decade. During the same period, economic sanctions and diplomatic pressures proved to be completely ineffective in enforcing international law, and the Security Council followed the example set by the worst traditions of the League of Nations in the 1930s.

The "Totality of Circumstances" Standard

THE STRONGEST OF THE ARGUMENTS against the conclusion that Operation Iraqi Freedom was a lawful act of anticipatory self-defense is the contention that, historically, the doctrine has been applied to settings in which the specific attack anticipated was clearly identified and was *imminent.* This time there were no tanks ranged along the border with Kuwait, as there were in 1990 (but recall that even then, the official U.S. position was that no invasion was imminent). Circumstances have changed dramatically, and the time may have arrived when claims of anticipatory self-defense need to be judged by the totality of the circumstances.

Saddam Hussein was the only head of state in the world who had engaged in unprovoked flagrant armed aggression against no less than four sovereign states.

In 1990, the U.N. Security Council recognized by Resolution 678 Saddam's Iraq to be a threat to the peace, and, acting unanimously under Chapter VII of the Charter, authorized member states to use military force not merely to eject Iraqi forces from Kuwait but also to "restore peace and security in the area." Not only has that resolution never been repealed, but it also has frequently been reaffirmed by the Council.

In 1991 the Security Council predicated its cease-fire with Iraq upon Iraqi acceptance of a variety of conditions that were evidently deemed essential to keep Iraq from remaining a threat to the peace. To be sure, the actual language of Resolution 687 required only that Iraq "accept" the cease-fire terms, but actual compliance must have been an implicit element in the agreement unless it was intended to have no practical meaning.

There is some force, therefore, in the American argument that when the Security Council unanimously concluded that Saddam's Iraq had materially breached Resolution 687, the legal effect was to breach the cease-fire agreement and leave in place the authority of Resolution 678 to use force to restore peace and security to the region through the use of armed force. (As noted above, however, the general principle of the law of treaties is that a material breach does not terminate the agreement but merely creates a right in the injured party—in this case, ostensibly the Security Council—to declare the agreement void.)

Nor was the breach a mere technicality. As a repeat offender with a long history of cavalierly using illegal weapons of mass destruction against his neighbors and his own people, Saddam Hussein had been required by the Security Council to rid Iraq of all such weapons and delivery vehicles under international supervision. This was obviously because the Council believed if he were allowed to develop such weapons he would once again use them.

The Council had unanimously and repeatedly passed legally binding resolutions under Chapter VII—a section of the Charter reserved for "Threats to the Peace, Breaches of the Peace, and Acts of Aggression"—not only noting that Iraq was in material breach but also demanding compliance. Even without explicitly authorizing a further use of armed force, these resolutions weigh heavily in favor of effective international action to enforce the law against a clear and recognized threat to peace.

The "totality of the circumstances" test I am proposing also mitigates against requiring certain knowledge that a specific attack is imminent before defensive force may be used. The secretive nature of the Iraqi regime made such certain knowledge unlikely to be obtained, while the potential consequences of one or possibly multiple simultaneous WMD attacks weigh against any legal rule that would permit a repeat offender—who is in material breach of more than a dozen Chapter VII Security Council resolutions—still one more "free kick" before potential victims may lawfully defend themselves.

Finally, Saddam's known connections with international terrorist organizations—also in violation of Chapter VII Security Council Resolutions—create the strong possibility of an Iraqi attack that might not leave any traceable fingerprints at the scene, as chapters 1, 2, 3, and 7 suggest. As the world changes, international law must adapt to address new realities. In early 2003, the United States knew that Saddam Hussein was a repeat offender responsible for numerous acts of blatant international aggression against several countries. He was a man who had gone to great lengths to obtain weapons of mass destruction, and he had repeatedly been found by the Security Council to be in flagrant breach of measures designed to eliminate such weapons and neutralize him as a threat to world peace. His totalitarian brutality made it very difficult to gain reliable intelligence about his intentions, but it was understood that, armed with WMDs, he could attack at a time and place of his own choosing—perhaps against multiple targets and quite possibly without even being clearly identified as the source of the attacks. In such a setting, to suggest that international law limits defensive responses to passively awaiting the next attack before reacting makes little sense.

The failure of the United States to provide leadership in the Security Council in the years after the 1991 Gulf War no doubt contributed to the current problem. Year after year, the Security Council would solemnly draw a new line in the sand and threaten Saddam that—*this* time—there really would be the most serious consequences if he didn't clean up his act. And each time that he ignored them—trying to convert his legal obligation to disarm under international supervision into a new "shell game" in which U.N. inspectors were challenged to "find the pea" in his vast, totalitarian country, or Iraq would be presumed to be in compliance—they would take a few more steps backward, pass a new resolution, and draw yet another line in the sand.

The Growth of International Humanitarian Law and the Right to Use Armed Force in Humanitarian Intervention

IN THE CASE OF OPERATION IRAQI FREEDOM, the totality of circumstances must also take into account the nature of the Iraqi regime: its monstrous and unrelenting abuse of its citizens' most basic rights, and the fact that its continued existence was itself a function of this pattern of heinous abuse.

One of the most dramatic changes in international law during the last half of the twentieth century was the increased recognition that international law creates rights not merely for states but also for individual human beings. Historically, for a state even to take notice of the abuse that occurs when a foreign state elects to mistreat its own nationals was considered a wrongful act—an interference in another state's "internal affairs." Prompted in part by Hitler's genocide of millions of Jews, gypsies, and other "undesirables" during World War II, states increasingly recognized that international law had to provide some level of constraint on gross violations of human rights.

The underlying debate reflects the divergence of opinion among legal "positivists"—who argued that there was no law beyond that accepted by sovereign states through treaty or custom—and advocates of "natural law," who contended that certain behavior was so inherently evil as to be prohibited by God or nature. Natural law champions have included in their number Francis Bacon, Hugo Grotius, John Locke, and, of course, Thomas Jefferson, who helped found a remarkable new country on the theory that all men were "endowed by their Creator" with "unalienable Rights."

Beginning with some general language in Article 1 of the United Nations Charter, which establishes as a purpose of the organization "promoting and encouraging respect for human rights and for fundamental freedoms for all," in 1948 the U.N. General Assembly passed the (nonbinding) Universal Declaration of Human Rights. The Declaration affirmed that the "inalienable rights of all members of the human family is the foundation of freedom, justice and peace in the world." Numerous human rights conventions—which, unlike the Universal Declaration, were intended to be legally binding upon parties—would become part of international law in the decades that followed.

Humanitarian Intervention and the Security Council

THE SECURITY COUNCIL HAS ON SEVERAL OCCASIONS acted to address major humanitarian catastrophes. On December 3, 1992, the Security Council passed Resolution 794, which read in part: "Acting under Chapter VII of the Charter of the United Nations, authorizes the Secretary-General and Member States cooperating to implement the offer referred to in paragraph 8 above to use all necessary means to establish as soon as possible a secure environment for humanitarian relief operations in Somalia." The U.N.-sanctioned intervention in Somalia established the legal principle—long recognized by many international lawyers—that force could legitimately be used to prevent egregious violations of international humanitarian law within a single state that threatened the lives of large numbers of human beings.

Less than two years later, the Security Council authorized the use of force in order to restore democracy to Haiti. On July 31, 1994, the Council adopted Resolution 940, expressing "grave concern" over the "further deterioration of the humanitarian situation in Haiti" and "reaffirming that the goal of the international community remains the restoration of democracy in Haiti." Acting under Chapter VII, the Council authorized member states "to use all necessary means" to bring about "the restoration of the legitimate authorities of the Government of Haiti." While the resolution did make references to "humanitarian" problems, the situation was not in fact measurably worse than the dismal circumstances that had plagued Haiti for decades under prior dictators. The goal of the Council was not that of addressing genocide or other egregious human rights violations, but rather that of restoring "democracy" to Haiti.

The Case of Kosovo

ON SEPTEMBER 23, 1998, the Security Council passed Resolution 1199, which asserted that "the deterioration of the situation in Kosovo, Federal Republic of Yugoslavia, constitutes a threat to peace and security in the region," and acting under Chapter VII, the Council demanded "that the authorities of the Federal Republic of Yugoslavia and the Kosovo Albanian leadership take immediate steps to improve the humanitarian situation and to avert the impending humanitarian catastrophe." Russia, however, announced the intention to veto any resolution designed to authorize military force.

On March 24, 1999, NATO launched Operation Allied Force and for seventy-seven days carried out air attacks against Yugoslavia in order to persuade President Slobodan Milosevic to withdraw his troops from Kosovo. The following day, Russia introduced a resolution in the Security Council declaring the NATO bombing to be a "flagrant violation" of the U.N. Charter and a threat to international peace. The Russian resolution failed to pass by a vote of 3 to 12, and the 80 percent opposition strongly suggests that the members of the Security Council were not outraged at the idea of pursuing a humanitarian intervention outside the framework of the Security Council when Council action had been blocked by the threat of a veto.

On March 26, the British representative to the Security Council noted that the policies of the Milosevic government in Kosovo had already been declared a "threat to the peace" by the Security Council and reasoned: "In the current circumstances, military intervention is justified as an exceptional measure to prevent an overwhelming humanitarian catastrophe."

It is worth noting that both France and Germany actively supported NATO's humanitarian intervention in Kosovo, despite the fact that

Article 53 of the U.N. Charter prohibits "regional agencies" like NATO from taking "enforcement action" other than self-defense without Security Council authorization. France, Germany, Belgium, and the United States attempted to distinguish the Kosovo operation as a unique incident, asserting that

> they had never stopped attaching crucial importance to the central role of the Security Council. The armed attack was initiated only as an exceptional measure justified by the failure of that body to act. However, as soon as the Security Council was in a position to take the issue into its own hands, they would discontinue any military action.[268]

History, however, shows that Kosovo was not unique. Scholars have recently drawn parallels between Operation Allied Force and Operation Iraqi Freedom.[269]

Humanitarian Intervention Outside of the U.N.

LEGAL SCHOLARS HAVE BEEN DIVIDED on the issue of whether force could be used outside of the Security Council process to protect a defenseless populace against truly egregious and widespread violations of fundamental human rights by its own government. Few scholars, however, have criticized the Kosovo intervention on moral grounds. The similarities between the use of armed force to prevent the slaughter of innocents by an aggressor state in another state, and the use of force to prevent tyrants from using force to slaughter or egregiously abuse their own citizens, are obvious. In both cases, the balance being determined by the law weighs the rights of sovereign states to be free of external interference in their affairs versus the importance of preserving human rights to life and fundamental freedoms.

In March 1999, a publication of the American Society of International Law reasoned with respect to the NATO intervention in Kosovo:

There are two possible arguments for intervention without Security Council authorization, but they both require an extension of recognized principles beyond the limits heretofore applied to them. The first is based on a limited right of humanitarian intervention to aid groups held captive or subjected to grave physical danger. The justification for humanitarian intervention is strongest when the intervening states are acting to protect their own nationals, as in the case of Israel's 1976 raid to release its nationals being held hostage at the airport in Entebbe, Uganda. The extended argument would be that in exceptional cases where peaceful means of alleviating a humanitarian crisis inflicted by a state on its own nationals have failed, and where the Security Council has recognized a threat to international peace, forceful intervention would be lawful so long as it is proportional to the situation.[270]

Consider for a moment the alternatives. If international law provides that *only* the Security Council may authorize the use of force if another Adolf Hitler emerges and starts slaughtering millions of innocent people, then it empowers any of five permanent members with an absolute veto to immunize such conduct. In such a case, international law would become part of the problem rather than an instrument for preserving peace, justice, and human life. As Jefferson recognized, we should not sacrifice the end to the means.

The dilemma was put well by U.N. Secretary General Kofi Annan in 1999 when he wrote of the "important questions" raised by the Kosovo conflict: "On the one hand is it legitimate for a regional organization to use force without a U.N. mandate? On the other, is it permissible to let gross and systematic violations of human rights, with grave humanitarian consequences, continue unchecked?"[271]

At the U.N.'s founding, the U.S. delegation in San Francisco in fact anticipated that the veto might be exercised to prevent Security Council action to stop armed aggression and refused to sign the Charter until it was clarified that traditional rights of individual and collective self-defense were preserved. The goal in both situations is the same: to prevent governments from unlawfully destroying large numbers of innocent human lives.

It is important to understand the basic values at stake in the humanitarian intervention debate. In deciding that force could not be used to redress economic or political disputes, the writers of the Charter placed great value upon the sanctity of human life. In permitting force in self-defense, they recognized that force may be justified in certain circumstances when, in the absence of defensive force, human lives would also be lost. When acting in humanitarian intervention, once again the use of force is intended to protect human life. The value that must be balanced against the desire to protect those lives is national sovereignty—a very important value in its own right, which is recognized in Article 2(7) of the Charter.

Professor Richard Falk, of Princeton University, was perhaps the foremost legal scholar in opposition to U.S. intervention in Vietnam and has been a critic of most other American interventions in the past half-century as well. But he was more supportive of intervention when the goal was protecting important humanitarian values. Writing in the *American Journal of International Law*, he concluded that a "normal textual reading" of the Charter would prohibit the NATO intervention in Kosovo, but he reasoned:

> to regard textual barriers to humanitarian intervention as decisive in the face of genocidal behavior is politically and morally unacceptable, especially in view of the qualifications imposed on the unconditional claims of sovereignty by the expanded concept of international human rights.[272]

Expressing concerns about the "self-marginalization of international law and international lawyers," Professor Falk notes that

> [I]t is often argued that the failure of the United Nations itself to evolve a collective security system justifies greater latitude in interpreting the occasions on which it is reasonable for a state to use force. This latitude allows for uses of force to uphold vital security interests or to serve the cause of humane governance that the Charter appears on its face to foreclose. In this regard, Articles 2(4) and 51, although

important guidelines, are no longer dispositive in relation to inquiries as to legality.[273]

More fundamentally, with respect certainly to a situation like Iraq, there is the question of where national "sovereignty" resides. Do we really believe that Saddam Hussein, by virtue of killing off much of his opposition and terrorizing the people of Iraq into submission, acquired the sovereignty of Iraq as his personal legal property? That would have been an accepted view many centuries ago, but the overwhelming majority view today is that sovereignty resides in the *people* of a country. If other states intervene for the limited purpose of restoring sovereignty to its rightful place by removing a tyrant who is slaughtering his people, it is difficult to contend that this violates the sovereignty of the people of Iraq.

Nor, for that matter, is it clear that such an intervention violates the use-of-force provisions of the Charter. Humanitarian intervention does not necessarily involve a threat to the "territorial integrity" or "political independence" of the state in question, and promoting human rights can hardly be considered "inconsistent with the Purposes of the United Nations."

Many experts believe that humanitarian intervention is already clearly lawful under the Charter. Others believe that, though moral, it is not yet easily reconciled with traditional interpretations of the Charter. At a minimum, it would appear that humanitarian intervention, as a matter of customary international law, is well on its way to becoming a recognized right—in certain exceptional circumstances.

When the Security Council has previously made a determination that a "threat to the peace" exists, and when it has then been prevented (by veto or threat of veto) from approving "measures necessary to maintain international peace and security" (per Article 51), the legal case for multilateral action outside the Council framework is a strong one.

Humanitarian Intervention and Iraq

THE SECURITY COUNCIL HAS REPEATEDLY RECOGNIZED the existence of serious humanitarian problems in Iraq. In Resolution 688, passed on April 5, 1991, the Security Council expressed its "grave concern" over the "the repression of the Iraqi civilian population in many parts of Iraq, including most recently in Kurdish populated areas, . . . which threaten international peace and security in the region."

In Resolution 778, of October 2, 1992, the Security Council reaffirmed "its concern about the nutritional and health situation of the Iraqi civilian population, and the risk of a further deterioration of this situation," and noted that previous resolutions had "provided a mechanism for providing humanitarian relief to the Iraqi population." The Council deplored "Iraq's refusal to cooperate in the implementation of resolutions 706 (1991) and 712 (1991), which puts its civilian population at risk, and which results in the failure by Iraq to meet its obligations under relevant Security Council resolutions."

On December 17, 1999, the Council passed Resolution 1284, expressing its "concern" about "the humanitarian situation in Iraq" and its determination "to improve that situation." Acting under Chapter VII, the Council called upon the government of Iraq to take "all steps to ensure the timely and equitable distribution of all humanitarian goods, in particular medical supplies, and to remove and avoid delays at its warehouses."

On November 8, 2002, when the Security Council gave Iraq "a final opportunity" to comply with its disarmament obligations, it also deplored "that the Government of Iraq has failed to comply with its commitments pursuant to . . . Resolution 688 (1991) to end repression of its civilian population and to provide access by international humanitarian organizations to all those in need of assistance in Iraq."

Although passed after the start of Operation Iraqi Freedom, Security Council Resolution 1472 of March 28, 2003, is also relevant. It reaffirmed "the right of the people of Iraq to determine their own political future," a right that was obviously far more likely to be achieved after the fall of Saddam Hussein's government.

Saddam's Record of Abuse of the Iraqi People

THE WORLD COMMUNITY REALIZED that the embargo begun in August 1990 could have disastrous consequences for the long-suffering people of Iraq, and over the years the Security Council tried hard to prevent or at least mitigate this harm. But Saddam Hussein, so far from desiring to mitigate harm to civilians, counted on the evident suffering of Iraq's civilian population to compel the Security Council to terminate the embargo that was complicating his military ambitions. Between the end of Operation Desert Storm and the start of Operation Iraqi Freedom, Saddam Hussein appropriated vast sums of money that could have been used to buy food and medical supplies for his people, and spent it instead on no less than forty-eight new "presidential palaces."

By the time Operation Iraqi Freedom began, more than half a billion dollars' worth of medical supplies, delivered to Iraq under the "oil-for-food" program, remained undistributed. According to Amnesty International, more than half a million children under the age of five died in the decade following the first Gulf War because of acute poverty and malnutrition, arising from corruption in Iraq.[274]

On August 15, 2001, Amnesty International (scarcely a "tool" of the U.S. or British governments) issued a report titled *IRAQ: Systematic Torture of Political Prisoners*, which recounted shocking stories of "gouging out of the eyes . . . severe beatings and electric shocks to various parts of the body.[275] The report noted that women had been tortured "simply because of family links," and noted the introduction in the mid-1990s of "judicial punishments such as amputation of hand and foot." The following excerpt provides a flavor of life under Saddam's Iraq:

Torture victims in Iraq have been blindfolded, stripped of their clothes and suspended from their wrists for long hours. Electric shocks have been used on various parts of their bodies, including the genitals, ears, the tongue and fingers. Victims have described to Amnesty International how they have been beaten with canes, whips, hosepipe or metal rods and how they have been suspended for hours from either a rotating fan in the ceiling or from a horizontal pole often in contorted positions as electric shocks were applied repeatedly on their bodies. Some victims had been forced to watch others, including their own relatives or family members, being tortured in front of them.

Other methods of physical torture described by former victims include the use of *falaqa* (beating on the soles of the feet), extinguishing of cigarettes on various parts of the body, extraction of fingernails and toenails, and piercing of the hands with an electric drill. Some have been sexually abused and others have had objects, including broken bottles, forced into their anus. In addition to physical torture, detainees have been threatened with rape and subjected to mock execution. They have been placed in cells where they could hear the screams of others being tortured and have been deprived of sleep. Some have stayed in solitary confinement for long periods of time. Detainees have also been threatened with bringing in a female relative, especially a wife or mother, and raping her in front of the detainee. Some of these threats have been carried out.

Consider as well this Amnesty International account of how the Iraqi judicial system under Saddam Hussein dealt with an accused critic of the government:

[A] 29-year-old theology student from Saddam City, was arrested in June 1999 and was tortured for long periods in the building of Saddam Security Directorate. His wife, father and mother were reportedly brought to the building in August 1999 and were tortured in front of him to force him to confess to being one of those responsible for the disturbances in Saddam City. He was said to have confessed in order to spare his parents and his wife any further torture. They were released following his confession but he was sentenced to death later and was executed at the beginning of 2001.[276]

Other accounts in the Amnesty report included that of a Baghdad obstetrician who was beheaded in October 2000 for complaining about corruption in the health system, and the twenty-five-year-old wife of a man accused of antigovernment activities who had managed to flee the country. The Amnesty report recounts:

> Men belonging to *Feda 'iyye Saddam* came to the house in al-Karrada district and found his wife, children and his mother. Um Haydar was taken to the street and two men held her by the arms and a third pulled her head from behind and beheaded her in front of the residents. . . . The security men took the body and the head in a plastic bag, and took away the children and the mother-in-law. . . . The fate of the children and the mother-in-law remains unknown.[277]

The fate of a large number of Iraqis "remains unknown." According to United Nations Commission on Human Rights figures, Iraq has "the highest number of disappearances reported" in the world.[278]

According to Amnesty International, in mid-2000 a new sentence was approved "by the authorities" to punish those accused of making remarks critical of Saddam or his family: "amputation of the tongue."[279] In 2001, the United Nations Commission on Human Rights condemned Iraq for the "widespread, systematic torture and the maintaining of decrees prescribing cruel and inhuman punishment as a penalty for offences."[280]

Nor were innocent children spared punishment. A health coordinator in Yemen's refugee health program reported in January 2002 that an Iraqi child under her care had needle scars on its wrists and forearms. The child had been injected with an agent designed to cause severe mental retardation, in retaliation for the father's "suspected" opposition to Saddam's regime.[281]

One of the many damning reports about human rights in Saddam's

Iraq was submitted to the U.N. General Assembly by Secretary General Kofi Annan on October 14, 1999. It was prepared by a distinguished Dutch diplomat, Ambassador Max van der Stoel, in his capacity as the Special Rapporteur of the U.N. Commission on Human Rights on the human rights situation in Iraq. Among his findings was that the under-five mortality rate in the south and center of Iraq (home to 85 percent of the population) grew from 56 deaths per 1,000 live births prior to 1989 to 108 per 1,000 during the five-year period ending in 1999. In contrast, in the autonomous northern region of Iraq, where Saddam was not in control, the mortality rate *declined* 20 percent during the 1990s.[282]

Discussing Saddam's refusal to cooperate with the "food-for-oil" program, Ambassador van der Stoel noted that under phase IV of the oil-for-food program, "$15 million was allocated for the targeted feeding programme for children under five and for lactating mothers. Despite repeated requests made by the United Nations at different levels, as of 31 July only one application, for high-protein biscuits, at a value of just under $1.7 million, had been received by the Office of the Iraq Programme and approved by the Security Council. No application for therapeutic milk has been submitted to the Office of the Iraq Programme."

Apparently, Saddam's government felt that Iraqi children had *too much* milk: on August 11, 1999, Kuwait intercepted a boat traveling from Basra, Iraq, smuggling seventy-five cartons of infant milk powder and twenty-five cartons of infant feeding bottles. The captain of the boat confessed that he had in the past made half a dozen similar trips.[283]

The U.N. report provides a good summary of Saddam's refusal to cooperate with the oil-for-food program:

> After the imposition of international sanctions in August 1990, the Government of Iraq decided not to take advantage of Security Council Resolutions 706 (1991) of 15 August 1991 and 712 (1991) of 19 September 1991, adopted by the international community in response to the specific needs of the Iraqi people. These Security Council resolutions allowed Iraq to sell $1.6 billion worth of oil every six months,

with the aim of importing humanitarian supplies. Instead, the Government of Iraq decided to rely only on domestic production to meet the humanitarian needs of its people, preferring to let innocent people suffer while the Government manoeuvred to get sanctions lifted. Indeed, had the Government of Iraq not waited five years to decide to accept the "oil-for-food" agreement proposed as early as 1991 in the above-mentioned resolutions to meet the humanitarian needs of the population, millions of innocent people would have avoided serious and prolonged suffering.[284]

The report quotes the executive director of the Office of the Iraq Program as saying in May 1999 that most of the $570 million worth of medicine and medical supplies that have arrived in Iraq under the oil-for-food program remained in government warehouses, which "are literally overflowing."[285] Although during the six-month period prior to the 1999 report an increase in oil prices had increased Iraq's income under the oil-for-food program to $3.86 billion, the government of Iraq had only budgeted $6.6 million in nutritional supplements for mothers and small children—less than half the 1996 sum.[286]

The conclusions of the 1999 U.N. report are ominous and warrant quotation at length (emphasis added):

[T]he situation of human rights in Iraq is worsening and the repression of civil and political rights continues unabated. . . . At the beginning of 1992, the Special Rapporteur concluded that the gravity of the human rights situation in Iraq had few comparisons in the world since the end of the Second World War. The Special Rapporteur regrets that since then he has had no cause to change his view. The prevailing regime in Iraq has effectively eliminated the civil rights to life, liberty and physical integrity and the freedoms of thought, expression, association and assembly; rights to political participation have been flouted, while all available resources have not been used to ensure the enjoyment of economic, social and cultural rights. *Indeed, the Special Rapporteur has concluded that the political-legal order in Iraq is not compatible with respect for human rights and, rather, entails systematic and systemic violations throughout the country, affecting virtually the whole population.* . . . [T]here is no freedom of speech or action since the mere suggestion that someone is not a supporter of the President carries the prospect of the death penalty; and there is no freedom of information on radio or television, the most popular public media. The . . . Iraqi people do not enjoy, and will not enjoy in the foreseeable future, respect for their human rights. . . .

Without firm determination on the part of the international community to respond substantially and meaningfully to the extremely serious violations referred to in the present report, the tradition of impunity which prevails in Iraq will almost certainly continue. Its unfortunate consequences will be, inter alia, to encourage the continuance of human rights violations, to dash hopes for the re-establishment of the rule of law, including accountable government, and to jeopardize efforts to establish peace and stability in the region. . . .

Considering the gravity and the complexity of the situation and on the basis of the foregoing, the Special Rapporteur reiterates all the conclusions and recommendations formulated in his previous reports. . . . [T]he Special Rapporteur observes no improvement in the situation of human rights in Iraq. In sum, the prevailing regime of systematic human rights violations is contrary to Iraq's many international obligations and, as determined by the Security Council in its resolution 688 (1991), remains a threat to peace and security in the region.[287]

These chilling human rights reports have now been confirmed over again, as people liberated by Operation Iraqi Freedom have come forward to tell their individual stories.

The Human Costs of Saddam's Regime

WHEN A SENIOR OFFICIAL of the United Nations Commission on Human Rights asserts that there have been few comparisons since World War II to the human rights deprivation in Saddam's Iraq, it is clear that the situation was extremely serious—and that a consequent case existed for international humanitarian intervention. Sanctions had been tried for more than a dozen years without visible success, as Saddam and his cronies were largely able to externalize the costs to the families and children of Iraq while hoarding scarce supplies for their own friends.

Measuring the extent of the humanitarian crisis is difficult. The total human costs of the 1980 Iraqi invasion of Iran and the 1990 invasion of Kuwait probably exceed one million deaths. Estimates of the numbers of Kurds killed by Iraq over the years range from 50,000 to 200,000, including 30,000 to 60,000 deaths due to unlawful chemical weapons, used against more than forty Kurdish villages in the 1980s. Human Rights Watch estimates that the number of "disappearances" in Iraq—that is, people who were taken off by government agents and never heard from again, or just "vanished" without explanation—is between 70,000 and 150,000, and many of these are presumably now dead.

Amnesty International alleges that Saddam's Iraq is also responsible for most of the "hundreds of thousands" of disappearances in the Middle East and North Africa in recent years, and estimates that an additional 500,000 children have died in Iraq in the past decade or so. An estimated 3 to 4 million Iraqis have fled their country and become refugees, ranking Saddam's regime second only to the Taliban's Afghanistan in the number of displaced persons it has created.

In January 1994, the Council of Europe passed Resolution 1022 declaring that the survival of Iraq's Marsh Arabs was threatened by Saddam Hussein's government. Human Rights Watch is one of several groups to conclude that the widespread killing of Iraqi Kurds violated the 1949 Genocide Convention and constituted "crimes against humanity."

Just as the case for anticipatory self-defense was clearly strengthened by the U.N. Security Council's numerous resolutions declaring Saddam Hussein's regime in Iraq to be a "threat to the peace" and in material breach of Chapter VII resolutions, the Security Council and other U.N. organs' documentation of Iraq's gross violations of internationally recognized human rights clearly strengthens the case for humanitarian intervention.

Discussing the NATO use of force in Kosovo in 1999, Professor Antonio Cassese of the University of Florence argued that the operation was probably unlawful under traditional interpretations of the Charter, but he noted that "a new customary rule" was most likely "in the process of emerging in the world community." Professor Cassese observed that "only very few states contended that the action on the part of NATO countries was contrary to the United Nations Charter in that it violated Article 2(4)," identifying fewer than ten dissenters. "Furthermore," he wrote, "the military action was also regarded as warranted in that it had been preceded by repeated pronouncements of the Security Council to the effect that the atrocities committed in Kosovo by the FRY against its own citizens amounted to a threat to the peace." He concluded: "This rule would legitimize the taking of forcible countermeasures by groups of states in the event of failure of the United Nations Security Council to authorize the use of force in response to gross, systematic and large-scale breaches of human rights amounting to egregious crimes against humanity."[288]

The point is a compelling one, and the pertinent question is whether the "emerging principle" had achieved the status of customary international law at the time of Operation Iraqi Freedom.

No friend of human freedom and dignity can favor a rule of international law that grants each of five states the legal power to immunize the kinds of appalling humanitarian abuse instituted in Iraq under Saddam Hussein's regime; but this is in fact the import of the claim that humanitarian intervention is impermissible without prior Security Council approval. If it is argued that customary international law had not yet reached the point where such an operation was clearly lawful in the absence of Security Council approval, it is perhaps all the more important that humanitarian coalitions engage in such operations in the interest of furthering the progressive development of such a customary rule.

The Proper Balance of Values

In the end, the United Nations' attempts to deter aggression and remove threats to the peace through nonforceful means failed. President Bush and Prime Minister Blair agreed to assemble a coalition of the willing to enforce the purposes of the Charter. There seems to be overwhelming consensus that this was the right thing to do; a strong case can be made that it was also a legal thing to do.

The fear, of course, is that Operation Iraqi Freedom will establish a precedent for other states, in less justifiable circumstances, to resort to force. Here again, the proper approach is to evaluate each situation in light of the totality of the circumstances: Saddam Hussein had created a thoroughly and uniquely malevolent regime, intentionally starving children and routinely engaging in the most brutal forms of torture imaginable not only against his political enemies but also against the friends and relatives of people even suspected of disloyalty. If the course of human history someday brings forth a comparable regime, Operation Iraqi Freedom may serve as a valuable precedent. Prior to that point being reached, Saddam's fate may serve as a valuable deterrent to budding tyrants who believe that emulating the behavior of Stalin or Hitler may be an acceptable means of maintaining political power.

Legal scholars will no doubt continue to debate for decades to come issues posed by Operation Iraqi Freedom. Evaluating the operation in the light of the totality of the circumstances, I would conclude that it probably was a lawful use of force. And to the extent that it stretched the edges of previously accepted permissible conduct, it may contribute to the progressive development of rules necessary for the maintenance of peace, security, and the rule of law in the modern world.

And since the very first "purpose" set forth in Article 1(1) of the U.N. Charter is to act collectively to "remove" threats to the peace—a status the Security Council repeatedly conferred on Saddam Hussein's regime each time it denounced his unlawful behavior pursuant to Chapter VII of the Charter—one cannot with a straight face contend that the effort of replacing this brutal tyrant has undermined the "purposes" of the Charter. While the Security Council may not have clearly authorized Operation Iraqi Freedom (an issue regarding which there is room for debate), the Council has formally made most of the factual findings necessary to justify the use of lethal force to remove Saddam Hussein from power.

In the end, the reaction of the Security Council to Operation Iraqi Freedom is noteworthy. Rather than condemning the operation as unlawful aggression, on May 22, 2003, the Security Council by a vote of 14–0 (with the representative of Syria absent) approved Resolution 1483, recognizing that the United States and Great Britain constituted "the Authority" in Iraq and supporting "the formation, by the people of Iraq with the help of the Authority and working with the Special Representative [of the U.N. Secretary General], of an Iraqi interim administration as a transitional administration run by Iraqis, until an internationally recognized, representative government is established by the people of Iraq and assumes the responsibilities of the Authority."

Thus, as this book goes to press, after the heavy lifting has been accomplished by the United States, Great Britain, and their allies, the world community seems once again united on the issue of Iraq. Rather than demanding the restoration to power of the regime of Saddam Hussein, the Security Council has formally endorsed "efforts by the people of Iraq to form a representative government based on the rule of law that affords equal rights and justice to all Iraqi citizens without regard to ethnicity, religion, or gender"—which is precisely the goal of the coalition that removed Saddam's regime from power. It is difficult to believe that this unity would have been possible had the world community honestly felt that Operation Iraqi Freedom was an unlawful act of international aggression.

As we move further into the twenty-first century, an appropriate test for evaluating use-of-force situations when the Security Council is deadlocked is this: under the totality of the circumstances, was the force used aggressively (e.g., for conquest or perhaps to resolve some political, diplomatic, or economic dispute) or defensively (either in defense of the state resorting to the use of force, in the defense of another state requesting assistance in collective self-defense, or in the defense of other human lives, made necessary by an extraordinary pattern of unlawful violation of fundamental human rights). Any *anticipatory* claim must be required to overcome a very high hurdle of presumptive illegitimacy. But that hurdle can surely be vaulted in a case in which a repeat offender has been expressly identified as a threat to the peace, and has violated numerous Chapter VII resolutions of the Security Council in a sustained effort to develop weapons of mass destruction.

Properly understood, Operation Iraqi Freedom reflects a proper balance of values in the twenty-first century.

Professor Turner holds both professional and academic doctorates from the University of Virginia School of Law, where in 1981 he cofounded the Center for National Security Law. A former Charles H. Stockton Professor of International Law at the U.S. Naval War College, he is the author of more than a dozen books and for several years chaired the American Bar Association's Standing Committee on Law and National Security. The views expressed are his own.

CONCLUSION

MOST OF THE AMERICAN PUBLIC understands why the United States went to war with Iraq: 52 percent believe that Iraq (and Saddam Hussein personally) were involved in the September 11 attacks. A decisive majority—74 percent—support President Bush's handling of the situation in Iraq, and nearly as many—70 percent—say he has strong leadership qualities.[289] In Bush's words, "A president has to be the calcium in the backbone."[290] Nothing has tested those qualities of leadership more thoroughly than the shocking events of September 11, 2001.

Far worse scenarios were possible, however. Iraq had already admitted to having a huge biological weapons program that was never turned over to the U.N. weapons inspectors. As the president and other senior administration officials reiterated, in the lead-up to the war among the greatest dangers to the country was the possibility that Saddam Hussein could provide biological agents to al Qaeda (or other terrorists), and thus inflict enormous damage without U.S. authorities being able to determine who was responsible.

Leaky Sanctions and Iraq's Rearmament

THIS CONCERN MARKED A COMPLETE REVERSAL of the thinking that had dominated U.S. policy during the 1990s, when Saddam was said to be in his "box"—even his "cage." Sanctions were the primary instrument the Clinton administration came to rely on to prevent Saddam's rearmament, and otherwise "contain" Iraq.[291]

The sanctions, however, were Swiss cheese, as President Bush remarked soon after taking office. Saddam and his regime had become enormously wealthy by diverting the stream of oil revenues, legitimate and illegitimate; only the Iraqi people were poor. Saddam's grandiose palaces were already familiar from 1998, when fruitless weapons inspections were conducted among them. We saw them again, closer up, when U.S. forces defeated the regime, occupied the country, and took over the palaces for their own use.

That the Iraqi regime had access to incredible wealth was also demonstrated by the bank heist carried out by Saddam's younger son Qusay just before the war began. With a letter from his father and in the company of several other senior Iraqis, Qusay seized $1 billion from the Central Bank, and had it hauled away in three tractor-trailer trucks.[292] Although most of it was recovered by U.S. forces, some forty-five boxes of one-hundred-dollar bills—totaling millions—are still missing.[293] The cash in Iraq's Central Bank did *not* include money from Iraq's main source of revenue, U.N.-supervised oil sales—funds that were kept in foreign banks. This was money obtained from activities that circumvented sanctions, including Iraq's illegal oil sales as well as the kickbacks it demanded and received from some suppliers involved in the U.N. oil-for-food program. U.N. officials later acknowledged that Baghdad was skimming $2 to $3 billion a year from that program. "Everybody knew it, and those who were in a position to do something about it, were not doing anything," Benon Sevan, the program's administrator, affirmed.[294]

Sanctions represented an easy policy solution for the United States, but they could not stop Saddam from engaging in terrorism. Nor did the sanctions—or the inspections—prevent Iraq from developing and producing proscribed weapons of mass destruction. As Secretary of Defense Donald Rumsfeld put it, shortly before the war began, "Iraq has designed its [weapons] programs in a way that they can proceed in an environment of inspections."[295]

Where Are the Weapons?

THE TWO MOBILE BIOLOGICAL WEAPONS production facilities found in Iraq after the war concretely demonstrate Rumsfeld's point. The two tractor-trailer trucks closely matched the description of Iraq's mobile BW labs provided by an Iraqi defector, evidence that Secretary of State Colin Powell cited in his prewar presentation to the Security Council.[296] After the war, the CIA and DIA carefully examined the vehicles and concluded that "the only consistent, logical purpose for the vehicles was the production of biological weapons."[297]

As for the remainder of Iraq's large proscribed weapons programs, it is impossible at this point to know what happened to that material. The Iraqis may have succeeded in hiding some portion of it; shifting it to another country like Syria; or destroying it, as U.S. officials have suggested. As the editors of London's *Daily Telegraph* affirmed,

> The failure to produce definitive evidence of WMD is scarcely surprising. What the Pentagon says on this matter is *prima facie* true: Saddam might have hidden, destroyed or dispatched his weapons to a safe haven in Syria before or during the war.[298]

Even if the weapons cannot be found, however, it may be possible to determine what the Iraqis did with them by interviewing the Iraqi scientists and intelligence officials now in custody, and by examining documents that have been seized. This process began only in early June, with the dispatch of the Iraq Survey Group. Consisting of more than one thousand government officials from the United States, Britain, and Australia, including a number who served with UNSCOM, the ISG has significantly greater expertise than the military intelligence teams who first searched for banned weapons.

That material certainly did exist—in gross violation of the U.N.-sponsored cease-fire to the 1991 war. That conclusion is not based on speculative or dubious sources. It is based on information that first came from the Iraqi regime itself. After Hussein Kamil defected in August 1995, the Iraqis panicked, fearful of what he might reveal, and UNSCOM chairman Rolf Ekeus played skillfully on their fears. It was then that the Iraqis acknowledged having produced much more advanced and much larger quantities of their most dangerous chemical and biological agents than they had revealed over the previous four years.[299]

The Iraqis also claimed they had destroyed that material, but they could provide no documents to support their claim, nor did they provide any coherent account of that destruction, as for example through interviews with the individuals who were supposed to have carried it out. UNSCOM concluded that the material remained in Iraq, as it stated in every report it issued from October 1995 forward.[300]

In June 1998, UNSCOM chairman Richard Butler (Ekeus's successor) made a lengthy presentation to the Security Council. He explained that following the discovery of equipment from Iraq's nuclear program in June 1991, Iraq resolved on a means to conceal key elements of its other programs by destroying them unilaterally, even though Resolution 687 called for UNSCOM-supervised destruction. This Iraqi maneuver had the effect of obscuring whatever material was *not* destroyed. As Butler explained (emphais added),

> It is important to note the order of magnitude of the weapons retained by Iraq: ⅔ of the operational missile force, more than half of the chemical weapons and *all of the biological weapons.* . . . This unilateral destruction was conducted by Iraq in such a manner as to hide the

existence of these weapons and to some extent to cover the level of achievement of its weapons programmes.[301]

Nor did anything change subsequently. The Iraqis relinquished nothing between then and the end of UNSCOM's presence in Iraq six months later; and the Clinton administration consistently maintained that Iraq retained significant amounts of banned weapons. UNSCOM's successor, UNMOVIC, did not even enter Iraq until November 2002, and it received virtually no proscribed material, although it did find and destroy eighteen empty chemical warheads for 122mm rockets, reinforcing the impression that proscribed agents remained in Iraq.

That the Security Council itself implicitly accepted this assessment is reflected in the fact that it maintained sanctions on Iraq. France, Russia, and China were all advocates for Iraq on the Security Council, but none ever claimed that the weapons programs had been destroyed.[302] The debate in the Security Council, before the war began, was not about whether Iraq retained such weapons, but rather about the most appropriate way to get Iraq to surrender them and how much time should be allotted for that project.

Similarly, within the United States, there was no debate among the national security agencies about whether Iraq retained significant amounts of proscribed weapons, as a knowledgeable source close to the administration affirmed.[303] The only real debate concerned the circumstances under which Saddam was likely to use that material, and therefore the nature of the threat he posed.

Gotcha!

DESPITE THIS GENERAL CONSENSUS about Iraq's retained weapons, a radically new account of that assessment suddenly appeared after the war, when U.S. forces did not immediately find weapons stockpiles.

Some who had opposed the war now suggested that the weapons did not exist, and that the administration's rationale for war was therefore based on faulty—even cooked—intelligence. *The New Yorker*'s Seymour Hersh published an extreme version of that claim in an article titled "Selective Intelligence"—a title that aptly describes the article itself.

Hersh writes, "What has been in dispute is how much of that capacity [the proscribed weapons], *if any*, survived the 1991 war and the years of United Nations inspections, no-fly zones, and sanctions that followed" (emphasis added). He claims that information supplied by Hussein Kamil "became a major element in the Bush administration's campaign to convince the public of the failure of the U.N. inspectors." But he also quotes Kamil as saying that "all chemical weapons were destroyed" before UNSCOM got to them.[304] In short, he was claiming the administration had made it up.

Kamil had indeed made that claim—but on that point he was lying, as UNSCOM knew, if only because UNSCOM itself had destroyed large quantities of Iraq's chemical agents. The key information about the weapons programs came not from Kamil but from Baghdad. After reading Hersh's piece, a former UNSCOM member remarked, "It appears that 1984 is alive and well."[305]

As war approached, five retired CIA officials, claiming to represent the "steering group" for a national network of CIA analysts, began writing memos on the subject, which were posted on the Internet. They called themselves the VIPS (Veteran Intelligence Professionals for Sanity). Their first note, issued immediately after Powell's presentation to the U.N., complained about his "narrow focus" on Iraq's lack of compliance with Resolution 1441 (which the Security Council had passed in November 2002, demanding that Iraq disarm). After all, they noted, by the same token, wasn't Israel in violation of Resolution 242 (the formal cease-fire to the 1967 Arab-Israel war)?[306] These analysts opposed the war, and maintained that containment was still an effective strategy.

Notably, even these CIA analysts did not claim that Iraq's weapons had been destroyed. Rather, they asserted, "It has been the judgment of the US intelligence community for over twelve years that the likelihood of such use would greatly increase" if the United States went to war, and they warned, "Clearly, an invasion would be no cakewalk for American troops, ill equipped as they are to operate in a chemical environment."[307]

In their next letter, the retired analysts cited the account of a debriefing of Hussein Kamil posted on the Internet by Glen Rangwala, a lecturer in politics at Cambridge University. Rangwala opposed the war (and had made a name for himself in 1999 by protesting the visit of Israel's dovish Shimon Peres to the university, demanding Peres's arrest for breaches of the Geneva convention and calling him "a murderer"[308]). Posting the transcript of the debriefing, Rangwala claimed that Kamil was the source of the information upon which the United States had made its claims about Iraq's weapons. That story then made its way into Hersh's *New Yorker* piece.[309]

VIPS subsequently cited Rangwala's comments, as reported by the left-of-center antiwar British paper *The Independent:*

> Mr. Rangwala said much of the information on WMDs had come from Ahmed Chalabi's Iraqi National Congress (INC), which received Pentagon money for intelligence-gathering. "The INC saw the demand, and provided what was needed," he said. "The implication is that they polluted the whole US intelligence effort."[310]

Apparently these analysts had conveniently forgotten their own assertion, of just three months earlier, that the consensus in the intelligence community was that Saddam retained proscribed weapons, as well as their warning of the dangers of U.S. troops having to fight in a chemical environment.

Nonetheless, this charge too made it into "Selective Intelligence," along with the assertion that Adnan al-Haideri, an engineer who fled Iraq in 2001 with the help of the INC, was prominent among those spreading false stories. Al-Haideri was behind Powell's claim about Iraq's mobile biological production facilities, according to Hersh, a claim that had already been confirmed by the discovery of one of those facilities![311]

Equally flawed was the accusation by Rangwala, echoed by the former CIA analysts and Hersh, that the INC's Information Collection Program was a rogue operation run by Pentagon hawks. The program was in fact established in 2000 under the Clinton administration, and was initially run by the State Department. Because State's Near Eastern Affairs despised the INC and sought to kill its programs (as discussed in chapter 4), the ICP was shifted to the Pentagon and run within the Defense Intelligence Agency by the Defense Humint Service (the same organization now directing the Iraq Survey Group). DHS considered the "outtake" (the information the defectors provided) from the INC "excellent," according to a knowledgeable administration official.[312]

These wild stabs are not a matter of policy debate—legitimate criticism designed to clarify an issue or provide alternative points of view. This is strictly a game of "Gotcha!" in which any stick will do to go after an opponent.

Many people were stunningly wrong about the Iraq war.[313] It was not the catastrophe that had been so widely predicted. The military planning proved to be brilliant, swiftly and expertly executed. Casualties, among both coalition forces and Iraqi civilians (and perhaps even Iraqi military) were strikingly limited. Iraqis, in their overwhelming majority, welcomed the war, and with it the American soldiers. Nor did the "Arab street" prove a tinderbox, ready to explode in fury or support the Iraqis on the ground in any significant way.

There have been no public reassessments of those predictions of catastrophe, however, because that is not how the game of "Gotcha!" works. This phase of the Beltway battle appears, if anything, harsher in tone. No misstep on the part of the Bush administration will be interpreted as mere error by these committed critics—who include not only journalists and commentators but also the intelligence analysts who had insisted that "containment" was an adequate strategy for dealing with Saddam.

The charge of "cooking the intelligence" on Iraq's weapons should never have been accorded any significant degree of credibility. It is certainly possible that mistakes were made in some details—common enough in the world of intelligence. But the international consensus before the war was, undeniably, that Iraq held significant quantities of proscribed weapons, a consensus based on the work of the U.N. weapons inspectors themselves.

For the administration, this campaign of falsification creates a double-edged problem. On the one hand, it is forced to invest time and energy in addressing such malicious and ill-founded criticisms, lest they acquire respectability through reiteration. On the other, it will need to take due note of legitimate criticism of its ongoing efforts, and make necessary policy adjustments.

A Major Intelligence Failure

THERE WAS, INDEED, a major intelligence failure in regard to Iraq, and it is highlighted in this book: the failure to recognize that Iraqi intelligence began working with Islamic militants to attack the United States, starting with the 1993 bombing of the World Trade Center. The CIA accepted and promoted another theory, favored by the Clinton White House, to explain this new Islamic terrorism: namely, that it was the work of a "loose network" operating without state sponsorship—although the lead investigative agency, the New York FBI, believed that the bombing was an Iraqi "false flag" operation. As more terrorism followed, the "loose network" theory became the paradigmatic explanation, and al Qaeda became the premier example.

In early September 2001, as we've seen, the Pentagon's newly completed review of counterterrorism policy had already given the administration reason to doubt that explanation. Within a few weeks after the September 11 attacks, a number of senior administration officials were convinced that Iraq had been involved. Most of the bureaucracy, however, including the CIA, remained committed to its long-held position, dismissing such important information as the Iraqi defectors who reported the training of Arab militants to hijack airplanes, as well as the Czech report tying Mohammed Atta to Iraqi intelligence.

Some information linking Iraq and al Qaeda did, nonetheless, survive the CIA's campaign and the formal interagency vetting process. Starting in the fall of 2002, as the United States prepared for war with Iraq, senior U.S. officials began to articulate six key points showing ties between the two organizations. But every time a senior official, including the president, cited that information, a series of anonymous leaks to the media followed, asserting that there was "no evidence" of any meaningful connections.

This occurred largely because of egos and careers. *New York Times* columnist William Safire wrote about the leaks that were still occurring as war with Iraq approached, leaks that undermined the administration's efforts to mobilize support. He summed them up as the work of "an angry minority" of CIA analysts "to justify years of mistaken estimates."[314]

As the nation's premier intelligence agency, the CIA has great authority over intelligence. It decides what information to collect, what such information means, and whether it can be publicly released. Moreover, the agency can veto the judgment of others. As one official explained, a handful of analysts—who had strongly rejected the notion that Iraq was involved in terrorism—dismissed virtually all evidence linking Iraq to al Qaeda or to the September 11 attacks as "fragmentary and inconsequential," while at the same time insisting that the information was sensitive and had to remain classified.[315]

Disgruntled bureaucrats even raised the explosive charge that the administration was "politicizing" the intelligence, the same charge that has become the core of the postwar campaign regarding Iraq's weapons.

Hamstrung by this systematic discrediting of the evidence suggesting Iraq's links to terrorism, the administration based its public case for war on the dangers posed by Saddam's weaponry. As Paul Wolfowitz, the Pentagon's second-in-command, later explained, "The truth is that for reasons that have a lot to do with the U.S. government bureaucracy, we settled on the one issue that everyone could agree on which was weapons of mass destruction as the core reason."[316] Little could Wolfowitz and other senior administration officials have imagined when making that decision that a time would come when they would be accused of "politicizing" the weapons issue as well.

It Is So Bad

THE MOST PROMISING EVIDENCE TYING Iraq to the September 11 attacks is still not being actively pursued. With the intensified investigation into al Qaeda after September 11, a radically new picture emerged of the decade of Islamic terrorism: a handful of Pakistani Baluch are the architects of most of those attacks. They include, among others, Ramzi Yousef, mastermind of the 1993 Trade Center bombing; Abdul Hakim Murad, Yousef's supposed childhood friend; and Khalid Shaikh Mohammed, supposedly Yousef's maternal uncle. Yousef and Murad were arrested in the mid-1990s, but Mohammed escaped and went on to head al Qaeda's military committee, in which capacity he masterminded the September 11 strikes as well as several other major attacks.

Iraqi intelligence has longstanding ties to the Baluch, whom it used as agents against Iran. Because the identities of these Baluch terrorists are based on Interior Ministry files in Kuwait that *predate* Kuwait's liberation in February 1991, it is urgent that these identities be investigated to determine whether or not they are "legends" created by Iraqi intelligence during Iraq's occupation of Kuwait. Yet this simple task has not been done—because of very strong bureaucratic obstructionism.

One intriguing document that emerged after the war may help illuminate this matter. In October 2002, Iraq finally returned Kuwait's national archives, which it had seized over a decade before. Among the documents that has since come to light is a secret memorandum from Saddam's office, dated April 30, 2000, and distributed to all intelligence directorates. It instructs them to "prepare the documents present at your directorates that belong to the Kuwaiti archive, *except those documents that went into intelligence pursuits*" (emphasis added). It further orders, "Remove all written comments and suggestions in the margins that were done by those at the service [Iraqi intelligence] and remove any markings or anything to do with the work of the service."[317]

Clearly, then, Iraqi intelligence had gone over Kuwait's archives with some care. This does not in itself demonstrate that the identities of the Baluch terrorist masterminds are false, of course, but it does establish that Iraq used documents that it obtained in Kuwait for intelligence purposes. Creating "legends" may well have been among those purposes.

Regaining Control of the System

HISTORIANS WILL LIKELY VIEW THE strategic intelligence failure that led to the 9/11 attacks as a blunder on the order of Pearl Harbor. As such, it is almost certainly the CIA's most serious error since its founding in 1947. Yet no one has been held accountable, nor have basic mistakes been corrected. In this respect, government bureaucracy is fundamentally different from the private sector. Herb Meyer was right: it never hurts to be fashionably wrong in Washington, D.C.

If a mistake on this scale had happened in the private sector, the company involved would be bankrupt, with key executives possibly indicted or facing lawsuits. After a government bureaucracy makes a horrific blunder, however, the typical response is simply to throw more money and other resources at it—and that has certainly happened. Although there is now, at long last, an emerging debate within the intelligence community about the involvement of Iraq in the Islamic terrorism of the 1990s, those responsible for this very costly policy error are not likely to be held accountable. The mistaken analysts have not even been called on to acknowledge and correct the fundamental misconceptions that caused them to regard as criminal matters attacks that were essentially acts of war carried out by a state.

The administration has so far shied away from the confrontation that would be entailed in correcting this mistake. Concern about establishing the truth, as important as that is, is often lost sight of in Washington, where players are satisfied just to achieve their critical policy objectives without taking on the underlying issues.

Yet if this fundamental error is not corrected, it only increases the chances that something similar can happen again in the future. Some other enemy may come to the same recognition that Saddam did: that the way to fight the world's only superpower is not through the clash of armed forces, but through a campaign of subterfuge and terror in which the United States does not even recognize the enemy it is fighting. And if the situation in postwar Iraq should turn sour, the administration will wish it had presented a much clearer explanation than it has of why this war had to be fought.

As Senator Fred Thompson of the Senate Intelligence Committee suggested shortly before leaving Washington, probably the single most pressing item in repairing the country's national security apparatus is intelligence reform. It is commonly said that everything begins with intelligence. If you do not understand what is happening, your ability to deal with events is compromised, your response is less effective, and—as with the United States' handling of terrorism—the result may prove not merely ineffectual but disastrously so.

As Thompson indicated, there needs to be far more accountability within the intelligence community. With regard to Iraq, the CIA made the same error again and again over the course of a decade. A mechanism needs to be developed within the agency for more effectively evaluating its analysts' basic assumptions and estimates—but before that can even begin to happen, the agency must first acknowledge that a mistake was made.

The president should establish a "Team B" to examine the question of Iraq's involvement with al Qaeda and the September 11 attacks. The congressional inquiry into September 11 focused only on tactical issues: Why didn't the CIA immediately inform the FBI that two al Qaeda terrorists had entered the United States? Absent from the congressional review was any consideration of the fundamental strategic blunder made by the CIA (and the FBI) in accepting, and *insisting* on, the explanation that this terrorism did not involve states. (The congressional oversight committees, it should be noted, share some complicity in the matter; if ever they questioned this assumption, they nonetheless failed to press it with any vigor.)

Other offices within the administration have already developed significant information that shows far more conclusively than has yet been publicly revealed that Iraq and al Qaeda are, indeed, intimately intertwined. More such information, particularly regarding the question of the identities of the terrorist masterminds, has been presented here. Yet the government's information has been withheld from public view by the effective veto power of a handful of analysts who face personal embarrassment in any thorough critique of the agency's performance. Nothing could better illustrate the gross inefficiencies of government bureaucracy than the fact that these individuals are still in a position to have a decisive say on this issue.

It is commonly said that one lesson of September 11 is the need for greater centralization of intelligence.[318] That view reflects the implicit assumption that if a government agency has made a serious error, the way to address it is to provide that agency more resources—in this case, more authority for the CIA. Certainly, information needs to be exchanged more freely and efficiently among the bureaucracies than it was before September 11, or than it is even now. The results of the FBI investigation into those attacks, for example, are still extremely tightly held. Although Zacarias Moussaoui and his lawyers have free access to it, outside of the Justice Department that information is only readily available to the CIA's Counter Terrorism Center—the same office whose errors made us so vulnerable to the September 11 attacks.

What the events of September 11 actually underscore is the need for *competing* intelligence analysis. Centralization of analysis leads to conformity, and conformity can lead to error. Better to let several competing hypotheses exist side by side, than to have the analytic community embrace an erroneous hypothesis as dogma—a development more likely to occur in an environment of centralized rather than competitive intelligence.

The Future of Iraq

As Operation Iraqi Freedom began, U.S. authorities basically looked to the old regime to form the basis of the new regime, as detailed in chapter 4. While they planned to remove the top of the Ba'athist power structure, they expected that most institutions of the Iraqi government would survive, and that the establishment of a postwar government would not be an overly onerous task. It would simply entail replacing one set of top officials with another. This judgment, however, papered over deep divisions between the State Department and the CIA on the one hand, and the Pentagon on the other, which thought that a more thoroughgoing cleansing of the regime would be necessary.

As it turned out, when the old regime fell, its institutions fell along with it. And because Saddam's government and its infrastructure collapsed so quickly, the United States did not really have a plan in place to address the problem of Iraq's postwar governance. A new U.S. agency, the Office of Reconstruction and Humanitarian Assistance (ORHA), was created for that purpose before the war began. But ORHA was the object of tremendous bureaucratic infighting even before it left Washington, again revolving around the competing views of the State Department and CIA versus the Pentagon. ORHA reports to the Pentagon, but it is administered as an interagency organization; now the battles of the Beltway have been transferred to Baghdad, where they are compromising U.S. efforts to establish a viable postwar order. Major and minor requests are regularly rejected by the State Department if they are perceived as Defense Department initiatives. One close observer pointed out that Secretary Powell could have no idea of the level of this harassment, as it is so petty and mindless.

Initially, ORHA was headed by a retired army general, Jay Garner, who had been involved in Operation Provide Comfort in 1991, when the United States helped Kurdish refugees return to their homes after the first war with Iraq. Although affable and well-intentioned, however, Garner was soon judged to be too ineffectual for the position, and in early May he was replaced by former U.S. State Department official. L. Paul Bremer, known as a hard-nosed, extremely effective bureaucratic player.

ORHA is a large organization, with some eight hundred U.S. officials posted to Baghdad. They are camped at the former Republican Palace, and it is not clear what many of them do. Considering the importance of ORHA's task, it is, by all accounts, already far too bureaucratic an enterprise, a "beast, seemingly unable to respond to actual conditions on the ground," in the words of the *Wall Street Journal*'s Robert Pollock. As Pollock notes, ORHA has actually blocked the efforts of private entrepreneurs to provide basic services like cell phones and air transport (claiming that more studies were needed).[319]

The United States has decisively settled the debate over whether the institutions of the old Ba'athist regime can provide a basis for the new government in Iraq. The answer is an unambiguous *no*, and a firm policy of "de-Ba'athification" has been laid down. But it remains unclear what is to replace it.

Initially (under Garner), the United States planned to move rather quickly to an interim Iraqi authority, in which Iraqis would basically be in charge, working with coalition forces. The realization of that objective, however, looks to be increasingly elusive as of this writing. The United States faces a radical choice: it can either govern Iraq itself for an extended period, or it can work to develop an Iraqi partner to serve at least as a transitional authority in conjunction with the United States. The first option requires a great deal of manpower and an intimate knowledge of the country, along with the effective use of both; it is far from clear, however, whether the United States has such resources, or is prepared to commit them. The other option would seem more promising—and the Iraqi National Congress, at least in this writer's view, presents a key element of the potential partnership. As of this writing, however, that does not seem to be the way the situation is developing.

Moreover, the war itself has not really ended, as the top Allied commander in Iraq, Lieutenant General David McKiernan, has affirmed.[320] U.S. forces remain targets, and some kind of Iraqi national security force, with Iraqis policing the country under U.S. command, is needed to limit the exposure of U.S. troops to attack. It would be a mistake for the United States to assume that the generally warm welcome it now enjoys among most of the Iraqi population will last indefinitely. The Israeli (and the U.S.) experience in Lebanon in the early 1980s is worth recalling in this regard: Lebanese initially welcomed the expulsion of the PLO, and even the Israeli forces that brought that about. But the welcome did not last long, particularly once Syria and Iran became involved in organizing resistance. The U.S. experience in Somalia holds similar lessons.

Saddam Hussein is almost certainly alive, despite the two U.S. attempts during the war to kill him (each of which the CIA initially reported as successful). Ba'ath party loyalists remain in Baghdad and in Sunni areas north and west of the city. Small groups regularly carry out hit-and-run attacks on U.S. forces. Parts of Iraq remain "a combat zone," as General McKiernan has explained, and "we're still in the process of removing the regime."[321]

It is entirely possible that Saddam and the top Iraqi leadership had developed a postdefeat strategy aimed at retaining as much of the Ba'athist structure and organization as possible, with the goal of eventually forcing the United States to leave in disgrace. Such a strategy would focus on making the U.S. occupation of the country difficult, through strategic sabotage, even down to the level of preventing restoration of basic services. That, indeed, may well be one reason the United States has encountered such problems in restoring electricity and phone service to Baghdad. Such an effort on the Ba'athists' part would be designed to sow discontent among the population toward the Americans, and it would include guerilla-like attacks on U.S. forces. Though it is virtually impossible to tell to what extent these actions constitute an organized resistance, such events already seem to be ongoing in Iraq.

Moreover, the neighboring country of Iran is not eager to see a stable, pro-American Iraq. Tehran too is doing what it can to destabilize the situation, even as it seeks to operate below the threshold that is likely to produce a strong U.S. response. Nor can it be precluded that Syria will not also become involved in instigating anti–U.S. violence.

Were the United States to succeed in its stated objective of establishing a democratic, constitutional government in Iraq, it would constitute an enormous achievement. This new Iraq would not have to look exactly like America, Britain, or Canada. It need only be respectable by the none-too-high standards of the Middle East. Even a flawed democracy would be a tremendous improvement over the horrific misery that Iraqis suffered under Saddam. It would also constitute an enormous challenge to the sclerotic Arab establishment, with its kings and potentates, who, once having taken power—even as presidents of a "republic"—regard it as a lifetime tenure.

Operation Iraqi Freedom is the most challenging war that the United States has fought since Vietnam. In war, some things will invariably go wrong, and they have. But by all relevant standards, this conflict has gone astonishingly well—so far. Those who favored fighting it were correct, not only in their view of the urgent need to do so, but also in their view of the war's likely course. Yet it is not over. So-called nation-building is not easy, and as a country whose technical skills now regularly outstrip its political skills, the United States still must exercise considerable thought and attention to ensuring that the noble gains of the war itself are not lost in the aftermath.

Notes

1. "U.S. Decision on Iraq Has Puzzling Past; Opponents of War Wonder When, How Policy Was Set," *Washington Post*, January 12, 2003.

2. CBS News, September 4, 2002; Agence France-Presse, September 5.

3. For relevant background see Laurie Mylroie, *Study of Revenge: Saddam Hussein's Unfinished War Against America* (Washington, D.C.: American Enterprise Institute, 2000), which carried endorsements from Richard Perle, Paul Wolfowitz, and James Woolsey, updated and revised as *The War Against America: Saddam Hussein and the World Trade Center Attacks, A Study of Revenge* (New York: HarperCollins, 2001).

4. Bob Woodward, *Bush at War* (New York: Simon & Schuster, 2002), p. 99; "U.S. Decision on Iraq Has Puzzling Past; Opponents of War Wonder When, How Policy Was Set," *Washington Post*, January 12, 2003.

5. Ibid.

6. Ibid.

7. Ibid.

8. "CIA Letter to Senate on Baghdad's Intentions," *New York Times*, October 9, 2002.

9. Press conference, March 6, 2003.

10. Clinton interview, *Newshour* with Jim Lehrer, January 21, 1998.

11. "U.S. Fears Nephews May Succeed Captive," *Washington Post*, March 4, 2003.

12. Major General John Parker, commander at Fort Detrick, where the tests were performed, "A Nation Challenged: The Response," *New York Times*, October 26, 2001.

13. October 7 was a Sunday and October 8 was Columbus Day, with no mail service. Thus, the letter could have been mailed at any time after the last mail collection on Saturday, October 6, and before the last mail collection on Tuesday, October 9. It is likely, then, that the letter was posted that Sunday or Monday, shortly after the U.S. campaign in Afghanistan began.

14. "A Terrorist's Fragile Footprint," *Washington Post*, November 29, 2001.

15. "Washington Wire," *Wall Street Journal*, May 2, 2003.

16. Ibid.

17. The spores that resulted in cutaneous anthrax had not gone through that process.

18. Lieutenant Colonel Edward Eitzen, M.D., M.P.H., chief of the Preventive and Operational Department of the U.S. Army's biological defense laboratory at Fort Detrick, Maryland, cited a 1970 World Health Organization study titled "Hypothetical Dissemination by Airplane of 50 Kilograms of Agent, along a 2-kilometer Line Upwind of a Population Center of 500,000 People" (Testimony before the Permanent Subcommittee on Investigations, Committee on Governmental Affairs, United States Senate, October 31, 1995). Another study estimated that 100 kilograms of anthrax, disseminated by an airplane flying upwind of Washington, D.C., on a clear, calm night, could kill between one and three million people (U.S. Congress, Office of Technology Assessment, *Proliferation of Weapons of Mass Destruction: Assessing the Risks*, OTA-ISC-359. U.S. Government Printing Office, Washington, D.C., August 1993, p. 54).

19. Testimony of Attorney General John Ashcroft before Panel 1 of a hearing of the House Judiciary Committee, September 24, 2001.

20. "A Nation Challenged: Aviation Precautions; Crop-Dusters Are Grounded on Fears of Toxic Attacks," *New York Times*, September 25, 2001. See also Marilyn W. Thompson, *The Killer Strain: Anthrax and a Government Exposed* (New York: HarperCollins, 2003) for more details on Atta's visits to South Florida Crop Care.

21. If Jarrah was an Islamic militant, he was apparently a recent convert who still maintained aspects of a more relaxed lifestyle. He lived in Germany with his Turkish girlfriend before coming to America. His great uncle, Assam Omar Jarrah, who had lived in East Germany since 1983, worked for the Stasi (East German intelligence), an organization with which Iraqi intelligence maintained links.

22. "Memo on Florida Case Roils Anthrax Probe; Experts Debate Theory Hijacker Was Exposed," *Washington Post*, March 29, 2002; Thompson, *Killer Strain*, p. 58.

23. Bob Woodward, *Bush at War*, p. 248.

24. Ibid.

25. "The New Cases: 2 New Anthrax Infections Found; Previous Cases Share Same Strain," *New York Times*, October 20, 2001.

26. "Additive Made Spores Deadlier; 3 Nations Known to Be Able to Make Sophisticated Coating," *Washington Post*, October 25, 2001.

27. ABC *World News Tonight*, October 26, October 28, November 1, 2001.

28. The FBI did link Iran to the 1996 bombing of the U.S. base in Saudi Arabia responsible for enforcing the no-fly zone over southern Iraq (although Iraq was the more obvious candidate). In my experience, the FBI simply did not want to hear about Iraq. In May 1993 I met with two FBI agents with a Pentagon official in attendance and explained why Iraq might have been behind the 1993 World Trade Center bombing, based solely on the *New York Times* reports. Though the meeting was very friendly and we agreed to talk again, subsequent calls were not returned. In following years I was repeatedly urged to brief the FBI (by, among others, a CIA official, an official in the State Department's Office of Diplomatic Security, and Jim Fox, former director of New York FBI). It became clear that the FBI did not want to talk to me—until after the 9/11 attacks.

29. "Response to Terror: The Anthrax Threat," *Los Angeles Times*, November 10, 2001.

30. "FBI's Theory on Anthrax Is Doubted; Attacks Not Likely Work of 1 Person, Experts Say," *Washington Post*, October 28, 2002.

31. Amerithrax Press Briefing, November 9, 2001.

32. Edward Epstein, "FBI Overlooks Foreign Sources of Anthrax," *Wall Street Journal*, December 24, 2001.

33. "Deadly Anthrax Strain Leaves a Muddy Trail," *Washington Post*, November 25, 2001.

34. Prepared testimony before House International Relations Committee, December 5, 2001.

35. "Anthrax Investigators Open Letter to Senator Leahy," *New York Times*, December 6, 2001.

36. The United Nations Monitoring, Verification, and Inspection Commission (which was dubbed "Unmoving" by wags, mocking its perceived tendency to operate out of its New York headquarters).

37. "Suspected Weapons Lab Is Found in Northern Iraq," *New York Times*, May 10, 2003.

38. "Iraq Said to Be Stashing Arms," *Washington Times*, January 17, 2003.

39. It was thought prior to the experience of fall 2001 that once symptoms appeared the disease was invariably fatal.

40. Saddam Hussein, October 29, 2001.

41. Arguably, a similar risk existed in blaming the attacks on the lone American of the FBI theory, but this account was quickly rejected by a number of journalists and experts. The theory would have seemed even less plausible following a full-scale BW attack.

42. Address of President Bush, October 7, 2002, Cincinnati, Ohio.

43. "Weighing the Risks of Terror," *Washington Post*, February 16, 2003.

44. "Preparing for Terror in Washington Area," *Washington Times*, March 2, 2003.

45. "G.I.s Search, Not Alone, in the Cellar of Secrets," *New York Times*, May 9, 2003.

46. Press conference, March 6, 2003.

47. For the argument that the anti-U.S. terrorist attacks of the 1990s were substantially the work of Iraqi intelligence, working through Islamic militant organizations including al Qaeda, see Laurie Mylroie, *Study of Revenge: Saddam Hussein's Unfinished War Against America* (American Enterprise Institute Press, 2000), revised as *The War Against America: Saddam Hussein and the World Trade Center Attacks: A Study of Revenge* (HarperCollins, 2001).

48. CBS News, September 4, 2002.

49. The definitive account is Anthony Cave Brown, *Bodyguard of Lies* (New York: HarperCollins, 1975).

50. The definitive account of this operation is John Cecil Masterman, *The Double-Cross System in the War of 1939 to 1945* (New Haven: Yale University Press, 1972).

51. Brown, *Bodyguard of Lies*, p. 667.

52. Rick Atkinson, *Crusade: The Untold Story of the Persian Gulf War* (New York: Houghton Mifflin, 1993), p. 332; the book contains a good description of the overall deception operations in Desert Storm. Also Defense Department, "Conduct of the Persian Gulf War" (U.S. Government Printing Office, Washington, D.C., 1993).

53. Personal communication.

54. Unclassified Version of Director of Central Intelligence George J. Tenet's

Testimony Before the Joint Inquiry into Terrorist Attacks Against the United States, June 18, 2002.

55. "In Hindsight CIA Sees Flaws That Hindered Efforts on Terror," *New York Times*, October 7, 2001.

56. "NSA Intercepts on Eve of 9/11 Sent a Warning," *Washington Post*, June 20, 2002.

57. "Some Hijackers Identities Uncertain," *Washington Post*, September 20, 2001.

58. Internet website at http://www.edwardjayepstein.com/nether_WWDK4.htm.

59. The sloppiness is detailed by Joel Mowbray, "Visas That Should Have Been Denied: A Look at 9/11 Terrorists Visa Applications," *National Review Online*, October 9, 2002. The website, http://www.nationalreview.com/mowbray/mowbray100902.asp, includes four of those visa applications.

60. "Hanjour: A Study in Paradox," *Washington Post*, October 15, 2001.

61. Ibid.

62. "A Trainee Noted for Incompetence," *New York Times*, May 4, 2000.

63. Ibid.

64. "The Terrorists Next Door," *St. Petersburg Times*, October 3, 2001.

65. This was an argument strongly promoted by the Clinton White House and was generally accepted. Many have written along these lines, including two former Clinton White House staffers who worked on terrorism, Daniel Benjamin and Steven Simon (*The Age of Sacred Terror*, New York: Random House, 2002).

66. Mylroie, *Study of Revenge*.

67. Ibid.

68. In November 1994, at Fox's suggestion, I conducted a brief and somewhat strange telephone interview with a retired official from New Jersey FBI. I began with what I thought was an unobjectionable statement, explaining that I worked on Iraq and admitting to having been "tricked" by the Iraqi regime. As I began to raise the question of Yasin, the man began immediately to say that I was dangerous and that he was going to hang up, his voice growing ever shriller. Speaking in the calmest of tones, I tried to keep him on the line but failed. If he was merely protecting an ongoing investigation, he had only to say that he was unable to help me on that account. My impression was that he may have understood that Fox had been right, and he was unwilling to acknowledge the mistake or even to address the question.

69. Gil Childers, comment at panel discussion of *Study of Revenge: Saddam Hussein's Unfinished War Against America,* at American Enterprise Institute, October 6, 2000.

70. Moussaoui was already in custody on U.S. soil, having been detained on immigration charges, when the September 11 strikes occurred.

71. Childers, panel discussion, *Study of Revenge,* October 6, 2000.

72. Iraq Television, September 15, 2001.

73. Ibid.

74. *Frontline,* "Gunning for Saddam" interview conducted in association with the *New York Times,* October 14, 2001. Transcript posted at: http://www.pbs.org/wgbh/pages/frontline/shows/gunning/interviews/general.html.

75. *Frontline,* "Gunning for Saddam" interview transcript posted at http://www.pbs.org/wgbh/pages/frontline/shows/gunning/interviews/khodada.html.

76. Ibid.

77. Ibid.

78. *Frontline,* "Gunning for Saddam" map sketch posted at: http://www.pbs.org/wgbh/pages/frontline/shows/gunning/etc/map.html.

79. "Satellite Photos Believed to Show Airliner for Training Hijackers," *Aviation Week & Space Technology,* January 7, 2002.

80. Jeffrey Goldberg, "The Unknown: The C.I.A. and the Pentagon Take Another Look at Al Qaeda and Iraq," *The New Yorker,* February 10, 2003.

81. *Frontline,* "Gunning for Saddam" interview.

82. A retired CIA official later stated that Salman Pak had been used for counterterrorism training in the mid-1980s. Apparently, the United States was involved in some of that training. Seymour Hersh, "Selective Intelligence," *The New Yorker,* May 12, 2003. However, it is entirely possible that the area had another purpose in the 1990s. Indeed, Space Imaging analysts described the entire facility as a terrorism training camp, as did the marines who occupied the area during the Gulf War.

83. Jim Hoagland, "CIA's New Old Iraq File," *The Washington Post,* October 20, 2002.

84. "U.S. Searches Shattered Iraqi Guard HQ," AP, April 6, 2003.

85. Edward Epstein, http://www.edwardjayepstein.com/2002question/saddams_actswalking_vanishing.htm.

86. Reuters News Service, March 2, 2003.

87. *The Prague Post,* June 5, 2002.

88. "Czechs Confirm Iraqi Agent Met with Terror Ringleader," *New York Times,* October 27, 2001.

89. Unclassified Version of Director of Central Intelligence George J. Tenet's Testimony Before the Joint Inquiry into Terrorist Attacks Against the United States, June 18, 2002.

90. Testimony in *Katy Soulas and Raymond Anthony Smith vs. Islamic Emirate of Afghanistan, Al Qaeda; Osama bin Laden; and the Republic of Iraq*, March 3, 2003.

91. "Saddam and the Next 9/11," *Wall Street Journal*, March 2, 2003.

92. Woodward, *Bush at War*, p. 99.

93. "Yemen, an Uneasy Ally Proves Adept at Playing Off Old Rivals," *New York Times*, December 19, 2002.

94. "President Broadens Anti-Hussein Order, CIA Gets More Tools to Oust Iraqi Leader," *Washington Post*, June 16, 2002.

95. "New Clue Fails to Explain Iraq Role in September 11 Attack," *New York Times*, December 16, 2001.

96. Michael Isikoff, "The Phantom Link to Iraq," *Newsweek* Web Exclusive, April 28, 2002.

97. Walter Pincus, "No Link Between Hijacker, Iraq Found, US Says," *Washington Post*, May 1, 2002.

98. *Prague Lidove Noviny*, "The United States Casts Doubt on the Czech Information on Atta," May 3, 2002.

99. Personal communication, October 2001.

100. No fewer than eight officials in different parts of the U.S. government told me about some aspect of this in the period from September 2002 through March 2003.

101. U.S. official, to author, October 2002.

102. Donald Rumsfeld, press briefing, January 30, 2003.

103. David S. Cloud, "Bush's Efforts to Link Hussein to al Qaeda Lack Clear Evidence, U.S. Intelligence Can't Affirm President's Claims, Despite His History with Other Terror Groups," *Wall Street Journal*, October 23, 2002.

104. Walter Pincus, "Alleged Al Qaeda Ties Questioned," *Washington Post*, February 7, 2003.

105. Walter Pincus and Dana Priest, "Bin Laden Hussein Link Hazy: US Officials Qualify Statements on Possible Terrorist Ties," *Washington Post*, February 13, 2003.

106. See, for example, Jimmy Carter, "Just War—or a Just War?" *New York Times*, March 9, 2003.

107. Personal communications.

108. UPI, January 21, 1996.

109. Lawrence F. Kaplan and William Kristol, *The War over Iraq: Saddam's Tyranny and America's Mission* (San Francisco: Encounter Books, 2003), p. 48.

110. *Civil War in Iraq,* A Staff Report to the Committee on Foreign Relations, United States Senate, May 1, 1991, p. 28.

111. Edward Jay Epstein, "Raymond Rocca: The Trust Breaker," February 6, 1976, at www.edwardjayepstein.com/diary/rocca.htm.

112. David Wurmser, *Tyranny's Ally: America's Failure to Defeat Saddam Hussein* (Washington, D.C.: American Enterprise Institute Press, 1999), p. 24.

113. This was the theory of Rifaat Shirwany, a Kurdish collaborator with Saddam's regime who headed the Iraqi Peasants Union in Baghdad during the Gulf War. When I interviewed him in northern Iraq in the summer of 1992 and asked if he understood why Schwarzkopf allowed the helicopters to fly, he replied, slapping his knee for emphasis, "Because the Americans thought they would make a coup, but that would never happen."

114. "Refugees Tell of Turmoil in Iraq; Troops Recount Allied Onslaught," *Washington Post,* March 4, 1991; "This Time, Say Iraqis, No Uprisings Until Baghdad Is Besieged," *Financial Times,* March 29, 2003.

115. "After the War: Stirring the Iraqi Pot," *New York Times,* March 21, 1991.

116. "U.S. Seen Lacking Policy on Postwar Goals," *Washington Post,* March 24, 1991.

117. "Wait and See on Iraq; Bush Views Aiding Rebels as Potential Morass," *Washington Post,* March 29, 1991.

118. "U.S. Fearing Iraqi Breakup Is Said to Rule out Action to Aid Anti-Hussein Rebels," *New York Times,* March 27, 1991.

119. This perverse view was indeed the opinion of the majority of Iraq experts, and their successors would play a major role in the U.S. occupation of Iraq twelve years later.

120. Paul Freeburg to author, March 1991; reconfirmed in October 28, 1993, interview; Ambassador Peter Galbraith relates a similar story from that time.

121. Interview with a Pentagon official during the 1991 Gulf War, November 1993.

122. Laurie Mylroie, "Help the Iraqi Resistance," *Wall Street Journal,* March 26, 1991.

123. Agence France-Presse, March 17, 2003.

124. Jim Hoagland. "Not a Vichy Option," *Washington Post,* March 23, 2003; another informed Washington source reported that the Saudi ambassador was boasting of the operation.

125. This is detailed in Peter Jennings, *ABC News Special,* February 7, 1998, and in Robert Baer, *See No Evil: The True Story of a Ground Soldier in the CIA's War on*

Terrorism (New York: Three Rivers Press, 2002). Also see David Wurmser, *Tyranny's Ally*, and Jim Hoagland, "How CIA's Secret War on Saddam Collapsed," *Washington Post*, June 26, 1997.

126. Richter had created serious difficulties for CIA operations in Iran, particularly when he pressed for more reports from U.S. agents there. The ill-conceived request led to a surge in communications from CIA assets in Iran, which Iranian intelligence observed. It then proceeded to round up many CIA assets there. Nonetheless, Richter was reportedly the leading candidate for director of operations, once Tenet became director (Hoagland, "How CIA's Secret War on Saddam Collapsed.")

127. Jim Hoagland, "How CIA's Secret War on Saddam Collapsed."

128. Wurmser, *Tyranny's Ally*, p. 21.

129. Interview with General al-Salhi, November 4, 1999.

130. Hoagland, "How CIA's Secret War on Saddam Collapsed."

131. Wurmser, *Tyranny's Ally*, p. 25.

132. Niels Frenzen, memo, March 15, 1998.

133. "Evidence to Deny 6 Iraqis Asylum May Be Weak, Files Show," *New York Times*, October 13, 1998; Andrew Cockburn, "The Radicalization of James Woolsey," *New York Times Magazine*, July 23, 2000.

134. The CIA accusation against Arras Karim was determined by the Defense Intelligence Agency to be false, as discussed below.

135. Hoagland, "How CIA's Secret War on Saddam Collapsed."

136. Lawrence F. Kaplan, "Rollback: America's Iraq Policy Collapses," *New Republic*, October 30, 2000.

137. "Firing Blanks: The Plot to Oust Saddam and the Constant Pounding from U.S. Jets Are Going Nowhere," *Time*, November 8, 1999.

138. Jim Hoagland, "Virtual Policy," *Washington Post*, March 9, 1999.

139. "Smearing Mr. Chalabi," *Wall Street Journal*, April 10, 2003.

140. The report is available at: http://oig.state.gov/documents/organization/15006.pdf.

141. Personal communication, November 5, 2002.

142. Indeed, Jordan was so close to Iraq in that period that it actually sided with Iraq following the invasion of Kuwait. Saudi and Kuwaiti officials even went so far in their suspicions as to suggest that Saddam's ultimate aim included the breakup of Saudi Arabia and that King Hussein had been promised the Hijaz, the western province of the kingdom containing the holy cities of Mecca and Medina, which the king's grandfather had once ruled.

143. This has a long, complex background. Other Chalabis owned a bank in

Geneva, MEBCO, with a related trading firm, SOCOFI. In April 1989, Swiss banking regulators took over the bank, charging that three loans, which formed over 20 percent of MEBCO's loan portfolio, lacked proper collateral (the loans were subsequently recovered in full).

At the time, Barzan Tikriti, Saddam's half-brother, was Iraq's ambassador to the U.N. in Geneva. Iraq had billions of dollars of deposits in Swiss banks and it was not the outlaw state it would become a year later, after it invaded Kuwait. Some suggest that Barzan was involved in getting the Swiss to look into MEBCO.

Whatever the case, SOCOFI, the trading firm, had been the target of a substantial fraud, carried out by a group that included its manager, Paul Mouawad, and a Greek shipping magnate. Two individuals were sentenced to prison in Switzerland for the fraud.

The Swiss takeover of MEBCO and the fraud against SOCOFI put pressure on Petra Bank, although, as the Chalabis explain, the situation at Petra had stabilized by July 1989.

Meanwhile, in Jordan, a new government took over following serious economic problems there that resulted in political unrest, including riots. The new governor of the Central Bank imposed the stiff regulation that all banks deposit 35 percent of their foreign currency reserves with the Central Bank. The governor was opposed to Chalabi, and when Chalabi had some difficulty meeting that requirement, rather than using administrative measures to address the problem, he used martial law to seize the bank.

144. Editorial, "Jordanian Justice," *New York Sun*, April 28, 2003.

145. Personal communication, November 2000. My impression was that this official was simply following his instructions; after September 11, he was a strong advocate of going to war with Iraq.

146. Personal communication from a source close to the administration.

147. Ben Miller was removed from his White House post in early 2003 and returned to the CIA (to be replaced at the White House by another CIA official). Miller was posted to Qatar during the war, where he advised Centcom; one has to wonder what sort of advice he could have been providing.

148. Source close to the administration, March 2003.

149. Kanan Makiya, "The Wasteland," *New Republic*, May 5, 2003.

150. Ibid.

151. Kanan Makiya, National Press Club, April 23, 2003.

152. Makiya, "Wasteland"; "U.S. Tells Iran Not to Interfere in Iraq Efforts, *The New York Times*, April 24, 2003.

NOTES **239**

153. Martin Indyk, "Back to the Bazaar," *Foreign Affairs*, January–February
2002.
154. "Rabin Slams Iran for Anti-Peace Violence," Associated Press, November 12, 1994.
155. Figures like Saddam or Qaddafi who, though not Islamic extremists, still remained unreformed (in spite of attempts by the Peres camp to bring them into negotiations) were considered too weak to cause significant harm.
156. *New York Times*, May 5, 2002.
157. Nachman Tal, "Islamic Terrorism in Egypt," *Strategic Assessment*, March 1998. *Strategic Assessment* is a publication of Tel Aviv University's Jaffee Center for Strategic Studies, Israel's leading institution in that field. This was by no means a fringe view: Tal is a retired officer of the Shin Bet, Israel's domestic security force.
158. The Iraqi threat in the highly regarded annual volume *The Middle East Contemporary Survey* diminishes as the issue of Iraq fades into insignificance. The 1992 volume presents a sober and realistic assessment: "For Iraq, the Gulf War did not end with the cease-fire of February 1991, but continued on in various ways throughout 1991 and 1992. . . . One of the greatest puzzles concerning Iraq's political stance from the end of the Gulf War through 1992 was the motive behind its persistent defiance of the U.N. cease-fire resolutions despite the severe social, economic and political dislocation this stand entailed. . . . [Baghdad] reached the conclusion early on that for various external reasons—fears in the West of the disintegration of Iraq, the perception in the West of Iraq as a balance against Iran, and a certain weakening of spirit among the Arab allies members—the possibility of another major military confrontation against Iraq was quite remote. It also calculated that it could weather the economic crisis without having to bend to the U.N." From Ofra Bengio, "Iraq" in *Middle East Contemporary Survey: 1992*, Ami Ayalon, ed. (Boulder, Colo.: Westview Press, 1993), pp. 447, 484–85. But three years later, even after Hussein Kamil's defection revealed how dangerous Saddam still was, Bengio writes only, "Iraq's cherished hope that the U.N. sanctions regime would be lifted in 1995 was frustrated yet again." ("Iraq," in *Middle East Contemporary Survey: 1995*. Boulder, Colo.: Westview Press, 1997, p. 337.)
159. e.g., Daniel Pipes, "Stupid Is as Stupid Does," *Wall Street Journal*, October 11, 1994. Even four years later, Ely Karmon writes of "the complete Iraqi defeat" in 1991 ("Why Tehran Starts and Stops Terrorism," *Middle East Quarterly*, December 1998).
160. Personal communication, March 1998.

161. Author's interview with senior Saudi official, Washington, D.C., February 29, 1996.

162. Of the twenty-one members of the Arab League, at the critical August 10, 1990, summit, only twelve voted against Iraq: Egypt, Syria and Lebanon, Saudi Arabia and the five Gulf sheikhdoms, along with Morocco, Somalia, and Djibouti.

163. Even now, after the war, neither the U.N. inspectors, nor the U.S. (so far) has managed to obtain a single microbe from Iraq's BW program.

164. A *Washington Post* reporter recounted this exchange to me several years later.

165. The resolution had actually been passed on April 14, 1995, after UNSCOM had reported, on April 10, that Iraq had an undeclared BW program. It was implemented in 1996.

166. Tal, "Islamic Terrorism in Egypt." An expert on Egypt, Ami Ayalon, puts the turning point in 1996 ("Egypt," in *Middle East Contemporary Survey: 1996*. Boulder, Colo.: Westview Press, 1998, p. 260).

167. "Egyptian Militants Turning Away from Violence," *Washington Post*, May 12, 2002.

168. Fouad Ajami, *Wall Street Journal*, April 10, 2002.

169. Statistics from Tal, "Islamic Terrorism in Egypt."

170. Reuters, December 12, 1997.

171. Ami Ayalon, "Egypt," in *Middle East Contemporary Survey: 1997* (Boulder, Colo.: Westview Press, 2001), p. 228.

172. Mary Anne Weaver, *A Portrait of Egypt: A Journey Through the World of Militant Islam* (New York: Farrar, Straus & Giroux, 1998), p. 269.

173. *New York Times*, November 19, 1997.

174. Weaver, *Portrait of Egypt*, p. 248. Indeed, it is even possible that the six men found dead in the cave were not the six gunmen, or that some were and others were not. The only thing that is really known about them is that the six men in the cave were dressed in the same black clothing as the six gunmen.

175. *New York Times*, January 11, 1998.

176. Ayalon, "Egypt," *Middle East Contemporary Survey: 1998*, p. 228.

177. Personal communication, April 29, 2002.

178. *Washington Post*, June 27, 1995.

179. *Washington Times*, October 19, 1995.

180. A full three years after the 1993 plot to bomb the U.N., New York's Federal Building, and two tunnels, U.S. authorities disclosed for the first time the involvement of two Sudanese intelligence agents employed at Sudan's U.N.

mission, as part of a broader effort to get the Security Council to impose sanctions on Sudan (*Washington Post*, April 11, 1996).

181. *Washington Times*, June 27, 1995.

182. Iraq News Agency, July 6, 1995, citing *Al-Thawrah*, July 6.

183. Reuters, June 27, 1995.

184. It was Ahmad Chalabi, head of the Iraqi National Congress, who first told me that Egypt believed Iraq was behind this attack (December 2001). Richard Miniter gave a similar account to me in April 2002, with the added detail that the Egyptians did not believe the assault was meant to kill Mubarak.

185. Senior Saudi official, Washington, D.C., February 29, 1996.

186. An Egyptian who participated in the 1993 World Trade Center bombing, Mahmud Abu Halima, fled to his hometown in Egypt after the attack. He was quickly picked up by Egyptian authorities and questioned under torture. From that interrogation, the Egyptians concluded that Iraq was probably behind that attack, and they were puzzled why the U.S. did nothing about it. (Personal communication, Christopher Dickey, then *Newsweek* bureau chief in Cairo.)

187. Agence France-Presse, November 21, 1995.

188. *Financial Times*, November 20, 1995.

189. Professor Ghanim al-Najjar, of Kuwait University, was part of a delegation of Arab professors that met then-Foreign Minister Tariq Aziz in the 1980s, in the latter stages of the Iran-Iraq war. The professors asked Aziz why Iraq attacked tankers carrying oil from Iran, even when they belonged to countries that were friendly to Iraq, like France. Aziz explained that Iraq wanted more international pressure put on Iran to end the war and that "people did want you want when you hurt them." Al-Najjar emphasized the importance of that statement (personal communication, 1996).

190. Cited in Hedrick Smith, *The Power Game: How Washington Works* (New York: Ballantine Books, 1996).

191. A Pentagon analyst first described this tactic, explaining that it was done to him, as well as to foreign intelligence agencies, not to mention individuals with no official standing. When I subsequently discussed this with a retired CIA analyst, he laughed in sympathy, it was so common and familiar.

192. Personal communication, December 2002.

193. Paul Pillar, *Terrorism and U.S. Foreign Policy* (Washington, D.C.: Brookings Institution Press, 2001), p. 50.

194. Ibid., p. 217. Compare the view set forth in Laurie Mylroie, *Study of Revenge: Saddam Hussein's Unfinished War Against America* (Washington, D.C.: American Enterprise Institute Press, 2000), which argues that Iraq was work-

ing with Islamic militants, including al Qaeda, to attack the United States, and that the danger of terrorism on a massive scale was therefore very real.

195. "Senior Intelligence Officer Blasts Bush's Axis of Evil Speech," *Insight Magazine*, February 22, 2002.

196. Personal communication (a chance exchange in the Fox News green room).

197. Journalists and independent researchers can, however, discern patterns and even examine detailed evidence in the public domain. *Study of Revenge* pointed to many of the pressing questions surrounding the 1993 terrorist attack on the New York World Trade Center, and in particular questioned the identity and affiliation of the key terrorist as a probable Iraqi plant.

198. Personal communication, February 2003.

199. Personal communication, October 2002.

200. Senator Fred Thompson, Center for Security Policy address, December 12, 2002.

201. Personal communication, November 25, 1998.

202. The first hint of a change in the Clinton administration's declaratory policy was a meeting of NSC Adviser Sandy Berger with Senate Majority Leader Trent Lott on November 13, at which Berger told Lott that the White House would adopt the ILA.

203. Martin Indyk, who served in senior Middle East positions throughout the administration, later explained that the real policy toward Iraq was sanctions, not overthrowing Saddam and not even weapons inspections. (Indyk served the Clinton administration, as NSC adviser on the Middle East, as ambassador to Israel [twice], and as assistant secretary of state for Near East Affairs.) Martin Indyk, "Don't Ignore the Sanctions," Iraq Memo #2, Brookings Institution, October 15, 2002.

204. In the 1992 presidential campaign, Clinton had been tougher than former President Bush, saying that Bush should have removed Saddam during the 1991 war. After the elections, however, Clinton's position changed entirely, as signaled in an interview he gave Thomas Friedman (*New York Times*, January 13, 1993), in which Clinton asserted that, as a Baptist, he believed in the possibility of conversion.

205. Personal communication.

206. Jim Hoagland, "Saddam Prevailed," *Washington Post*, September 29, 1996.

207. Personal communication, July 2002.

208. Patrick L. Clawson, ed., *Iraq Strategy Review: Options for U.S. Policy* (Washington, D.C.: Washington Institute for Near East Policy, 1998).

209. Ibid., p. 11.

210. Ibid.

211. Ibid., p. 115.

212. Ibid., p. 158.

213. Ibid., p. 88.

214. Ibid., p. 158. The author, Max Singer, sent me a draft of his chapter for my comment. The appendix, under Clawson's name, includes the note, "With profound thanks for the detailed assistance of Max Singer, who dissents from the analysis presented here," p. 149.

215. Personal communication, September 1998.

216. Daniel Byman, Kenneth Pollack, Gideon Rose, "The Rollback Fantasy," *Foreign Affairs*, January/February 1999.

217. In a later book, Pollack links the offer to a change at the NSC, in which a new director for the Near East was appointed, with whom he had previously worked. It coincided, roughly, with the declared change in policy. Pollack maintains that it was seriously meant and that the campaign in Kosovo got in the way (others, including some on the White House staff, contradict that). Pollack claims that he was hawkish on Iraq and that the *Foreign Affairs* article showed some people at the White House that he would be "realistic" in seeking a change of regime—which is pretty much the point his critics make (although, they wouldn't describe him as being particularly tough in that period). *The Threatening Storm: The Case for Invading Iraq* (New York: Random House, 2002), p. 90.

218. Lawrence F. Kaplan, "Rollback: America's Iraq Policy Collapses," *New Republic*, October 30, 2000.

219. Pollack, *Threatening Storm*, p. 82.

220. Hoagland, "Saddam Prevailed."

221. Pollack, *Threatening Storm*, p. 77.

222. Ibid.

223. Ibid., p. xi.

224. Ibid., p. 179.

225. Ibid., p. 236.

226. David Benjamin and Steven Simon, *The Age of Sacred Terror* (New York: Random House, 2002), p. 169.

227. Ibid.

228. Personal communication, 1995.

229. Kamil, personal communication, September 1995. He also told me what he told UNSCOM, that Iraq had no banned weapons.

230. Personal communication, March 2003.

231. "U.S. Fears Nephews May Succeed Captive: Mohammed's Relatives Are Also Involved in Attack Planning, Officials Believe," *Washington Post*, March 4, 2003.

232. Agence France-Presse, August 18, 1990.

233. "Bold Tracks of Terrorism's Mastermind Khalid Sheik Mohammed Carried Al Qaeda's Hope for Revenge, Renewal," *Washington Post*, March 9, 2003.

234. "The CEO of al-Qaeda," *Financial Times*, February 14, 2003.

235. This point is discussed in greater detail, with illustrating documents, in Laurie Mylroie, *The War Against America: Saddam Hussein and the World Trade Center Attacks: A Study of Revenge* (New York: HarperCollins, 2001).

236. A Kuwaiti official was kind enough to obtain this information for me. As he read from a summary of the file, I wrote down this information, and when he was through speaking, I looked up and asked, "What is that information doing in your file?" His jaw dropped. Of course, that information did not belong in a Kuwaiti file. November 1994.

237. Yousef obtained the passport on which he fled by going to Kuwait with *photocopies* of Karim's expired 1984 passport and his current 1988 passport. The latter document gives Karim's height as five eight.

238. Mylroie, *Study of Revenge*, pp. 51–65, 176–81, 208–12.

239. BBC News, September 18, 2001.

240. "Al Qaeda and Iraq: How Strong Is the Evidence?" *The Guardian*, January 30, 2003.

241. Personal communication, November 1, 2001.

242. Personal communication; former U.S. official involved in investigation and prosecution of Yousef, November 2001.

243. *New York Times*, January 9, 1998.

244. "The Plot: How Terrorists Hatched a Simple Plan to Use Planes as Bombs," *Los Angeles Times*, September 1, 2002.

245. "Qaeda Aide Slipped Away Long Before Sept. 11 Attacks," *New York Times*, March 8, 2003.

246. "Bold Tracks of Terrorism's Mastermind: Khalid Shaikh Mohammed Carried Al Qaeda's Hope for Revenge, Renewal," *Washington Post*, March 9, 2003.

247. Jim Hoagland, "9/11 Mysteries in Plain Sight," *Washington Post*, March 9, 2003.

248. Personal communication, December 1994.

249. For a more extensive discussion of this see Mylroie, *Study of Revenge*, pp. 195–96.

250. Personal communication.

251. Personal communication, U.S. official, April 2003.

252. Patrick E. Tyler and Felicity Barringer, "Annan Says U.S. Will Violate Charter If It Acts Without Approval," *New York Times*, March 11, 2003, p. A8.

253. Jefferson to Colvin, 12 *The Writings of Thomas Jefferson*, 419 (Mem. ed. 1903).

254. Donald Kagan, *On the Origins of War* (New York: Doubleday, 1995), p. 351.

255. Sun Tzu, *The Art of War* (New York and Oxford: Oxford University Press, 1963), p. 77.

256. According to local time zones; it was still August 1 in the United States.

257. The U.N. first authorized the sale of oil in a resolution in the late summer of 1991, which Iraq rejected.

258. Mary Ellen O'Connell, "Addendum to Armed Force in Iraq: Issues of Legality," *ASIL Insights*, April 2003, available on the Internet at: http://www. asil.org/insights/insigh99al.htm.

259. Ibid.

260. While a full discussion of the constitutional issue is beyond the scope of this chapter, it should be noted that Operation Iraqi Freedom was clearly authorized by Congress when it enacted into law the "Authorization for the Use of Military Force Against Iraq Resolution of 2002" (Pub. Law 107–243, 116 Stat. 1501), which expressly provided in Section 3: "The President is authorized to use the Armed Forces of the United States as he determines to be necessary and appropriate in order to—(1) defend the national security of the United States against the continuing threat posed by Iraq; and (2) enforce all relevant United Nations Security Council Resolutions regarding Iraq."

261. Kagan, *On the Origins of War*, p. 412.

262. Ibid.

263. State Department lawyers might arguably have strengthened their hand by observing that Resolution 949, of October 15, 1994, had expressly "reaffirmed" previous resolutions on Iraq, "in particular paragraph 2 of resolution 678 (1990)." That paragraph provided that, "*[a]cting under* Chapter VII of the Charter," the Security Council:

> 2. *Authorizes* Member States co-operating with the Government of Kuwait, unless Iraq on or before 15 January 1991 fully implements, as set forth in paragraph 1 above, the foregoing resolutions, to use all necessary means to uphold and implement resolution 660 (1990) and all subsequent relevant resolutions and to restore international peace and security in the area;

By specifically *reaffirming* the use-of-force authorization language from the earlier resolution—irrespective of the subjective intentions of its members (which are only relevant if a textual interpretation is "manifestly absurd or unreasonable")—one might easily argue that the council had once again authorized the use of armed force. The argument against this interpretation would be that, while Resolution 949 did invoke Chapter VII of the Charter, the language reaffirming paragraph 2 of Resolution 678 occurred *prior* to the invocation of Chapter VII. Thus, the argument is still not likely by itself to carry the day.

264. The requirement of unanimity is theoretical at best. A majority of the Security Council, in the absence of a veto, has independent authority under the Charter either to terminate Resolution 687 or simply to authorize the use of force again. Here the distinction made by Professor O'Connell is important.

265. Robert F. Turner, "Military Action Against Iraq Is Justified," 44(4) *Naval War College Review* (2002), 72, 73.

266. See, e.g., Marc Weller, "The Legality of the Threat or Use of Force Against Iraq," *Journal of Humanitarian Assistance*, June 3, 2000. Available on-line at: http://www.jha.ac/articles/a031.htm at 6.

267. George K. Walker, "Anticipatory Collective Self-Defense in the Charter Era," 31 *Cornell International Law Journal* (1998), 321, 375–76.

268. Quoted in Penelope C. Simons, "Humanitarian Intervention: A Review of the Literature," Ploughshares Working Paper 01–2, available on-line at: http://www.ploughshares.ca/CONTENT/WORKING%20PAPERS/wp012.html, p. 10.

269. Ibid., p. 4.

270. Frederic L. Kirgis, "The Kosovo Situation and NATO Military Action," *ASIL Insights*, March 1999.

271. Quoted in Simons, "Humanitarian Intervention."

272. Richard Falk, "Kosovo, World Order, and the Future of International Law," 93 *American Journal of International Law* (1999), 847, 853.

273. Ibid., 853, 855.

274. Amnesty International, *IRAQ: Systematic Torture of Political Prisoners*, August 15, 2001, p. 2, available on-line at http://web.amnesty.org/library/Index/engMDE140082001?OpenDocument&of=COUNTRIES%5CIRAQ?OpenDocument&of=COUNTRIES%5CIRAQ.

275. Ibid.

276. Ibid., p. 3.

277. Ibid., p. 5.
278. Quoted in van der Stoel, p. 3.
279. Ibid., p. 6.
280. Quoted in ibid.
281. Bureau of Democracy, Human Rights, and Labor, U.S. Department of State, *Iraq: A Population Silenced* 9 (December 2002). Available on-line at: http://usinfo.state.gov/products/pubs/silenced/.
282. Max van der Stoel, Special Rapporteur of the U.N. Commission on Human Rights on the Situation of Human Rights in Iraq, Gen. Assembly Doc. A/54/466, October 14, 1999, p. 5.
283. Ibid., p. 6.
284. Ibid.
285. Ibid., p. 7.
286. Ibid.
287. Ibid., p. 8.
288. Antonio Cassese, "A Follow-up: Forcible Humanitarian Countermeasures and *Opinio Necessitatis*," 10 *European Journal of International Law* (1999) 791–93.
289. CBS News/New York Times Poll, cited in *The Bulletin's Frontrunner*, May 14, 2003. A February 2003 poll found that 72 percent of Americans believed Iraq was probably involved in the 9/11 attacks. Cited in Seymour Hersh, "Selective Intelligence," *The New Yorker*, May 12, 2003 (posted May 5).
290. Woodward, *Bush at War*, p. 259.
291. Martin Indyk, "Don't Ignore the Sanctions," Iraq Memo #2, Brookings Institution, October 15, 2002.
292. "Hussein's Son Took $1 Billion Just Before War," *New York Times*, May 6, 2003.
293. "Boxes of Cash May Be Hussein's Plunder; Most of Stolen $1 Billion Found, U.S. Officials Say," *Washington Post*, May 15, 2003.
294. ABC News, May 20, 2003.
295. "Iraq Said to Be Stashing Arms Underground, in Residences," *Washington Times*, January 17, 2003.
296. The secretary's presentation, including illustrations, can be found at: http://216.239.39.100/unclesam?q=cache:9rPxueCVFNIJ:www.state.gov/secretary/rm/2003/17300.
297. CIA Report, "Iraqi Mobile Biological Warfare Agent Production Plants," May 28, 2003, on-line at http://www.cia.gov/cia/publications/iraqi_mobile_plants/index.html.

298. "Why Did We Go to War?" *Daily Telegraph*, May 30, 2003.

299. Recall that Iraq was supposed to declare all elements of its banned weapons programs within fifteen days of the April 3, 1991, passage of UNSCR 687, and UNSCOM was to destroy them within the next ninety days.

300. The UNSCOM reports can be found at http://www.un.org/Depts/unscom/.

301. Richard Butler, presentation to U.N. Security Council, June 11, 1998.

302. Indeed, French president Jacques Chirac and German chancellor Gerhard Schroeder, who opposed the war, received similar estimates regarding Iraq's weapons from their own intelligence agencies. Jim Hoagland, "Clarity: The Best Weapon," *Washington Post*, June 1, 2003.

303. Personal communication, May 2003.

304. Hersh, "Selective Intelligence."

305. Personal note, May 7, 2003.

306. "Memorandum for the President," Veteran Intelligence Professionals for Sanity, February 7, 2003.

307. Ibid.

308. "Protest at Peres Visit," *Varsity Online*, January 28, 1999. Rangwala received unmerited credibility by catching the office of the British prime minister in something it should not have done—using large parts of an on-line article on Iraq's intelligence services in one of its papers on Iraq.

309. http://middleeastreference.org.uk/kamel.html.

310. "Revealed: How the Road to War Was Paved with Lies," *The Independent*, April 27, 2003; cited in "Intelligence Fiasco," Veteran Intelligence Professionals for Sanity, May 1. This memo was subsequently cited by Nicholas Kristoff, "Save Our Spooks," *New York Times*, May 30, 2003; "Interview: Larry Johnson Discusses the Allegation That the Defense Department Deliberately Skewed the Facts to Convince the Bush Administration to Go to War with Iraq," *All Things Considered*, National Public Radio, May 30; and "Tenet Defends Iraqi Intelligence," *Washington Post*, May 31, among others.

311. The first reports that such a facility had been discovered emerged in late April, e.g., "Truck Is Tested for Biological Agents," *Los Angeles Times*, April 29, 2003.

312. Personal communication with administration official, May 2003.

313. "They Said What?" is a lighthearted review of a number of those erroneous predictions. *Wall Street Journal*, April 23, 2003.

314. William Safire, " 'Irrefutable and Undeniable,' " *New York Times*, February 6, 2003.

315. Personal communication, October 2002.

316. Deputy Secretary Wolfowitz interview with Sam Tanenhaus, *Vanity Fair,* May 9, 2003, posted at http://www.defenselink.mil/transcripts/2003/tr20030509-depsecdefo223.html.

317. Provided to the author by the INC, which obtained a large number of Iraqi documents, which it is analyzing in coordination with the DIA.

318. Reportedly, Brent Scowcroft, NSC adviser under Bush 41 and now head of the President's Foreign Intelligence Advisory Board (PFIAB), has prepared a still-classified study which advises just that.

319. Robert Pollock, "Great Expectations: Iraqis Embrace Freedom," *Wall Street Journal,* May 30, 2003.

320. " 'War Has Not Ended' in Iraq, Says Top Allied Commander," *Wall Street Journal,* May 30, 2003.

321. Ibid.

INDEX

DATE DUE
